DATE DUE

GENERAL ALEXANDER LEBED

GENERAL ALEXANDER LEBED

My Life And My Country

Regnery Publishing, Inc.
Washington, D.C.

Library of Congress Cataloging-in-Publication Data
Lebed ' , Aleksandr.
    [Za derzhavu obidno—.   English]
    General Alexander Lebed : my life and my country / Alexander
Lebed.
        p.   cm.
    Includes index.
    ISBN 0-89526-422-6 (alk. paper)
        1. Lebed ' , Aleksandr.   2. Generals—Soviet Union—Biography.
3. Politicians—Russia (Federation)—Biography.   4. Soviet Union—
History, Military.   I. Title.
DK275.L43A3   1997
947.086'092—dc21
    [B]   97-33323
                                                                                                    CIP

Published in the United States by
Regnery Publishing, Inc.
An Eagle Publishing Company
422 First Street, SE
Washington, DC 20003

Distributed to the trade by
National Book Network
4720-A Boston Way
Lanham, MD 20706

Printed on acid-free paper.
Manufactured in the United States of America

10 9 8 7 6 5 4 3 2 1

Books are available in quantity for promotional or premium use. Write to Director of Special Sales, Regnery Publishing, Inc., 422 First Street, SE, Suite 300, Washington, DC 20003, for information on discounts and terms or call (202) 546-5005.

CONTENTS

CHAPTER 1:
ADMIT HIM ON PROBATION

IN MY CHILDHOOD I never dreamed of becoming an army officer. In our family there were no career officers, but we were soldiers. My mother's father Grigory Vasilievich achieved the highest rank among my relatives. He came back from World War II a much-wounded master sergeant. His wounds were so severe that he died of them in 1948. But because he died in bed rather than on the battlefield, my grandmother Anastasia Nikiforovna was denied a widow's pension.

My father Ivan Andreevich was a jack of all trades. But every job that passed through his hands was executed with calm professionalism. He returned from the war as a sergeant first class, and though the war left him prematurely aged, he did not die until 1978. My father lived through hard times. In 1937 he was sent to a labor camp for five years. His crime? Being late to work twice, by five minutes. When the Finnish War broke out, my father was sent to a penal battalion. He froze. He starved. It was so cold he had to cut his bread with a saw. He participated in attacks more than once; they didn't loaf in the penal battalions.

My father never shirked his duty; he had shown his bravery, and God preserved him from bullets and bayonets. But there was a catch—in order to be transferred from the penal battalion to a regular unit, you had to shed your blood, to redeem yourself. But after the Finnish War, wisdom won out, and he was assigned to a line unit.

He fought until 1942, spending the whole time in forward positions. So far unscratched, the wild thought occurred to him that he might have some charm against death and enemy bullets. That summer, while hitching a ride on a tank, a fragment of a lone enemy artillery shell smashed against his right femur. He didn't remember how he got to the battalion aid station, but he spent a whole year in hospital beds. They were able to save his leg, but it was shortened by five centimeters. He hobbled around the hospital grounds, and little by little, he became reattuned to civilian life until an order from Stalin decreed that a shortened leg should not be considered an obstacle to army service. He was sent to a line unit, and back to the front. He did not return home until 1947.

Ten years of lying on government bunks and eating government grub stripped him of any sociability he might have had. He always spoke briefly and to the point. If he saw that someone needed help— if our elderly neighbor needed her fence repaired, for example—he took his tools and fixed it. Silently. Free of charge.

In Novocherkassk my mother Ekaterina Grigorievna worked in the telegraph office from 1944 until her retirement. She met my father there and bore him two children—me and my younger brother Aleksei. We lived on part of an old aristocratic estate. Actually, the stable. No matter. We rebuilt it, and Father helped us erect a jungle-gym in the yard. If Father saw that we weren't using a tool just right, he would come over, silently take the instrument, and show us the right way to use it. He never yelled. He never hit us, although we sometimes gave him cause.

When I was fourteen years old, I became greatly interested in boxing. At the sporting academy, the trainer praised me as a promising fighter. I had long arms and a thick skull, and I wasn't afraid of being hit. I mastered the skills, built my endurance, and learned how to be a disciplined fighter.

Once, in training, we were vaulting the horse. We jumped for a long time, competing with each other, moving the springboard back, lengthening the jump until, at last, I jumped without gathering enough momentum and broke my collarbone. It was Saturday, and the clinic was closed, so they took me straight to the hospital. Perhaps the doctor was in a hurry, or maybe the nurse was inexperienced, but all they said were the traditional words, "He'll live to see his wedding," and put my arm in a sling.

I began to think seriously about what I wanted to do when I grew up. I felt a subconscious pull toward the sky, to be a military flier, the very symbol of courage.

In a week, when my collarbone knitted, it turned out to have shortened by 3.5 centimeters and I couldn't raise my arm. I had to accept the fact that they were going to break it again. After all, I thought, I couldn't become an officer with a collarbone like that—and it was while I was recovering that I decided to be a military aviator—so I'd have to stand the pain. And stand it I did. When my injury had healed, I went back to the sports academy, but my boxing group had broken up. I

> **"In 1937 my father was sent to a labor camp for five years. His crime? Being late to work twice—by five minutes."**

heard that there was a pretty good boxing team at the polytech, and I was right. But then another blow fell. They kicked everybody off the team who didn't attend the institute. I was forced to train in back alleys. I became a street boxer. As they say, "I've been through a hundred fights, but all on the streets." But I also took part in formal competitions, since trainers who knew me were willing to sponsor me as a promising boxer.

On my vacation after ninth grade[1], we went out to do farm work at the village of Bogaevskaya. One day, a team from our class was playing

---

[1] In the Soviet system, students generally started first grade at age seven instead of age six, as in the United States. Therefore, children coming out of ninth grade would have been fifteen or sixteen. Tenth grade was the final year of high school.

soccer with some of the local boys and we beat them pretty badly, scoring in double figures. Everyone parted on good terms, but as soon as it got dark, the sounds of a fist fight and breaking glass woke me. These local boys had come back to get even for the day's match. I jumped up and ran outside to help my classmates. But before I had time to make a fist, I was hit in the face with a board from a picket fence and lost consciousness. My nose was broken and pushed to one side, but I didn't let this bother me. I was no girl. I knew a man needed to be only slightly better looking than an ape, and that a man's true worth wasn't defined by the prettiness of his face.

When I first told my father that I wanted to become an officer, he took it calmly and didn't try to talk me out of it, but I felt he had no faith in my dream. In the tenth grade, I began to prepare for enrollment in a military institute, looked over some prospectuses, and chose the Kachinskoye Aviation School. A popular song at the time went, "Embracing the sky in his strong arms, the aviator climbs the heights." I shared a common dream with that aviator—the heights!

I put an application in to the registration and enlistment office. My examinations were easy enough; all that remained was the ear, nose, and throat doctor. The elderly doctor sat me down, questioned me, examined my tonsils and the curvature of my septum, then silently took my medical sheet and wrote, "Unfit for flight training." I felt beaten. But I went to the hospital, and within two weeks they had taken care of both my tonsils and the curvature of my septum. After the operation, I went back to the enlistment office, but they told me nastily, "Eat all your *kasha*[2] and get ready for next year."

Kasha is *kasha,* but you have to earn money to get it, and where can a seventeen-and-a-half-year-old find work? I went to one factory after another. "Too young," they would say. "You're not eighteen." Mama talked me into applying to the polytechnical institute—she

---

[2] Russian porridge made from oats, wheat, or most any type of grain.

saw me as an engineer. On my first entrance exam, in mathematics, I got a B. But I decided not to come back. I didn't want to spend my life staring at electronic schematic diagrams. The sky—the heights—were beckoning!

I went to the *raion*[3] committee of the *Komsomol* and asked them to give me a job in a factory. I was sent to the Novocherkassk Permanent Magnet Factory, where I was assigned to the department where they ground magnets. I remember my first day there very well. They showed me how to grind the most primitive of magnets, and I struggled with it the entire shift. As I was preparing to leave, a beautiful young woman walked up to me and said, "I am the secretary of the shop's *Komsomol* organization. And by the way, we pick up for ourselves around here—we don't have a maid." The girl's name was Inna, and, skipping ahead, I can say that, after four years of courting, she became my wife.

Soon, I was to understand another part of the calculus of the "period of stagnation."[4] It did not profit a man to work too hard: as soon as one's production rose, the norm-setter would come by and slash the piece-rate. The head of my work brigade, Zhenya Barskov, was a straightforward fellow who could work miracles on the job. He built a "night machine" that enabled him to grind ten to fifteen magnets simultaneously with a great degree of precision. But the brigade could use it only on the night shift, when the management wouldn't be around to see it. We would build up a great surplus, and then goof off on the day shift. I signed up with my work brigade immediately and passed the qualifying exams for my position, but I never stopped dreaming, and as summer approached, I again prepared to enroll in the Kachinskoye Aviation School. This time they rejected me because I was two centimeters too tall, but they recommended that I try the Fighter Pilot Training Institute in Armavir.

[3] The rough equivalent of an American county.

[4] The Brezhnev era is sometimes referred to as the period of stagnation.

I was so sure I'd get in that I ignored the shop foreman's advice and immediately submitted my letter of resignation to the factory. I went in for my medical exams, and again it was the ear, nose, and throat doctor who stopped me. This time, she found a darkening of my maxillary sinus and an enlargement of my nasal cavities. They treated me for a long time and cauterized my nasal cavities. Then they decided my antritis required a further operation.

> **"W**hen I told the medical examiner I wanted to parachute, she tapped at two big letters on an eye chart. 'Can you see them? Good. Go jump.'**"**

So my application was stalled. Inna thought I should return to the factory. But my pride wouldn't let me. Instead, I spent a year unloading grocery trucks before I could again face the medical commission. I went to Bataisk to see another panel of doctors. The surgeon started carping about my clavicle, and washed me out. I trembled with rage and exploded with shouts of frustration until the head of the medical commission waved his hand and said, "Go to Armavir. Let them decide what to do with you."

I arrived at the Armavir School on May 10, 1960, and found the gray-haired colonel in charge of medical services at the institute. I explained my situation. He was friendly, and invited in the surgeon. The surgeon asked me to do pushups. He noted that my clavicle had knitted in an ugly fashion, but was otherwise fine. The colonel cleared me to proceed with the rest of the required exam.

I began with the ear, nose, and throat doctor, thinking "If I get through this, I won't be afraid of the devil himself." But the doctor immediately detected evidence of several operations, and people who had two or more operations were automatically "Unfit for flight training." Again, I was beside myself, and went back to the head of medical services, who just shrugged his shoulders and said, "There's nothing I can do. It's an order from the minister of defense."

I left the institute in a blind rage. I walked through Armavir, hungry and angry, not knowing what I would do. I had to hitchhike back to Rostov.

They treated me sympathetically back at the registration and enlistment office. The major who had sent me to the institute calmed me down by saying, "Well, why do you have to go to aviation school? If you want to be an officer, we'll find someplace just as good!"

I leafed through their catalogue. I was too tall for a tank. Submarine duty didn't interest me, and neither did the artillery. Finally, somewhere toward the end, my glance fell upon the Lenin Komsomol Double Red Banner Ryazan Higher Airborne Command School, with the ungainly Russian acronym RVVDKDKU. I decided to take a chance. Although I wouldn't be in the pilot's seat, I'd still be in the sky. I went home and told my father.

"Well, son, if that's what you've decided, you should try it. But do you know what you're getting into?"

"I confess, only vaguely."

"It wouldn't be a bad idea to try it out first."

And so I did. When Father spoke, we jumped. I traveled to a little community on the Don River, sixteen kilometers from Novocherkassk, where there was an aeronautics club. I found some guys standing around the airfield.

I said, "How do you get to make parachute jumps around here?"

At first, they laughed. Then they took pity on me and pointed out the instructor. "There's Viktor Sergeevich. You need to talk him into it."

The large-framed instructor looked rough. He greeted me rudely: "What did you come crawling over here for? You wanna jump? Get out of here. Guys like you are always coming around."

I went back to my new acquaintances, who were now convulsed with laughter.

"Run and get some vodka," one of them advised me, "and everything will be all right. Three bottles should do it."

I brought back four—you could get them for kopecks then. The instructor rolled his head and said, "OK, go learn how to pack a parachute." In one day they taught me everything. I packed a parachute, went through the prejump training, and passed my medical exams.

In packing the chutes, the instructor would show us a step, then we would repeat it. The instructor's chute turned out beautifully. The others were fairly close. But mine had four strange tails. I asked my neighbors what I'd done wrong, but they had no idea. I didn't ask the instructor because "ass," "moron," and "cretin" were the nicest words in his vocabulary. I folded the tails accordion-style and closed up the pack. I found out later that I had intuitively done the right thing. It turned out the others were all packing parachute model D-1-8, while I was packing a PD-47 (Parachute-lander, 1947 model, square form, with tails for guidance).

A Pronichev training apparatus—a ten-meter-high tower with counterweights—was part of the training. You'd saddle your equipment, jump, fall about three meters, and then hang five or six meters off the ground. The instructor would command: "Turn right!" "Turn left!" "Parachutist! To the left, to the right, back!" But whose left, whose right? The trainees on the ground would laugh, and the instructor would bark, "You're an ass! Get down!" The assistant would release the lever, you'd hit the ground, and then try to make a dashing jump to your feet before he pulled you back up and dropped you again. Everyone got to laugh at everyone else, because inevitably we stubbornly repeated each other's mistakes.

I went alone to the medical commission; the others had passed it already. I was cautious and tense when I opened the door of the medical station. A young woman was sitting there reading a book. I coughed. Only then did she raise her head. When I explained what I wanted, she took a pointer and tapped at two big letters on an eye exam chart. "Can you see them?" she asked.

"Yes, I see them clearly!"

"That's it. Go jump!" she said, filling out my admittance papers.

I had theater tickets for the following evening, but warned Inna that I would be jumping in the morning. I stayed at the barracks that night but was anxious and couldn't sleep. Many of us stayed up until 2:30 AM, talking. Night was giving way to dawn when we arrived at the airport, where an Antonov-2 biplane stood ready for takeoff. On the field we saw our instructor and several other people. The air traffic controllers were arguing about the weather. According to procedure, if wind gusts arose, parachute jumping was forbidden. There had been some gusts overnight, but they had disappeared. We listened to our instructors arguing. They finally decided it was all right to jump. My feelings when I heard the words, "Fifth plane, cleared for takeoff," were indescribable. I was jumping into the abyss, the unknown, the future! In my mind, I already saw myself as a cadet at the Ryazan School, jumping behind enemy lines.

"Go!" I stepped, awkwardly, into the abyss. My headlong fall jumbled earth-sky-plane—then a bump, and I was bouncing from the shroud lines of a square chute, which looked like a giant handkerchief. I saw the other four in my group descending under round parachutes, and the feeling was remarkable. But about 125 meters off the ground, I was swept away in a gust. I remembered only one thing from pre-jump training: "Hold your legs along the angle of the drift." I held them in what seemed to be the correct fashion. "Experienced" jumper that I was, I didn't change position when the gust died. So I landed on my tailbone. Following Murphy's Law, I fell onto a hard-packed field road.

Colorful spheres and circles flitted before my eyes. The white parachute collapsed in front of me. I heard no wind, no sound, nothing. My ears rang with silence. As I sat on the road, with a wild pain in my tailbone, none of my comrades came running to me. They took their time, apparently thinking that I was just crazed with happiness after the jump. I tried my arms. They moved. I struggled to my feet and rejoiced. People with broken backs can't stand. I started gathering my parachute. The pain was intense, and the circles and spheres returned. I finally managed to hoist the parachute and shuffle about five hundred meters to a pack table and a doctor. It was the same woman who had waved me through the medical examination so cavalierly. She pronounced her diagnosis: "It's clear. He landed on his fifth vertebra. Get him to a hospital."

I was lifted into an old GAZ-51 truck. I stood in the truck bed, resting my hands on the cab for support. We had ridden to the jump site over the very same road. It seemed so smooth then. Now it seemed like some sort of crazy washboard.

The rest of it would have been funny if it hadn't been so painful. I was dropped off at the air club, where they called the ambulance, saying in the heat of the moment that a parachutist had crashed. The pain was overwhelming me. My ears were ringing, and my head was spinning. When the life-support ambulance arrived, I was leaning against a fence, not fully understanding what was going on. The ambulance doctor asked where the seriously injured parachutist was. When they pointed to me, leaning up against a fence, the doctor let loose a torrent of swear words. This damned oaf needed life support? He threw me rudely onto a stretcher and into the ambulance. At the October Settlement Hospital in Novocherkassk, they discovered that not only was my coccyx broken in three places, but I had severed tendons in my left arm.

I was in pain and weary from not having slept in twenty-four hours. The hospital bed with its thick mattress was a deliverance. But they quickly took the mattress away and replaced it with a felt-covered board. I howled.

"You have a fracture," they told me. "Don't even think about getting up, or it might go badly for you." I collapsed in exhaustion. When I opened my eyes the next morning, I realized my parents probably didn't know where I was. I raised myself, put on some pajamas, and hobbled into the corridor, looking for a telephone. The orderlies caught me, stripped my pajamas, and put me back on the board. They warned my neighbors, "Anyone who gives him pajamas will be confined to the ward." As it was a warm, sunny spring, no one wanted to be trapped inside.

My immediate neighbor was an old man who had cut his hand on a table saw. I convinced him to call my parents. When my mother arrived, she was too scared to speak. It turned out that the conversation between the old man and my mother had gone something like this:

"Ekaterina Grigorievna?"

"Yes."

"Do you have a son?"

"Yes."

"Did he go sky jumping?"

"Yes."

"Well, he crashed." A long silence. Then: "Don't worry. He's still alive." And he hung up.

That "he's still alive" part showed a real knack for words—and for hanging up the phone—leaving my mother to imagine a rickety bag of bones might live... a day? an hour? I wanted to pound a lesson into the old man, but instead, we two invalids had a fierce argument.

When I was finally released from the hospital, I discovered I had to learn to walk all over again. My normal gait had become a pigeon-toed shuffle.

At the military reception center, all the applicants for the military school were received coldly. They warned us immediately: "Tomorrow you'll go before the medical commission, and after that, we'll talk with those who are pronounced fit."

Well, I thought, here we go again. I've no sooner gotten here than I'll have to turn around and go back.

All the same, I decided to fight it out to the end.

The next morning, I began with the surgeon. A young second lieutenant was sitting in the surgeon's office, looking as though he didn't give a damn about any of us. He ordered ten of us to take off our shorts.

"Anybody here got a hernia?"

No one did, so he pronounced us fit for duty. Imagine my joy when, after three years, I was finally pronounced: "Healthy. Fit for service."

But my celebrations were cut short. Like a bucket of cold water, the words hit me, "Now you need to pass your exams."

> **"I** *brought my fist down on his jaw. His teeth rattling, he slid until his head collided with a door.* **"**

There was reason to be afraid. I hadn't cracked a book in the past two years. Various worldly-wise elders had told me, "The important thing is to get past the medical commission. After that, even if you're dumb, they'll take you." Now I faced a battery of examinations with roughly six candidates competing for every slot.

My first exam was in mathematics. I got a D,[5] although that poor performance wasn't really my fault. The reception center was busy as an anthill: everyone running around, fussing, making crib sheets, looking for people from their hometowns—preferably smart ones. I found a guy from somewhere in the Kuban. Although it might have been far away on the map, he was still like a neighbor to me. He was strong, happy-go-lucky, perhaps a bit too talkative, but everyone has his faults. He was stuck on the idea that he was a pure-blooded Kuban Cossack, and the Don and Kuban Cossacks were brothers, and all that. I'm not sure how he decided that I was the smart one, but he kept buzzing around trying to convince me that I should display my brotherly feelings during the exams. Finally I gave up and said, "All right. Sit in front of me. We'll work something out." At first, everything went according to plan. He sat immediately in front of me. They gave us all two sheets of paper, with the stamp: "Education Department" in

---

[5] Literally, a "two." Russian tests are graded from five to one instead of A to F. One and two are both failing grades (unlike an American "D"), but one is almost never given.

one corner. The assignment turned out to be in two parts—two models, and one problem in geometry with trigonometric applications. I'm not quite sure how, but I solved the two models almost instantaneously, and the geometric part of the problem seemed to solve itself, but then I got stuck. I remembered that there was a formula you needed to apply to get the answer in this type of problem, but I'd forgotten what it was. I looked around, and everybody had their noses buried in their tests, breathing heavily, straining, not wanting to ask anybody, much less copy someone else's answer. I had the feeling that I was just about to remember it, just a little bit more and it would come back to me. Then the fellow from the Kuban popped up and said, "Well, how are you doing?"

"I've got the two models and half of the problem. I'll get the rest of it in a second."

"Let me see what you've got."

"Here."

I pushed the sheet with the answers to the front of the table. He whipped it off, tore his second sheet of paper into strips, copied my models onto the strips, jauntily rolled them into balls and threw them right and left, to his buddies. I took my sheet back, but the formula was still elusive. My second sheet began to irritate me, and I pushed it to the edge of the table. The guy from the Kuban had finished writing, and, with a satisfied grunt, sat up and relaxed. The proctor of the exam, Mathematics Department Chairman Ivan Ivanovich Kuzin, walked toward him.

"Are you finished?"

"Yes!"

"Hand it in."

"Here you are."

"And where's your second sheet?"

Something distracted Ivan Ivanovich for a moment, and in one quick motion, the guy from the Kuban grabbed the sheet from the edge of my table.

"Here it is."

It all happened so quickly that I didn't understand what this would certainly mean. After torturing myself for another ten minutes, I decided that I wasn't going to remember the formula. I wrote out its approximation in words, what was needed in the equation, and what the answer should be. At the same moment, two rows ahead of me, a small scandal erupted. Ivan Ivanovich had found a young man using a crib sheet stamped "Education Department." Ivan Ivanovich took the sheet away from the young man, and showed him the door. I was captured between a sense of doom and disbelief. Ivan Ivanovich turned his glasses on me.

"Are you finished?"

"I'm finished."

"Hand it in."

I held out my one sheet.

"So it was yours." He put the sheet on the table, and with a thick red pencil wrote a D about eight centimeters high.

"If you please," he smiled, making a friendly gesture toward the door.

It would have been useless to plead that I was innocent, because I wasn't. I was choked with cold fury. I went silently to the door, and as it happened, the first person I saw on the other side was the guy from the Kuban. He was so happy, rubbing his hands together, telling someone a story. He turned to me, and fear flashed in his eyes. I brought my fist down on his jaw, putting into that punch all my overflowing emotions. His teeth rattling, he slid several meters until he was stopped by his head colliding with a door. I walked to the exit without a word.

I went back to the barracks and packed my suitcase before I was halted by a wild thought: "Let them kick me out officially." I had no basis for hope. That big, red D had been written right in front of me. I had been shown the door, and then I had laid out my partner in crime with a nasty blow. What hope could I have? Still, let them kick me out.

The next day at the reception center, they read off the list of people who had gotten a D. It was a long list that cut the crowd nearly in half. My name wasn't on it! I didn't believe my ears. I wanted to check, but I stopped myself. I was afraid they would answer, "Sorry, friend, I skipped your name. You're on the list." If they didn't read my name, that meant I should go study for physics.

I was ecstatic. I knew the D was there, but it didn't matter. I knew there were plenty of witnesses to my knockout the day before, but they must have thought I had a good reason, and kept quiet. And the guy from the Kuban had disappeared. The physics studying was coming along wonderfully. In fact, I had the impression that I knew the whole textbook, cover to cover.

The day of the exam came. This exam was proctored by the Physics Department chair, Igor Ivanovich Perrimond. Igor Ivanovich was famous for ranting about how all physics textbook authors were incompetent. The true nature of physics could be comprehended only through the textbook that he, Igor Ivanovich, was just finishing.

I selected quite an exam in physics[6]—the resolution of forces along a parallelogram, Faraday's second law, and a problem. The problem I solved immediately, and I also sketched out parallelograms loaded with all the various vectors around them, but Faraday's second law escaped me. I remembered it had the letters "a," "v," and "o" in it, and that it contained a fraction, but what did it all mean? That, I couldn't remember. I turned the page over and began to write out the letters, enumerating all the possible alternatives. I chose a moment when Igor Ivanovich was busy with one of his poor victims, and maneuvered to be examined by his assistant, Klavdia Ivanovna. She quickly determined that I had gotten the right answer to the problem, although by some method previously unknown to science. We came to Faraday's second law, and I turned the page over. She saw

---

[6] Tests in Russia are often given orally, with the students asked to draw a card with a topic. They are given a few minutes before being examined by the professor.

my copious notes and asked, for some reason in a whisper, "What on earth is that?" To maintain the conspiracy, I also whispered, "Faraday's second law, as I understand it."

"Oh, get out of here," she said, using her full voice now.

I left depressed, thinking that I had gotten another D, but this time for impudence.

At the next day's gathering, the "blacklist" was read again, and another third were "washed out." But I survived.

I didn't bother preparing for the upcoming composition. My high school teacher in Russian language and literature, Lyudmila Ivanovna, was a World War II veteran and the widow of an officer. She was a very strict and demanding person. Tall, skinny, primly dressed, she was absolutely merciless. Her demanding nature, which admitted no compromise, had so thoroughly beaten Russian grammar into me, that to this day if I ever see a document with a comma missing, I immediately add it. She was a remarkable teacher, but we understood that only later, when we were out in the real world. At the time, we used to make fun of her behind her back.

I got an A in composition. That meant I had nine points on three exams, which averaged out to a C. Again I wondered why I had survived when others had been washed out for far less.

The oral examination in mathematics was next. In school, I had always loved logarithms, both simple and decimal logarithms. I don't know why—I just did. I lazily leafed through my beloved logarithmic tables, and then went off to the exam thinking "Come what may." And what came? When I saw Ivan Ivanovich and looked at my ticket, it was a miracle. The whole exam was on logarithms. I was prepared to answer the questions at once, without making any notes. Here I made a crude tactical blunder. I should have put on a studious face, waited my turn, modestly collected my A, and left. Instead, I went up to answer without preparing, and what the panel of professors (there were three of them) must have thought I can only guess. They listened to my brilliant logarithmic computations rather absent-mindedly, and then began to ask me extra questions that had nothing to do with logarithms. Inspired, I managed to remember all sorts of things, even if I didn't express them very clearly. The result? I got a B.

When I went before the credentials committee, I discovered that Klavdia Ivanovna had given me a C after all. Then Ivan Ivanovich took the floor. He told the committee that I had been caught throwing crib sheets to other students. That was the first time he remembered this happening in all his years as an instructor. But since the answers were all correct, he recommended that I be enrolled at the institute on probation. The committee looked through my personnel file. I had worked for two years, and I had helped my comrades, although in a questionable manner. The credentials committee's decision was: "Admit him on probation."

CHAPTER 2:
UNDER A CADET'S PARACHUTE

MY FIRST REACTION to the credentials committee's decision was shock. I wandered around campus like a drunk, numb from happiness. At the barracks I took a sheet of paper and wrote an excited letter home.

But we cadets weren't allowed to remain euphoric for long. As summer ended we were put on alert, dressed in full kit, and walked five-and-a-half kilometers from the school to a pier on the Oka River. There we boarded a decrepit ferryboat, number 13. It took three hours, floating past fields and villages, before we disembarked in a desolate, low-lying area facing the village of Kuzminskoe across the river. We looked around—the place was deserted. We were still five kilometers from camp. For an experienced soldier, this is nothing, but many of us were wearing boots for the first time. None of us knew how to roll foot wrappings, and our feet were rubbed raw. Our column was a pathetic sight to behold—dragging our feet and gasping for breath.

The school's camp was small and located in a beautiful pine forest. Officers lived in one-story cottages, other full-time personnel lived in barracks, and we cadets slept in tents and were proud of it. Moving to the barracks was considered bad manners. The tents introduced a certain element of romanticism into our lives.

The next morning, despite our blistered feet and far-from-military mood, everyone had to get up, and training started. The training was tough, even cruel, but there was no hazing from the two companies of third-year cadets. They may have looked down on us plebes, but they didn't harass us.

The first one-and-a-half or two months were hard, sometimes very hard, but I still believe that this is the most important period in building the character of a young recruit. Either he overcomes himself and becomes a soldier, or he lags behind and is a misfit.

My company was under the command of Senior Lieutenant Nikolai Vasilievich Pletnev. He was the paragon of an exemplary officer.

Neat and elegant, he could walk up to the horizontal bar, wearing a tunic or even a greatcoat, and calmly perform the sequence of exercises required to pass the military's first-class fitness requirements. That was a challenge for us: eight sets of pull-overs, five sets of one- and two-hand kips, and eleven sets of legs up to the bar. Even wearing only boxers, we were panting and couldn't do it. Pletnev would look at our spasmodic attempts and show us all over again. Then, after getting off the bar, he would say, "Anyone who can repeat it after me will get a furlough." Since the cadets were not allowed to have furloughs, he was obviously sure that none of us could do it.

Pletnev was an excellent runner at any distance. We tagged behind him, struggling to keep up. In the evenings, we staggered to our tents and slept like dead men. I clearly remember our first attempt at the one kilometer forest trail in our heavy boots. The company's two best runners got a C rating; the rest of us got Ds. About fifteen cadets didn't even make it to the finish line. The trail was covered with sand, so our feet kept skidding.

Pletnev told us exactly what he thought of us. He used obscenities only rarely, but he was a forceful speaker whose unrehearsed eloquence was devastating. He was the kind of commander who lived by the rule "Do as I do," and as a consequence, inspired loyalty and respect.

By the end of September we had finished with classroom instruction in parachuting. The company commander announced that now it was time to move from "theory" to "practice." We were awakened early in the morning and put on alert.

The company was ordered to the landing field, where parachutes would be distributed. On the way we did combat drills, maintaining formation and repelling imaginary enemy attacks. The landing field was three kilometers away, but our route made it twice as far.

The first jump was without any weapons, so we checked them with a guard. I put on a D-1-8

> **"N**one of us knew how to roll foot wrappings, so our feet were rubbed raw. Gasping for breath, our column of cadets was indeed a pathetic sight.**"**

parachute, commonly called an "Oak," because it is bulky and heavy: the main chute alone is sixteen kilos; the reserve chute adds another seven kilograms.

A squadron of Antonov-2 biplanes was ready for takeoff. Nine paratroopers and one releasing officer boarded each airplane. I wasn't thinking about the jump. I had no doubt the chute would open—the D-1-8 was a reliable parachute—but there was no way to steer it. You had to land wherever it carried you. The only thought I had in my head was "How am I going to land?" Given my previous rough landing, I expected the worst.

Still, calmly, almost automatically, I pushed off with my left foot and jumped into the chill autumn dawn. This time, I lucked out. I landed in a soft, slightly bumpy, dried-out swamp. My fear of a hard landing vanished forever.

For a month and a half, until the middle of October, we ran in cross-country races and practiced demarches, in addition to our normal physical training. A trip to the bathhouse was like taking three baths. We would run there and back, taking a sweat bath each way.

What I remember most vividly from that period is the ever-present feeling of hunger. Seventeen cadets from our company filed formal requests to resign, and were washed out. Anyone who stayed on developed the hide and heels of a rhino. It was natural selection: all those who were looking for the easy romanticism of the officer's life dropped out, and the rest drew closer together. In a month and a half, we became different people, ready for any challenge.

We had to face our first challenge as early as October, thanks to a malefactor in the third-year class. A Makarov pistol had disappeared during target practice. For a whole day, the entire battalion searched for the lost weapon, combing the forest kilometer by kilometer. The pistol was finally found in the camp. Someone had gotten scared and ditched it in a trash can in the smoking room. As punishment, the battalion commander, Lieutenant Colonel Aleksei Stepanovich Karpov, ordered the entire third-year class to dress in full combat gear and make a fast demarche of about seventy kilometers. The first-year cadets stood there, goggle-eyed. The battalion commander pondered a bit, and then added that the first-year class would go along so that we would never be tempted to make a similar mistake and steal a firearm.

The battalion commander also ordered that part of the run would be done in a gas-mask and protective coveralls to train us for overcoming "contamination zones." If the third-year class was familiar with the routine, for freshmen, the challenge was close to impossible. Within twenty-four hours we covered seventy kilometers and finished near Ryazan. We were unable to run the last three kilometers, so we walked in threes—two persons on the flanks supported one in the middle. I remember how I entered the school campus proudly carrying two machine guns and a bazooka.

After completing the autumn physical training course, we found ourselves in a completely different world. We sat in warm classrooms attending lectures, turning from forced marches to math and physics textbooks. The calm, however, was only relative. As soon as the first snow fell, we started cross-country ski training. According to the academic plan, the company spent an average of two to three weeks once every two months in a training center. Just as Czar Nicholas I once drew a straight line to show where the first railroad from St. Petersburg to Moscow should be built, Pletnev took a ruler and traced the route the company would follow on the map. On each leg of the route, a different cadet would assume command. He was given a map, a compass, and sole authority. Nobody was allowed to help him—that was the ground rule. If he strayed from the prescribed route, the company would pick up some extra kilometers, and the unfortunate "commander" would feel the "warm" and "caring" looks of his subordinates on his back. That was how they cultivated a sense of responsibility in us.

At the end of my plebe year, we had a visit from the commander of the Airborne Troops, General Vassili Filippovich Margelov. He was the founder of the Airborne Troops, a hero of the Soviet Union, and a veteran of the Finnish War and World War II. He was an eagle of a man, who lived by the principle "There are no impossible missions." He made it the motto of the Airborne troops. For us, his visit was like the second coming of Christ. The sixty-year-old general entered the gym, and our platoon commander, Lieutenant Gerlein, reported: "Comrade Commander, cadets of the third platoon of the first company are conducting a physical training session." The cadets stood, dumbstruck, beholding the descent of their God to earth.

The commander gave us a fatherly look and said quietly:

"Plebes! What are you good at, sons? Can you handle the vault?"

Actually, the vaulting horse was a weak point. A good half of us were struggling with it, but we shouted, "Yes, sir!" in unison. The vaulting horse was set up and our three best athletes flew over it. I was the fourth, but before I could jump, Margelov asked, "How about a somersault? Can you do it?" We had never tried it before, but the answer was just the same: "Yes, sir!"

The horse was positioned crosswise, and a springboard was placed in front of it. I stepped back, and two cadets took off and did somersaults. Then my turn came. I remember that I completed one somersault and went for the second rotation, but the floor got in the way.

The blow was so strong that I passed out with a concussion. I came to in the hospital.

During the second year, Pletnev left us. He was promoted to captain and sent off to the regular troops. Captain Anatoly Ivanovich Ilyin replaced him, but not for long. He knew English fairly well and was soon appointed commander of the 9th Company of the Special Forces. Ilyin was replaced by Captain V. M. Zaitsev, who is worthy of special mention. Zaitsev used to be a reporter for the Military District paper. He was writing an "epic" novel about the airborne troops and asked the commander for an opportunity to command a company in order "to see things through the eyes of his characters." They gave him a company in the 105th Airborne Division, stationed in Fergana. Within two or three months he had failed everything he could. Then someone had the bright idea that he should be "promoted" to command a cadet company. They apparently assumed he would do less harm there. He was only thirty years old, but was already as bald as a cue ball. He was also an extremely inept administrator. He reminded me of a character from one of Saltykov-Shchedrin's satirical novels. He tormented our company for eight months. By then I was already a deputy platoon commander and a sergeant first class. Despite my experience and good discipline, I "earned" a total of twenty-three days of arrest from Zaitsev, but I didn't serve a single day. Zaitsev knew that he could punish cadets, but nobody had to do any time, because the company commander didn't have the strength of will to carry out his threats.

You could get a day under arrest for nothing at all! Once I came to the school office and started my verbal report about the day's classes.

Zaitsev interrupted me: "What were you doing hanging around the checkpoint yesterday?"

Dumbfounded, I replied: "My mom came to visit me."

"And who gave you permission to leave?"

"Nobody! I never left the perimeter."

"So you're talking back now, huh?"

"If you think that's talking back, then okay, I'm talking back!"

"Fine! Five days under arrest."

Zaitsev never did finish his book, and he was ultimately relieved of his command. God knows where he wound up, but I'm thankful I had the chance to experience a perfect example of a bad officer. The contrast between him and Pletnev was especially striking.

Gennady Ivanovich Fedorov, our English teacher, was another character, a short bow-legged guy with a nasty temper. During class, he would not say a single word in Russian. You could easily score five to seven Ds within forty-five minutes. That could result in the cancellation of all leaves and vacations, and extra brainwashing at Komsomol

> **I** *was the first in my class to get married, and though many years have passed, time has not blunted my feelings for my wife.*

and Party meetings. It was like a punishment from God, and we had to deal with it. We started looking for his weaknesses and found three: boxing, chess, and collecting pins with city names.

I was quite good at boxing. I remember one fight in my second year. In the second round, I knocked my opponent through the ropes and sent him toppling into the screaming fans. A heavyweight, I got to the semifinals of the school boxing championship. Gennady Ivanovich Fedorov sat in the first row and cheered passionately.

The next day, Saturday, English was my first class. As usual, Fedorov ran into the classroom and, after listening to someone give an oral report, announced a pop quiz. Naturally, I was unprepared. I honestly admitted it to Fedorov. Out of respect for me, he said in Russian: "Write down what I say!"

"I won't write it. I'm not ready!"

"Write!"

"Yes, sir!"

I took a sheet of paper, signed it "Sergeant First Class Lebed," and turned in a blank page.

When I got it back, it was filled out with calculations: "Today's dictation—an F. Yesterday's fight—an A. An A and a F would give you an average of a C minus; and that adjusted to the special co-efficient of double A would result in an A. Bravo!"

I also played chess fairly well. Fedorov would enter the class-room and find a chessboard "accidentally" left on the windowsill. He was unable to resist for longer than five minutes. He gave the platoon an assignment—read from here to here, translate from here to here—meanwhile ordering me in English: "Set up the board!" I could have beaten him easily, but my tactic was different: I would win the first game and throw the second one. Naturally, we'd have to play a tiebreaker. And that would usually take the rest of the class period. My platoon finally got a break.

The cadets also learned to exploit Fedorov's third passion: pins. Those who had given up hope of meeting his requirements in English directed all their energy to searching for the right kind of pins. Naturally, they failed the official exam, but on the oral make-up test, they would stuff their pockets, not with crib sheets, but with goodies to tempt him into giving higher marks. There was a certain trick to this. After introducing himself, the cadet would nonchalantly jiggle the pins in his pocket. Hearing the familiar sound, Fedorov would perk up: "What do you have there?"

"Just some pins."

"Come on, show them! Okay, what do we have? This is junk, this is also junk... oh, here is one—Pskov. That's an entirely different mat-ter! Is a C all right?"

The majority would be delighted with a C, but some of the brassier cadets would haggle! "Comrade Captain, I've aced every sub-ject but English. The company commander said that if I got a C, he wouldn't give me a furlough."

The plea would be accompanied by offering another handful of pins. Fedorov's eyes would dart, and he would wave his hand and say: "All right, I'll give you a B. Tell the company commander you can go on furlough."

I got married in the winter of my second year. Initially, I was going to wed in the summer, but due to financial difficulties, I had to postpone it for half a year. On February 20, 1971, I was married. All my high school classmates came to congratulate me. It was an exotic moment for them: I was the first one of our class to become a married man. Now my wife and I have three adult children, and though many years have passed, time has not blunted my feelings for her.

My twelve-day holiday flew by, and I had to return to school.

Nothing significant happened my second year, except that I got my only academic C. The second year final exam on firearm training was held at the army firing range in Seltsy. As a deputy platoon commander, I presented the platoon

"In the jump plane, greasy sausage and the smell of kerosene, anxiety, and inexperience took their toll. The puking contest began."

at the exam. The teacher, Lieutenant Colonel Filippov, sat the first four people down and declared: "Anyone who can present his topic without preparation will get a grade one notch higher." I loved firearm training and knew the subject well, so I decided to go ahead. I got an easy set of questions. I can remember them to this day. The first one was on the interaction of the parts and mechanisms of an automatic rifle during a single shot. The second one was on the design of a PG-7V recoilless gun, and the third one involved calculating the distance that a bullet shot horizontally from a machine gun would travel. The teacher gave me a minute to concentrate. I was ready to answer the first two questions right away, but I had to work on the third one. I started my presentation and got a B+ on the first question and an A on the second one. I handed in my work for the third problem. Lieutenant Colonel Filippov looked at it and said, "Wrong." I reviewed my answer. I was sure it was correct and pointed this out to him, but he advised me to think it over. It was time for the next cadet's turn. I saw a French curve lying on the table. I used it to draw the trajectory with multicolored pens and depicted a full height target. Basically, I did the same thing, it was just neater. I showed it to him and he said: "Now we are talking!" At that point I flipped out. For my tactless behavior, Filippov ordered me out and gave me a D. When the teachers, company commander, and platoon commander met to decide on final grades, they took into consideration my impressive delivery, but condemned my conduct. Their compromise? I got a C.

Lieutenant Colonel Filippov was a World War II veteran and had two serious combat wounds, so I hold no grudges. Soon after that exam he resigned.

My third year was stressful, but went smoothly. At the end of my third year, Zaitsev was replaced by Lieutenant Pavel Grachev, fresh from the Baltics, and a true professional. Grachev was a "Master of Sport" in cross-country skiing. He was neat, strict, and led by example. Our sporting nature and competitive spirit were renewed, and we left for our practical training in good spirits.

As part of our practical training, our company was sent to the 345th Airborne Regiment of the 105th Airborne Division located in Fergana. The purpose of the exercise was to immerse us in the hectic reality of army life. So we were sent to participate in regimental exercises. The regiment was supposed to be dropped in Kazakhstan near the village of Ush-Tabe. Our whole company joined that regiment, and the as cadet trainees we were assigned to various positions. I played the role of the battalion's deputy chief of staff. The battalion was under the command of Major V. A. Danilchenko. A sapper by training, he was abrasive, with eyes as sharp as his mocking tongue. He was a great teacher, but unfortunately none of his advice is printable.

In preparation for our exercise we had two training jumps. The first landing site made our eyes pop out. The surface was as hard as concrete, covered with gravel. Stones larger than a man's fist were piled up together.

"You use this as a landing site?"

"Yes, is that a problem?"

As it happens, we got used to it. We jumped off an Antonov-12 plane in two streams, in a frame pattern. In theory, jump in sequence. In practice, our rhythm collapsed and several of us felt our neighbor's boot on our faces.

The day before the exercise, Danilchenko brought a velvet banner with tassels and an embroidered profile of Lenin on it. He gave me the flag and explained my mission: "You'll fly it as soon as we take the high ground."

"Where is the flagpole? Am I supposed to fly it off my arm?"

"All right, wise guy," said the commander. "Go to the sapper company and get a mine probe to serve as a flagpole."

I got the probe, which had three sections, fifty centimeters each. I packed the flag in an empty gas-mask pouch. I had to stick the probe sections in my boots, since there was no other place for them. I took some extra bandages as well, thinking that, if I break my legs because of the damned probe, I could at least use them as splints.

They got us up before dawn. The entire regiment went on foot toward the airfield, where there were more than forty Antonov-12s waiting for us. On the plane, the releasing officer went from row to row, handing each of us a quarter-loaf of bread and a chunk of greasy sausage. Everyone was so hungry that all the food was finished at once. The company commander and two signalmen with portable two-way radios were sitting right in front of me. We had a two-and-a-half hour flight ahead of us.

The air in the cabin was stuffy and smelled like kerosene. According to the landing roster, two-thirds of the servicemen on the plane were new recruits and soon the "bouquet" of greasy sausage and kerosene, plus anxiety and inexperience took its toll. In about an hour the folks started fidgeting and calling the mechanic on board for a bucket. And the puking contest began. Invoking curses from heaven and hell, the mechanic brought a bucket. But it was tall and narrow, and the first, most "impatient" person to get his hands on the bucket missed the target. The kerosene vapors were enhanced by the acrid smell of vomit, causing a chain reaction. I had never in my life experienced nausea. Neither before that incident, nor after it, was I so close to disgracing myself. The mechanic realized the situation was out of hand and gave up trying to find more buckets. I sat looking at the pale green faces and bits of sausage on the floor. I prayed for the ramp to open so I could get out of there. For an hour and a half I was almost delirious, persuading myself to endure just a little bit longer. It was an incredible relief to leave that plane for the blue sky and fresh air.

On the ground, we discovered our mission had been changed. The high ground was nowhere in evidence. We were surrounded by a desert of sand and rock dotted by lonely bramble bushes. We were supposed to make a twenty-kilometer march under blistering heat. We had no more water in our canteens, but we knew that there were two wells along the way. We had special Pantacite water-purification tablets, which could make any water drinkable in twenty minutes.

When we got to the first well, our unit's doctor lowered a grappling hook and pulled out... a dead dog. He announced the water was not drinkable. So in stupefying and exhausting heat, we trudged seven more kilometers to the next well where we found... another dead dog instead of water.

We were all at our limit. When a water tank finally arrived, people rushed toward it, pushing each other. The water was spilling on the ground, but nobody could get any. It was necessary to pull everyone apart, before we could slake our thirst.

When we were back in Fergana, after our "walk" in the desert, the city seemed like a scene from an Oriental fairy tale. I remember Fergana as a noisy, hot, dusty, fun city. In its center was an Oriental bazaar with mountains of watermelons and sweets. Irrigation ditches flowed along the streets, donkeys stepped ceremonially, the people radiated tranquillity and contentment.

The most important lesson I learned in my training at Fergana was that if a man does something wrong, he should be punished strictly in accordance with regulations, but under no circumstances should a man's human dignity be assaulted. I also learned that an offi-

cer should never let his fists do the talking. If an officer can't moti-
vate his subordinates without beating them, he has no place in the
army. He should take off his epaulets and find another line of work.

I spent my fourth year working hard on my thesis. In addition to
the intense thesis work, we kept on jumping. I remember one day in
March, we flew over a landing site covered in snow. It was up to half
a meter deep, but melting under a spring thaw. My friend Yura
Lazarenko sat next to me. He looked out of the window and whistled.
"No way am I jumping into that!"

"So how will you get there?" I asked. "By submarine?"

Lazarenko cut his control cord from the KAP-3M safeguarding
device. He called for the releasing officer. "Look! My control cord's
loose. Is it too late to fix it?" he asked with feigned regret.

The releaser decided not to risk it and told him he wouldn't be
jumping. Lazarenko threw a dramatic fit, saying he was sure he could
fix it; he just had to jump with the rest of us. The releaser got mad,
yanked Lazarenko's parachute, and ordered him out of the pressur-
ized compartment. The "dejected" Lazarenko "grimly" retired, under
the envious gaze of his peers.

We landed, as expected, in knee-deep mush. My parachute was
immediately soaked and impossible to lift. A good half of us fell on
landing and had to walk, drenched from head to toe, about three
to five kilometers. I remember one cadet waving to the rest: "Come
over here where it's shallow—just up to the waist." We floundered
in ice-cold water all day, but no one got sick.

Under Grachev's command in our fourth year, we became so
strong that we were the only team in the school Spartakiad tourna-
ment to compete on equal terms with the 9th Company of Special
Forces. A few words about this company. In 1969 the Ryazan Airborne
School created an additional company for training platoon commanders for Special Forces. The process of was extremely rigorous. These
guys were the elite of the elite. The Spartakiads were tough. I remember the school's assistant director, Colonel Rodionov, always wore
thin black gloves because of his nervous eczema. We called him the

"Black Colonel." His views were clear-cut: "I do not believe in a technical loss. If you consider yourself a paratrooper, you must fight no matter whom you are dealing with—a master or a candidate master. If you don't have the backbone, don't bother to show up." And so we fought. Quite often, our will to win worked miracles. One picture that hung on the wall of the gym showed the finals of the school's heavyweight boxing—the fight is over and the referee is standing between two mighty boxers, holding each by the hand, waiting for the announcement of the winner. Both of them have their eyes closed and their heads hanging to the side. Even from the black-and-white picture, you can see their faces are most thoroughly smashed. The picture has an inscription under it: "This is how victory is achieved."

At the end of May, the entire school left for the training center. The departure, as always, was timed for the opening of the summer Spartakiad. It was just like a mini-Olympics: track-and-field competitions and team sports were the main events. The Spartakiad was organized in such a way that each company had to be represented by as many participants as possible. There was no chance for a few of the strongest athletes to lead the entire company to victory. The Spartakiad determined which units were really the strongest.

The finish of my academic marathon was much better than the start. I aced all my final exams, including firearms training. For my thesis, I designed a T-shaped depot for long-term storage of tanks, armored vehicles, and automobiles, and successfully defended it to the examiner. At the end of the year, it was decided that the two best graduates would stay in school to serve as platoon commanders. Initially the candidates were a master sergeant of the 1st Company, V. Poptsov, and a deputy platoon commander of the 1st company, I. Pankov. Grachev also asked me to stay, but I refused and got assigned to the 7th Airborne Division, stationed in Kaunas.

During the state exam in "scientific communism," Poptsov got in an argument with the evaluation board and got a D. That was a major mishap. After lengthy negotiations and a lot of noise and fuss, the board was swayed and replaced the D with a C. But the Chief Political

Officer, N. M. Kivaev, was categorically against keeping the trouble-maker in school.

Then, without any consultations, two days before graduation, they switched us around. When the director of the personnel section, Major Snegov, handed me the assignment, I was dumbfounded. I rushed to the company commander and, after that, to the battalion commander, Lieutenant Colonel V. I. Stepanov. They just threw up their hands: "What can we do? Who knew that Poptsov would fall through? It's too late to change anything." So I gave in.

Graduation was rather unusual. A film was being made about the school, and the director wanted to film our graduation.

Graduation was July 29, 1973—and it rained, developing into heavy thundershowers. Wearing our dress uniforms, we lined up on the parade ground. Because the film crew needed to shoot scenes several times, we had to stand an extra long time in the downpour and pass the reviewing stand five times. We were soaked, and our boots turned the parade ground into a giant mud pie.

CHAPTER 3: INSPECTION

MY LIFE AS AN OFFICER began on August 30, 1973, when I arrived in my new—I mean old—service location, Ryazan Airborne School. The first person I saw there was my company commander, Senior Lieutenant Grachev. When he saw me, he said:

"You're here! Great! You'll be serving as a platoon commander under me."

"I need to report to the battalion commander," I pointed out.

"Go ahead and report, but it's already a done deal. Report to the commander that I am taking you to lead a platoon."

Indeed, when I reported to Lieutenant Colonel Stepanov, he approved Grachev's decision and ordered: "At 1500 today we'll take two cars to the training center."

Stepanov became a battalion commander in my third year. He was big, sarcastic, strict, and versatile, and had exceptional control over the battalion. His authority was uncontested.

He had an iron will. In 1972, fulfilling the regular officer fitness requirements, he overstressed his heart. He was encouraged to resign and become a reservist, but he categorically refused, whatever the risk to his health. His courage made us respect him even more.

At 1500 we started off from the school's checkpoint. We used two compact Ladas. Stepanov, Grachev, and the commander of the 2nd Company, Tarlykov, were in the first car. I was in the second, together with the commander of the 4th Company, Captain A. S. Chernushich, and the commander of the 3rd Company, Senior Lieutenant V. A. Bobylev.

Since the rain had been pouring for the past few days, we chose the road passing Kriusha, which was once described by the poet Yesenin. The paved stretch was easy, but the broken dirt road that took over was pockmarked with craters full of water, typical for Ryazan. Instead of getting a ride, we had to give the car a ride, putting branches under the wheels and pushing the cars. It took us more than two hours to get through the most difficult three-kilometer stretch. When the road finally improved everyone was covered with dirt. The battalion commander assessed the situation and announced a rest.

> **"I**t turned out those four sleepless night had been a test of my endurance. "You're as strong as a moose," said my commander.**"**

I had two bottles of vodka with me, which I presented to my exhausted comrades. We started drinking, and Bobylev took out a first-rate Sauer shotgun, which he passed around. While Tarlykov held the gun, a large bird jumped on the road. He took aim and winged it. The bird dashed into the woods and all of us, including a lieutenant colonel with twenty-two years of service, gave chase, leaving two cars, a shotgun with ammo, and other army gear abandoned in the middle of the road.

The forest brush was remarkably thick, and darkness was setting in. We returned to the road empty handed, but covered with cobwebs and pine needles. We drank another bottle of vodka, packed up, and went on. Riding in the car, I dozed off. Suddenly, I heard shouting. I saw Vladimir Stepanov illuminated by the car's headlights, standing on a wooden bridge over a stream. The bridge was swinging and bending, as though ready soon to collapse. Strong rainfall had substantially washed out its supporting structure. What could we do? Stepanov got back in the car and shouted, "Follow me!" He backed the car fifteen or twenty meters, accelerated, and flew over the bridge. Chernushich did not have anything else to do but follow his example. After that, I dozed off again and woke up when the car was parked in front of the hotel at the camp.

I got out having only one thing on my mind—to get some sleep. Tomorrow promised to be exciting—I was going to be presented to my company.

The hotel building was new and still smelled of paint. Three of us shared a hotel room: Grachev, myself, and another platoon commander from our company, Vladimir Ivanovich Krotik. Right after we checked in, Grachev sent me to find a guy named Ivan Fedorovich Perepelitsa. Half-asleep, I forgot to ask where he was before I left our room.

Hoping to get lucky, I pushed the first door I came across and saw a captain who was asleep and dressed in jogging pants, shirt, and tie. I picked him up by the tie: "Are you Perepelitsa?"

Absurdly, the sleeping man opened his eyes and said, "Yes, I am. And who are you?"

I reported: "Commander of the third platoon of the first company, Lieutenant Lebed. Grachev's asking for you."

Ivan Perepelitsa returned with me to our room. He, Grachev, and Krotik settled down to play a card game called "snoring." I confessed I didn't know how to play, but Krotik exclaimed, "Nonsense. We'll teach you right now."

We started playing and got carried away. By 0545 I owed eighteen rubles to Grachev and seventeen rubles to Krotik. I broke even with Perepelitsa. Grachev, after taking a good long stretch, said it would be nice to take a nap for an hour or two.

Like a fool, I stretched and agreed: "Yeah. That would be great."

Grachev stared at me, surprised: "And what do you think you're doing? It's your turn to take the company out for P.T."

I was flabbergasted. In the first place, I was desperate for sleep. In the second, I had no idea where to look for the damn company. But within a few minutes, I brushed my teeth, put on my warm-up suit, and rushed out to look for my company. I found it quickly—Master Sergeant Oskin had formed them up on the drill ground in front of their barracks. At once, I introduced myself. The master sergeant and deputy platoon commanders were visibly surprised to see me. After the morning exercises, the battalion commander officially introduced me to the company. I was busy with assignments all day, and in the evening, I worked with my newly promoted sergeants, conducted the evening roll call, and finally returned to the hotel, more than ready to sleep.

But it was not to be. Our room started "snoring" once again. At 0545 sharp, we finished the game. I recouped some of my losses, but again there was no time for sleep. I ran off to lead P.T., worked out, and worked all day. When I got back to the hotel, the "snoring" started all over. At 0545, the previous two days repeated themselves. I returned to the hotel, and my "friends" tried to drag me into another round of "snoring." My fourth sleepless night in a row! I couldn't take any more, and I damned them all to hell. I didn't expect their reaction—applause and overflowing emotion. It turned out those sleepless nights had been a test of my endurance. Grachev announced I had passed the exam with flying colors.

"You're as strong as a moose," he said.

Fortunately, I was granted twenty-four hours' rest. But even under the normal regime I was kept busy. From 0530 till late at night, my schedule was full. Still, I enjoyed it.

One evening, at approximately 2230, I came to the checkpoint, wearing, as always, my tight sword belt. The warrant officer told me there was a brawl under way in the park across from the school building. The combatants were our Airborne commandos and the cadets of the Ryazan School.

The warrant officer told me that he had already notified the chief officer on duty and recommended that I not go out on the street.

I ignored him, thinking, "Get out of my way, and hide your fat ass behind closed doors!"

Either the fight had just approached its turning point, or, in the darkness, I was mistaken for the duty officer. When I yelled "Stop it!" it worked. The cadets rushed back to their school, and our guys took off between houses along Kalyaev Street toward the corner of the campus and were clearing the high stone fence without any trouble. I ran after them and grabbed someone by the collar. Before I could identify his company, out of the corner of

"One paratroop cadet had his head pierced by an anvil-shaped rock. Another was dragged toward the village; his eye hooked on a steel staple attaching a fence to a metal pole."

my eye, I saw a big fist heading for me. I pushed the collar away, turned, and blocked the fist. But then a stampeding crowd surged forward and slammed me into a stone fence. They took their best shots, so I was flattened pretty good.

I scraped myself off the fence, climbed over it, and ran to my company. I called an alert and lined the company up for inspection. There were no traces of fighting. Some guys were out of breath, but they explained it either as being caught in the middle of a workout or as their zeal to get to the line-up in time. I had to pretend to believe them.

The next day, a high-powered inspection board arrived from Moscow: two lieutenant generals, a major general, and up to ten colonels from the Interior Ministry and the Airborne troops. They wanted to get to the bottom of the brawl. The warrant officer, who had been on duty at the checkpoint, informed them that Lieutenant Lebed had been in the thick of the fighting.

I was immediately summoned before my superiors. As soon as I reported, I was asked bluntly: "Lieutenant, why didn't you take measures to prevent the fight?"

I thought it best to say nothing. So, for about thirty minutes, everyone took turns lecturing me and even accusing me of cowardice.

My crushed bones ached, and I hardly listened to them. I knew they were only looking for a scapegoat. I left the office with a deep sense of relief, not forgetting to ask for permission to leave and responding loudly: "Yes, sir!"

> *Here they can call you a cur,*
> *And strip you of virtue and honor,*
> *But we, having muttered "Up yours!"*
> *"Yes, sir!" will always holler.*

By 1976 I was the acting company commander. That May the school was scheduled to conduct its first group parachute jumps from an Antonov-22 "Antaeus" airplane. Since this was a new operation, technical problems inevitably came up in the "Antaeus."

At first they lined up streams of twenty-one people each, then seventeen, and finally nineteen. In this fashion, the cadets from both companies, the first and second, got mixed together.

I pointed out the streams needed to be reconfigured according to our organizational structure—platoons and squads—but the representatives of the Airborne service hissed that we would sort things out after the landing, which was asking for trouble.

We jumped in two streams through two doors—thirty-eight people in all. I jumped during the first fly-over and landed safely. It was a clear day, and the wind was blowing at a rate of about two to three meters a second. Soon, all thirty-eight people gathered at the assembly point.

The plane left for the second fly-over. Meanwhile, a truck from the garrison store drove onto the field and started selling soda, pastry and cigarettes. The cadets happily formed a line for this rare treat.

At last, the plane made its second pass for the next paratroop drop. Two strings, nineteen parachutists in each, hung in the air. When they were about two hundred meters from landing, an overpowering gust swept over us. The canopies of the parachutes, filled by the wind, turned into huge sails that towed the parachutists away from the landing field, dragging them parallel to the ground.

I ordered our cadets into the field toward which the paratroopers were heading, dispatched an ambulance, and threw the boxes out of the catering truck and sent it out. The frightened saleswomen from the garrison store started crying. I found another truck, but it wouldn't start, so I ran to the field. By this time, the garrison store truck was heading back. A cadet fell out of the truck. I looked in the truck bed and saw two boots under the bulk of an open parachute.

"Who's that?" I asked the cadet.

"It's Master Sergeant Oskin. He's dead."

I jumped in the truck and pulled back the parachute. I checked Oskin's ribcage. It was intact, but his skull gave in under my fingers. Later I found out he had crashed into the concrete support of an A-shaped electrical post. Death had been instantaneous. Oskin was twenty-one years old.

I sent the cadet with the body to the assembly point and ran to the field.

Soon I learned that three more people had died. Cadet Pertiukov's neck had caught between two suspension lines, strangling him. Another cadet crashed into an anvil-shaped rock that pierced his head. Cadet Nikolai Liutov was dragged for 3.5 kilometers through a field and meadow, over the river, and smashed into the riverbank, removing about a ton of dirt. Then he was dragged toward the village, where his eye hooked on a steel staple attaching a picket fence to a metal pole.

When they found Liutov, he had no boots, his coveralls were rubbed off well above his knees, and bare bones stuck out of his toes.

Two officers were also injured. One had broken his shoulder, the other had been knocked out, but saved from Liutov's fate by a shepherd, whose motorcycle collided with his parachute. The shepherd, his motorcycle, and the officer were dragged a little further, until the parachute got tangled around the bike and closed down.

Four seriously injured cadets were hospitalized. Because of the confusion at the airfield, that I mentioned before, we did not know who was dead and who was alive. We didn't even know who had jumped. In ten minutes, the windstorm died as unexpectedly as it had started.

Many of the cadets were married, and because the rumor instantly spread that at least half of the first and second companies had been killed, two expecting mothers had miscarriages. After she learned about the death of her only grandson, cadet Pertiukov's grandmother died of a heart attack.

The terrifying sound of the mournful crying of relatives lingered over the parade ground. Much later, death, funerals, and tears became common occurrences, but back then it was an extraordinary event.

That summer was marked by another unpleasant event. In July I took our cadets to their practical training at the Pskov Airborne Division, where we made a drop near the city of Chernigov. During the approach to the landing site, a technician on board warned us that the wind on the ground was extremely strong. After I cleared the airplane and looked down on the landing site, I realized that the term "extremely strong" was not strong enough. I saw hundreds of parachutists dragged across the site.

With gusts of ten or eleven meters per second, I flopped on a dusty road, heated by the generous Ukrainian sun. The dust softened the blow, but that was where my luck ran out. The wind caught my chute and sent me plowing through dust so deep I couldn't breathe.

We'd been trained to care for our parachute; cutting it was allowed only in emergencies. But this was one. I was about to slash the shrouds. Suddenly the road made a turn, and my parachute hit a big bush. I stood up, positioned myself against the wind, and deflated the parachute.

I looked around. Paratroopers freed from their harnesses were helping others deflate their canopies.

Meanwhile more Antonov-12 airplanes in groups of three were dropping paratroopers. I saw a soldier heading for me, not even trying to position himself to the wind. It was possible he had been injured clearing the plane. He hit the ground fifty meters away, but the wind caught his canopy and he came toward me at high speed. I grabbed the pilot chute and tried to turn the canopy against the wind. But the gusts were too strong. Not being able to turn the chute around, I crawled under the canopy, still holding the pilot chute with both hands. Getting up from under the canopy, I saw the soldier, on all fours and staring at me absentmindedly. "Come around fast!" I yelled to him, but he didn't react. I repeated my command. Still no reaction. A third time. I even tried to get his attention by gesturing: still no reaction. The wind picked up and tore the pilot chute out of my hands. I was caught between his suspension lines, and the chute, the soldier, and I were whisked across the field at incredible speed.

It would be hard to imagine a more ridiculous situation. After 120 meters, something caught the parachute. I slipped out of the trap and grabbed the pilot chute. The soldier finally came to his senses, gained his feet, and ran against the wind. The two of us deflated the canopy. I told the soldier, eloquently and colorfully, what I thought of him, and set off for the assembly point.

The drop was completed, and, fortunately, this time there were no casualties. But three people broke both legs, twenty broke one leg, and several people broke arms and collarbones. A major, who was an MD, managed to get a major portion of his upper lip ripped off. To a greater or lesser extent, everyone was beaten up.

Now the exercise began. At the edge of the landing site, a tank regiment revved its engines and launched an attack on our airborne regiment. A huge, tread-screeching, cannon-spewing cloud of dust rolled over our regiment. Everything disappeared in the haze and gloom. If it had been a real battle, it's hard to say how it would have come out. I could see no further than fifty meters to the left or right. I suspected that the tank crews under the red-hot armor could not see even that far. We were lucky no one was run over in that mess. The "fire" from both sides was intense, but the mediators, eventually, gave preference to the paratroopers.

> **"I** *forgot to give the command "At ease!" so they had to vote while standing at attention. Within the hour I was no longer a political officer.* **"**

After completing its immediate mission and getting to the meeting points, the regiment began licking its wounds. At the edge of a small forest there was a stump with a regular soldier's aluminum bowl full of iodine resting on it. Attending the bowl was a poker-faced medic holding a swab. He had a long line of injured folks. The medic was dipping his swab in the bowl and smearing the sores of each sufferer in turn. You could hear gnashing teeth, juicy Russian oaths, the usual soldiers' teasing, and comradely laughter.

The paratroopers spent that evening sprucing themselves up. In the morning, the regiment formed a big column and set out for Chernigov. The paratroopers were met with a band, and an ocean of flowers, smiles, and warm comments. Unfortunately for discipline, moms and dads, grandpas and grandmas, friends and acquaintances, classmates and school sweethearts literally snatched the soldiers away to homes and clubs, and for dates. Of course, all the things we lived through during the landing, coupled by the excitement of the reception, resulted in a good old Russian drinking spree. All evening and all night we had to pick up partying parachutists. But, I've got to give the soldiers credit. In the morning, everyone was accounted for and our regiment marched sharply for the train to Pskov. Those who had been seriously injured in the training exercise were left behind at a local military hospital. About thirty people who merely suffered broken bones were placed in a first class coach and sent home for treatment.

As a company commander, I graduated my first cadets in 1977. The vast majority of these officers endured the crucible of the Afghan War. Nine cadets from that graduating class came back in zinc coffins.

The academic year over, I filed a written request to be reassigned to active duty. I was sick of school. In response, I was called a careerist. I was told to wait another year before requesting a transfer.

After the year passed, I again requested a transfer and the battalion commander authorized it. Unfortunately, the transfer wasn't approved by the chain of command. It had already been decided who would be transferred, and my request vanished.

Another year passed. Under my new request for transfer, the school's director, Lieutenant General Chekrizov, wrote: "Send for active duty after graduation of the 1981 class." Thus, I became only the second person in the history of the school to command the same company all the way through the school, from beginning to end.

After the graduation of my second company, I found that, suddenly, I had gone from being a "youngster" to being an "old man." I was thirty-one years old, and a captain. I was considered an experienced company commander of cadets. Naturally I asked myself: "Whatever happened to the 'prime of life'? How did I—as a promising young fellow—go straight to the category of 'old folks' who were a burden on the personnel office?"

It still wasn't clear whether my transfer would be approved. In the meantime I was receiving job offers from others at the school. The director of the Department of Firearms Training, Colonel V. A. Bobrov, was the first to extend an invitation.

He explained to me that I was perfect for his department because I had a voice that could reach as far as a round of ammo. He offered me a job as a firearms instructor. I told him teaching is a God-given talent that I didn't have and I had no wish to be a mediocre instructor.

Bobrov was insulted and warned that I would yet regret my stupidity. Two days later, the director of the Department of Tactics, Colonel Khokhlov, offered me a job. It was tempting, but I refused.

The school principal came up with a third offer—to become the commander of the cadet battalion. It was a colonel's position, so I agreed. But then the appointment was rejected by General D. S. Sukhorukov. He told the school principal, "A colonel's position to a thirty-one-year-old captain? Are you crazy?"

After that I was told I would be assigned as a battalion commander to the Pskov division, but somehow that, too, went nowhere.

I conscientiously went to work every day, though I was no longer on the organizational chart. I had been replaced by a new company commander and officially had nothing to do. One day, the school principal invited me over. The political officer of the battalion, Major Grinevich was on vacation, so I was invited to substitute for him. I objected that I wouldn't make much of a political officer. But the school principal calmed me down: "Gods don't do men's work, men do." My first assignment as the new political officer was to elect the battalion's *Komsomol* committee. I spent the rest of the day compiling a list of committee members and getting it approved by the company commanders.

The next day I had my cadets assembled. I ordered them to line up on the parade ground immediately after lunch.

"Attention! Cadets so-and-so, so-and-so, and so-and-so, ten steps forward! Close ranks to the middle!" I announced that the cadets who stepped forward were going to be members of the battalion's Komsomol committee. "All in favor, say 'aye'!" I forgot to give the command "At ease!" so they had to vote while standing at attention. That was considered a travesty of democracy. Within the hour, I was no longer a political officer. Nevertheless, the Komsomol committee was functioning successfully. The main thing is who you get elected and not how you do it.

Next, my superiors assigned me to an evaluation board under the commander of the Airborne Corps. I flew to Bolgrad to inspect units of the 98th Airborne Division. It was a surprise inspection and allowed me to make some interesting observations—chiefly that there is no such thing as a "minor detail" in the army. Everything matters.

I inspected the 99th Regiment, whose commander was Lieutenant Colonel Yatsenko, a person with a clear bent for construction. Thanks to his energetic activity, the regiment had a nice club and barracks, and was building further improvements. Even the company commander, personally, cut glass.

Yatsenko's construction activities would have been welcome if we hadn't discovered that the regiment's combat readiness—the purpose of any military unit—had become a low priority. Soldiers could turn up late to the firing range or neglect other military training with impunity. But if a company or a platoon did not fulfill its daily construction requirements, Yatsenko would fly off the handle. During our inspection, one battalion was supposed to conduct a parachuting and target practice exercise. We ran out of paper making a list of their shortcomings, though the Airborne soldiers' pride showed through as they gritted their teeth and fought hard to overcome their inadequate training.

Before one of the combat exercises, I took a measuring tape out of my pocket and measured some of the targets. They appeared to be 1.5 or 2 centimeters wider and higher than they should have been.

The commanding colonel—Colonel Muslimov—was outraged. His division executive officer, Lieutenant Colonel Bondar, assured him he would investigate and punish the warrant officer responsible. But I knew Bondar was responsible. Any real warrant officer complies strictly with division executive officers' orders.

We left for the hotel near the training center. There, our dinner table was set up with exotic fruits and vegetables, crayfish, and a variety of other fish. Colonel Muslimov said in a colorless voice, "Bondar, are we going to dine like pigs again?"

"Comrade Colonel, why? It is just a regular setup."

"Bondar, you're already a lieutenant colonel and a division executive officer. You ought to know that only pigs dine without alcoholic beverages."

Bondar made sure that we did not sink to the level of pigs, so the dinner proceeded in a warm and friendly atmosphere.

The next morning it was raining.

I inspected the target range and found that none of the problems discovered the previous day had been addressed. After another friendly dinner, the officers from the combat training department explained to me that it would not be expedient to make the changes under the pouring rain. It was decided we would lower the battalion's grade by one point. Because of the nonstop rain and a strong wind, a scheduled parachute jump was canceled. The battalion was driven to the landing site and positioned as if they actually had parachuted. The exercise started.

Firearms training is an exact science. The battalion was fighting under especially bad weather conditions, but the men were obviously poorly trained. I checked two of the five target ranges, and gave the battalion two Ds.

I don't know who checked the other ranges, but, as a result of lengthy and complex calculations, it turned out that the battalion had passed the inspection with a C. Somehow the inspectors forgot to knock off a point for the failure to fix the targets.

This left me with a very unpleasant feeling. I remembered the officers who went out of their way to succeed. It was not their fault that nobody taught them the right way, it was just their misfortune. You don't make people better by lying about their performance. Handing out a passing grade to people who don't deserve it is an insult.

CHAPTER 4:
ON THE ROADS OF AFGHANISTAN

PART 1: A CALL TO THE FUTURE

I was sick to death of bouncing around without an assignment. That's why, in November 1981, I went for the umpteenth time to the head of the institute's personnel department. As usual, I listened to excuses. This time, I flew into a rage:

"Did you call about my transfer?"

"I did."

"Well, now let me call."

"Go ahead."

I picked up the receiver and ended up talking to a Colonel Kamolov.

"Who the hell are you?" he demanded.

"Captain Lebed, former cadet company commander."

"How long did you command a company?"

"Five years, two months."

"Are you willing to go south as a battalion commander?"

"Yes!"

"Don't you want to know where?"

"I don't care."

"Well, call me back in two hours."

I called back and was told that my orders were being drafted. I would be named the commander of the 1st Battalion of the 345th Detached Airborne Regiment.

There is a saying about fate: "If someone is fated to be hanged, he won't drown." I learned later that three people had been offered this job and turned it down. So, they needed a battalion commander immediately—and I just happened to call.

> "**M**y first week in Afghanistan, I felt I was in a bizarre, eastern fairy tale. I was not alone. But those who didn't snap out of it went home in zinc coffins."

At this time, the 345th Regiment was stationed in two locations: Fergana and Bagram, Afghanistan. The regiment had been trained in the forests and bogs of Lithuania, but were absolutely helpless in the mountainous territory of their new assignment. We had to retrain the regiment in the middle of combat operations, which cost us dearly.

I flew into Afghanistan in November 1981. The *Dushmani*[1] had Stinger missiles, so our Antonov-12 was flying at a high altitude. The ground seemed far away, the mountains like toys, and in the valleys and ravines, the ground seemed covered with irregular spider webs. At first I didn't understand what these were. Then Kudinov, the regimental political officer, explained to me that these were *duvaly*: wall-like fences made of clay that interconnected the houses in a village. In the course of the flight, he briefed me, explained where the *Dushman* nests were, and told me who controlled what territory.

My first week in Afghanistan, I had a strange unsettling feeling: on the one hand, I felt as though I had fallen into some eastern fairy tale (though, with clear traces of war), and on the other, I felt as though I were on a movie set.

[1] The slang word the Soviets used for Afghan freedom fighters; it comes from the Turkish word for "enemy."

I wasn't alone in this feeling. But those who didn't snap out of it quickly came home in zinc coffins on a "Black Tulips." [2] As the song goes:

> *In Afghanistan*
> *In "Black Tulip" Land*
> *Vodka in hand*
> *We're silently drifting along....*

PART 2: BRINGING MY TROOPS TO COMBAT READINESS

Our regiment was based at the Bagram airfield. The regimental commander, Lieutenant Colonel Yuri Viktorovich Kuznetsov, met the plane himself. He was a person of medium height and thickset; a real hothead. Kuznetsov told me quite frankly that my appearance was unexpected and not at all welcome, for he had been planning to name his regimental intelligence chief Volodya Nikiforov to my post. He went further, telling me that officers from academies and training units bore as much resemblance to "real" officers as training guns did to automatic rifles.

Kuznetsov introduced my predecessor Major Rembez, and gave him seventy-two hours to have me fully in control of all his duties.

The 345th Regiment had been in Afghanistan since June of 1979 at Hafizullah Amin's request[3], guarding the Bagram Airport. Its platoons and squads were spread over an eighteen kilometer perimeter. A soldier could serve his whole hitch in the regiment and not know comrades who were serving in his same company or even platoon. Divided into groups of seven or eight in each defensive position, the soldiers had no sense of belonging to a single military unit. They lived in primitively equipped dugouts and trenches. There were no forests

[2] A "Black Tulip" is a plane which carries dead bodies.

[3] Hafizullah Amin was prime minister and leader of the People's Democratic Party of Afghanistan. He overthrew President Nur M. Taraki and became ruler in September 1979.

in Bagram, so they were forced to build the dugouts with anything they could get their hands on, propping up the light, dusty earth so it wouldn't collapse.

My second day in Afghanistan, I was hit with the mysterious malady that catches every new arrival. It took me three days to recover and five days to become acclimated. Now it was time to put my own stamp on the battalion and remake it according to my own views.

> **"I** *grabbed an automatic rifle, four magazines of ammunition, two grenades, and two bottles of vodka, and headed for my twenty-four-hour leave.* **"**

It was a difficult job. After commanding cadets for eight years, I was used to a different level of interaction. The cadets had been much better educated and were, for the most part, polite, clever, and smart. Any interaction with them was based first on the intellect. Here, the intellectual level was lower, the rigors of service had left their mark, and a kind of bandit culture had grown up. This was where I learned the truth, which is as old as the world, that existence determines consciousness.[4]

The material and financial status of the battalion left much to be desired. When the supply platoon trucked soup around the perimeter, along those marvelous Afghan roads, somewhere around the tenth or twelfth kilometer it became difficult to say just what the slop was.

There was little opportunity to bathe. Bed linens were often missing, and, where they existed, were infrequently changed. Naturally, all of this brought about mass infestations of lice. Finding solutions to these problems was my first task, because if a soldier lives like a human being, he will behave like a human being, but if he lives like a pig. . . .

[4] A classical Marxist theorem.

In early December my brother, Captain Aleksei Ivanovich Lebed, called me and asked whether I could visit, as he was soon to be rotated home. At that time, he was commanding the reconnaissance company of the 103rd Airborne Division. He had been one of the first into Afghanistan, and had conscientiously served two years there. For the many battles in which he participated, he was decorated with the order of the Red Star and a medal "For Courage." Everyone acknowledged that he had earned much more, but by character my brother was obstinate and stubborn. Back then, such people were routinely left off the decoration lists.

When I brought my request to the regimental commander he hemmed and hawed a bit, because it was not an opportune time. But he understood, and generously gave me twenty-four hours' leave.

It was not very far from Bagram to Kabul: fifty-some kilometers by road. But in Afghanistan, fifty kilometers is a lot of territory. If you went two or three kilometers in any direction from our perimeter, you'd get all the fighting you could handle. The regimental commander recommended that I fly.

I grabbed an automatic rifle, four magazines of ammunition, two grenades, and two bottles of vodka, and went to the dispatch point. I lucked out. The dispatcher, a sprightly and, from all appearances, not-altogether-sober warrant officer, pointed out the window: "That Antonov-12 is flying a army exchange truck to Kabul in an hour."

The army exchange truck had already been loaded onto the plane. A picturesque crowd swirled around the aircraft: women in *chadors*,[5] bearded old men in turbans, children, goats, chickens, knapsacks, bags, crates. Somehow the engineer and the co-pilot found space for them all. After the chattering, bleating, cackling crowd settled down, the airplane took off. In about forty minutes, we touched down at the airport in Kabul. There we unloaded the

---

[5] A sheet-like garment that covers a woman from head to toe, leaving only a small opening for the eyes.

truck, and I was driven to the Bal-Khisar fortress, where my brother's reconnaissance company was based.

I arrived for a wild party of soldier's gossip and repeatedly filled shot glasses. The division was undergoing its first mass rotation. After spending two years fighting themselves silly, the officers and warrant officers were celebrating new arrivals. Everyone knows almost everyone else in the Airborne troops. All the officers are forged in the Ryazan Airborne School, and there is only one warrant officers' school. My brother's company, as he explained it to me, was celebrating seven "holidays" at the same time: first, the director of intelligence was leaving; second, a new one was arriving; third, the company commander (i.e., my brother) was leaving; fourth, a new company commander was coming; fifth and sixth, two new lieutenants had arrived to take the place of those who had died, to be platoon leaders; and, seventh, the senior technician of the company, a burly, balding, gloomy fellow named Edik, was having a birthday.

So the company offices, which doubled as a recreation area, were set up with a fitting banquet table. In addition to typical army fare like fried potatoes with beef, cabbage, and cucumbers, there were about thirty glass jars of black caviar, with an aluminum army spoon sticking out of each. There were also alternating bottles of Russian vodka, Cuban rum, and unlabeled mystery brews. Between hosts and guests, there were about twenty-five of us. I warned my brother that I hadn't flown here just to get drunk in an hour. We agreed to drink only a couple of toasts, but that was hard to follow in practice.

To understand these officers one needed to have done a lot of fighting, seen comrades returned to the Soviet Union in zinc coffins, frozen in the mountains, gone hungry, and endured the waiting for one's replacement. People drank, but didn't get drunk; the conversations just got hotter, the details even more picturesque. A captain sat next to me—he was a doctor who had been through the whole cycle. He looked at me—an alcohol-sodden man with completely sober eyes—and went on and on about how a land mine had blown a squad to bits. He and the captain had had to collect bodies.

"Stop!" I said.

But the captain didn't hear me. He raised his shot glass again and again. The scene flashed before his eyes: intestines, feet, hands....

I said to my brother: "Let's get some fresh air. You can show me around the fortress. There's a moon out tonight."

We walked around the fortress. My brother told me picturesque details of its capture, and pointed to where comrades had been killed or wounded. Along the way we wandered from party to party—each awash in vodka.

About 0300 the next morning, we finally returned to my brother's company. There were only nine people left at the table, no full bottles, and the jars of caviar were empty. But our return seemed to give the party a second wind. Reserve bottles were discovered and passed around. Somehow, we got to arm wrestling. How it started, the devil only knows. A big, self-assured senior lieutenant sitting across from me said something about the wimps from the 345th. I'd been serving in that regiment only a few days, but all the same this pushed my buttons. Dishes fell off the edge of the table as he and I set about trying to establish which regiment of the Airborne troops actually contained the most wimps. We appeared evenly matched, but I was considerably more sober. After two minutes of struggle, the back of his arm hit the table.

"Well, let's try the left arms."

He did even worse with the left arm: he was completely played out. Suddenly, he blew an emotional fuse, his eyes burning with a wild, unthinking flame. I socked him in the jaw, toppling him across a bed into some armor netting. He lay there, motionless.

"What the hell? How hard did I hit him? He's not batting an eyelid."

Surrounding the bed now, everyone grew quiet. In the ensuing silence, the gentle snoring of the senior lieutenant could be heard distinctly. The poor devil had been dead drunk, and it was as if he had said to himself, "You know, what I'd really like now is a punch in the jaw," and I granted his wish. He fell asleep before he hit the ground. Sensing the proper thing to do in this situation, the entire group broke out in laughter.

The next morning, I got ready for the return trip. The sobered senior lieutenant, who turned out to be a platoon commander, tried to mumble some apologies. His service buddies, not even letting him sleep off his hangover, had been buzzing in his ears all morning about

> **"When I confronted the leader of the hazing incident, he denied it, so I let him have it on the jaw."**

what a boor he had been to the battalion commander from the fraternal 345th. They told him that he had well deserved his punch in the jaw. Apparently, he didn't remember anything that had happened the night before. And that troubled his conscience all the more. But we buried the hatchet and shook hands.

The two bottles of vodka in my knapsack were bone dry. Now I knew where the reserve bottles had been found.

As I was leaving, I ran into the doctor-captain from the night before. He looked at me with glassy eyes, but was very glad to see me.

"Wait up," he said. "I'll finish telling you my story. The land mine, remember?"

My first impulse was to tell the captain to go to hell. But when he said the word "land mine," his eyes glowed with a special meaning, and his face took on such an expression of suffering, that it became clear to me what had happened. The captain was psychologically tortured by that bloody Afghan road, the land mine, and the pieces of corpses. He tried to free his mind the traditional Russian way: drowning his visions in vodka. As in most such cases, the vodka only aggravated his troubles. The nightmare became permanent. This was a person with a mental illness.

"Excuse me, old friend," I said. "I have to go. I'll be back soon; you can finish telling me about it then."

My brother and I said our good-byes, and wished each other success. Our good wishes came true: we both returned safely from the war, as did our cousin Mikhail.

The same Antonov-12 on which I had arrived flew me back to Bagram and to the problem of improving living conditions for my soldiers. It went very slowly, despite my best efforts, which was depressing, but I tried not to show it. Then I heard a rumor, which soon became an order, that my battalion was to be replaced by a special guard unit from the Soviet Union. The new battalion arrived at full strength, almost seven hundred people, with plenty of shining new equipment.

Over the course of three days, they took over our positions. It didn't go smoothly. My wild troops pinched the newly arrived beds, linens, night tables, and other accoutrements of civilization.

My new job was to bring my scattered battalion together and prepare it for combat. There again, their wildness took over. Having no unit cohesion, hardly knowing their comrades, they fought each other to establish a sort of animal hierarchy. Broken noses, cracked jaws, and black eyes became the norm. No one could stop them, and I couldn't keep tabs on my men all the time: two soldiers would go to the restroom; one would return; the other would come back later with a completely battered face.

Sitting for months in trenches rots the body, so I knew we needed to increase physical training. I organized the building of a sports complex. We welded horizontal bars and parallel bars and set them in concrete; and though it looked preposterous, we made weights and dumbbells from the tracks of tanks.

So far, my troops thought I was a "softy." But on the fifth day of my new regime, I ran across a group of wise guys who had gone up to another soldier and said: "Can you do a cartwheel?"

"No."

"But the battalion commander says you have to! We'll teach you."

They grabbed him, strapped him to a horizontal bar, attached his feet to a field telephone and turned the crank, shooting an electric shock that sent him flying to the ceiling.

When I confronted the leader—"Was this your bright idea?"—he answered me like any normal soldier would answer any normal battalion commander: "Sir, no, sir!"

I let him have it on the jaw. He went out cold, sliding across the floor into a corner. Then I went after the others. His "first deputy" fell across him. Nine more went down on top, along, or beside him. Only one proved tough. I had to hit him twice.

That evening my conscience tormented me. My long-held theories of how to handle men had fallen apart in practice. But the next morning, there was not one black eye. The fighting stopped. I was no longer a softy.

I gave the regimental commander a report, with a request to give me two weeks to bring the battalion up to combat readiness. He gave me ten days.

By the end of the ten days, I had a battalion I was ready to take into combat. They were proficient with their weapons, they had come together as a unit, and no one, from the battalion commander to the lowliest private, had an ounce of extra fat on him. But it still wasn't easy sledding.

The chief of staff of my battalion, before my arrival, had held onto four people who were supposed to be discharged to the reserves. I told them, "As soon as you dig the holes and build the outhouse I've planned, you're free." They were not happy, and demonstrated it by doing nothing. I pretended not to notice. The next day, tired of being ignored, they took up their picks, crow bars, and shovels and went to the spot I had marked off. At lunch, I went over to see how they were doing. It was a sad picture. The picks and crowbars bounced off the hard soil. The shovels were picking up milligrams at a time. Moreover, the soldiers' hands were covered with bloody blisters, and the soldiers grumbled and gave me the evil eye. Realizing that no good could come of this, I ordered the battalion to prepare for explosives work. Now the lads really came to life. Digging a prospecting shaft for explosives—well, that's entirely different from digging a latrine foundation ditch. Within two days, they were done.

The head of the engineering-sapper company, Volodya Garasyuk, complained that we had used too many of our explosives already. He suggested that we use some captured Italian antitank mines for digging the foundation ditch. I followed his advice. We placed a cordon around the area, and I pushed the button myself. The foundation ditch turned out perfectly. But all the glass in the regimental buildings facing the explosion—including the windows in the regimental commander's office—shattered.

The officers and warrant officers of the entire battalion spent the next two weeks trading for, buying, and otherwise acquiring and installing glass. Up until then, the regimental commander had relied on the reports of the deputy commander, Lieutenant Colonel Grachev, who had talked about the high quality of our battalion exercises. Now he decided to conduct the evaluative exercises personally.

Things turned out badly. Our equipment kept running out of gas at the least convenient times and in the least convenient places. The din of what the regimental commander said to me could be heard throughout the regiment. Still, he was good enough to say that I was doing the right things, but not following through sufficiently.

The transition from commanding cadets to commanding combat troops was rather difficult for me. By the end of December, however, the battalion had completed its first military operation, combing through a group of *kishlaks*, or Afghan villages.

The new year, 1982, approached. But four days before the holiday, we discovered that the regiment's food stores had been looted. The food stores were in a refrigerator, guarded by my battalion. Among the food that was taken were fifty cans of stewed meat and several kilograms of cookies, candy, and apples for the New Year's party. The compartment's seal had been cleanly cut. If the thief had had the brains to take the food from the back of the refrigerator instead of from the front, the storehouse manager might never have caught on.

I searched for the food until 0200 the next morning before taking a rest. But at 0300, the duty officer woke me and said that Private Gainulin had been brought into sick bay, with all five fingers of his right hand cut off.

On my way to the sick bay, I was told that Gainulin had gone into the bathroom. The light went out. He walked outside, lit a fuse, and it blew off all his fingers. It was a story that didn't make any sense.

I took a lamp to the accident site. There was blood, but not as much as I expected.

Again, I got an illogical explanation.

"Comrade Captain, he put his hand in his jacket."

I went to the sick bay and found Gainulin's jacket. The jacket turned out to be dry on the inside. Something wasn't right. I went to his company headquarters. In the sergeant's office hung a big picture of Leonid Brezhnev, covered in blood and pieces of finger and bone.

> **"A***fghanistan means pain. Afghanistan means tears. Afghanistan means remembrance. Afghanistan can mean anything, but not shame.***"**

Soon I was able to get the truth. The former "lions," seasoned officers near the end of their tours of duty, had asked some of their junior comrades to host a holiday luncheon for them. Their juniors, including Gainulin, thought for a while, and decided to take the food from the regimental refrigerator. The barracks were built of silicate bricks, and the soldiers simply bricked the food up into the wall. Then Gainulin began to be plagued by fears. Maybe someone would find out and catch him. He had heard somewhere that if you took the fuse out of a grenade, it could cause a minor trauma. He thought he would wound himself slightly, wind up in sick bay, and stay there until the whole thing blew over. About 0300, he put the fuse in his fist and jerked the pin out. And, of course, he blew all his fingers off. The blood had gotten onto Brezhnev, or more accurately, onto his portrait. I felt sorry for the soldier, who was really a decent fellow. In the hospital, he told me that his father was an invalid of the first group, and his mother and brother were invalids of the second group[6], and now he had become an invalid.

On New Year's Day, I was the regimental duty officer. The only thing I really remember is that at midnight Moscow time, the whole sky over the Bagram valley was spotted with tracers. The "limited contingent"[7] was celebrating the New Year.

In the few months following my telephone call, my life had changed to its very core. From that dead-end swamp of inactivity, I had been thrown into a military maelstrom and, despite the difficulties, I was happy to have made that trade.

PART 3: THE SEVERED "RING"

Afghanistan means pain. Afghanistan means tears. Afghanistan means remembrance. Afghanistan can mean anything you like, but not shame. It was politicians who made the decisions: some wise, others less so; some expedient, others not. For the unwise decisions, soldiers paid with their blood. The politicians who started and ran the war knew that neither they, nor their children, nor their grandchildren, nor their friends, nor anyone they knew personally would do the fighting. The "workers' and peasants' Red Army" fought there.[8]

---

[6] In the Soviet Union, people with disabilities were classified according to the severity of their injuries to determine, among other things, what types of work they were fit to do and what benefits they should receive.

[7] The Soviet authorities described their presence in Afghanistan as a "limited contingent" of troops. Later, the commander of the Soviet forces in Afghanistan, General Boris Gromov, wrote his memoirs of the Afghan War, and titled them *The Limited Contingent*.

[8] The original title of the Red Army was the "Workers' and Peasants' Red Army" (*Raboche-krestianskaya Krasnaya Armiya*).

I mean, literally, the children of workers and peasants. It didn't matter who they were: privates, majors, or colonels. No one ever saw the children of high-ranking Soviet officials in uniform in Afghanistan.

As in any war, we had all kinds there: cowards, scum, and rascals—but also those who exemplified the unseen soaring of the human spirit. There were incomparably more of the latter. Afghanistan was paid for with fifteen thousand lives, given honestly in a war they didn't understand. About forty thousand were wounded and maimed. No one ever counted how many tens of thousands of soldiers took ill with hepatitis, malaria, typhoid, or exotic fevers. Such people had their lives shortened by at least ten years.

In January 1982 we began preparing for a large-scale operation to comb out the Bagram valley. I was a battalion commander, so nobody bothered to fill me in on all the details, but the general idea was to take a territory of two hundred square kilometers with your troops, run a fine-tooth comb over it, liquidate all the Islamic committees and *Dushman* bands that resisted, and then disarm and sort out the rest at filtration points. The 345th Detached Airborne Regiment was one of the main strike forces, and consequently, it was assigned the liveliest sector.

Preparation for this operation took almost two weeks. Soviet forces cooperated with the Afghan army to conduct operations. In practice this meant that the area would be surrounded by Soviet soldiers, then combed twice: once by the Afghans, once by the Soviets. For this operation, the second battalion of the Afghan 444th Regiment, the "commandos," was given to my command. The regiment's name was covered in historical glory, but there were some anomalies. The real "commandos"—those who had given the regiment its glorious name—had either been killed or had run away. The regiment had been replenished by regular draftees, and had lost its traditional fighting spirit and military discipline. The commanders were all slippery characters.

I prepared the battalion for the operation according to plan. But three soldiers had boils on their legs, so I assigned them to whitewash the barracks and work on the battalion's sports complex.

About this time, Colonel General Merimski, whose nickname was "The Grey-Haired Death," came to check our readiness. He saw three soldiers whitewashing the barracks and immediately concluded that the battalion was not training for the upcoming operation, and that the battalion commander was a fool. He went to the regimental commander, Lieutenant Colonel Kuznetsov, and chewed him out. Experience had long taught me that the only thing to do was keep a military posture, wear your most serious face, preferably with an element of repentance in it, and say "Sir, yes, sir!" or "Sir, no, sir!" So I ordered the soldiers to report to sick bay.

In the end, my battalion was deemed—with many shortcomings, of course—to be ready.

Early in the morning of January 13 we began the operation, which was supposed to take two weeks. The much-praised commandos quickly exhausted all my feelings of internationalism. For one thing, they practiced what we called the "tea defense." In effect, it worked like this: we would surround a village or a group of villages and prepare to comb the area. Then the Afghan ring would move in, set up in the village, and inside the courtyard, a carpet would be unrolled, a tea pot would be set boiling, and their Afghan flat cakes would be laid out.

A couple of times, I tried to explain to them that I had nothing against tea in principle, but that the proper time for tea was after the operation had been completed. They didn't understand. The Afghans are a decent, manly people, forged by a rigorous upbringing and deeply rooted tradition and religion. It was ingrained in them that a real leader was strong and harsh. If he tried to talk his people into or out of something, then he was a poor excuse for a leader. When I tried to talk to them, they avoided my eyes and adopted sour expressions.

The third time, I changed my tactics radically. In a large home where about ten of the Afghans were engaging in "tea defense," I had riflemen secure all the exits, entered in my heavy shoes, trampled the food, and kicked the tea kettle into the nearest "tea lover." All without saying a word! They quickly picked up their automatic rifles and fell in without even a murmur. Their leader then came up to me and said they understood me, and requested permission to proceed with the operation. We smiled at each other, the soldiers behind us began to smile, and they marched out the door.

My battalion headquarters staff consisted of the commander, his chief of staff, two radiomen, an air transport officer with an assistant, and soldiers, but the Afghan battalion's administration dragged along a gang of so-called *anziboty* (orderlies). They were of no use at all during the day, but at night, like cockroaches, they would scatter in all directions, returning with all manner of carpets, rugs, and pillows, and provide the commander and his friends with a comfortable place to spend the night, leaving me not even a rotten blanket. I had to take drastic measures. I went into the Afghan staff quarters, thanked them for all their work on our behalf and their care for our comfort, and kicked them all out. Thrown out onto the grass to weep and gnash their teeth all night, the Afghans drew the appropriate conclusions. Thereafter, we built quarters side by side, and mine were always the best.

Operation "Ring" struck me, as a young officer, as not very well planned. For five days we encircled, combed, moved forward, and maneuvered. We were shot at; we returned fire. But for the most part, we were doing battle with an unseen, elusive foe. Our casualties, thank God, were small, but so were our results. We captured a few automatic and repeating rifles, some cartridges and grenades, but found no men in the villages—just women, children, camels, donkeys, frowns, hatred, and indifference.

On the morning of the sixth day of the operation, a mass of Afghan boys and men poured into our camp. By lunchtime, I had an enormous number of prisoners of war, if you could call them that, ranging from twelve to seventy years of age. With gestures, ingratiating smiles, and every means at their disposal, they tried to convince me that they had all arrived in our camp by coincidence. I ordered that boys under sixteen and the old men over sixty could leave the group and go home. Within an hour the crowd was cut in half, but a mob still remained.

Attempts to organize this seething mass of people were completely fruitless. They acted like idiots, wandering around. Finally, our interpreter Sergeant Azimov, a home-spun country boy and a Tajik by nationality, brought over two elders who were said to be *mullahs.*

An idea occurred to me: with all the respect I could muster, I asked these two old men to help me restore order and get them seated in rows of one hundred. They stroked their beards, clambered up on some rocks, and began shouting in shrill voices and clapping their hands. In about fifteen minutes, we had seventeen and a half rows of one hundred men each seated on the desert floor.

After thanking the elders for their help, I stopped and thought a moment. These men had been caught in our encirclement of the area, having retreated for five days. Some had probably put up a fight—most were big men—but nobody had been taken red-handed. To hold such a group in a field until dark and, even worse, after dark, was impossible. I wasn't sure where to put them.

At first, the regimental commander didn't believe my report, then he promised vaguely to do something about it. I realized I had to make a Solomon-like decision on my own. Looking around, I found a fortified house.

Here I must mention that the Afghans build houses by constructing a square of clay walls four to five meters high. The length of the walls depended on the wealth of the owners, in this case about 70 × 70 meters. The doors are low, wide, and solid. (I used to wear a helmet just in case I bumped my head.) All the rooms in the home adjoined the walls, and the roof had about one meter of wall sticking up above it, pitted with gun holes. Here, a man's home really was his castle. A couple of guys with automatic rifles, running from roof to roof within the square, could make such a fortress all but impregnable to infantry.

I checked out the fortress. It seemed fairly spacious to me. The people, in their groups of one hundred, went in. I followed. Now it no longer seemed so spacious. The people were packed like fish in a barrel. But, for want of anything better, I had to stand by my decision. I posted a guard, and a BMD (an airborne infantry fighting vehicle) good-naturedly pointed three machine guns at the entrance door. I had just begun to breathe easier when the next crisis hit.

Suddenly, hundreds of shouting, crying women seemed to spring up from under the ground—the wives, mothers, and sisters of the prisoners. They had all brought little improvised bundles with them. We had to calm them down and set up a check point to investigate the bundles before passing the goods along to those inside. At first we were worried about this new invasion, but I soon saw that they had come in the nick of time.

The men inside began to chant, and the translator told me the gist of it: "You captured us, imprisoned us, now feed us!" But what could I feed them, when my own battalion was fighting on an empty stomach? I thought about our situation. These prisoners were one of the goals of the operation. But, having captured them, we could not prove that they were who we thought they were.

At 0900 the following morning, a reconnaissance company, a sapper company, and a third company (I no longer remember what kind) arrived. I was ordered to turn the prisoners over to these units, which would take them to the little town of Charrikar, about nine kilometers away.

That very evening, the commander of the reconnaissance company reported that since the road, which lay between two *duvaly,* was narrow and winding, some of the prisoners had run away. Furthermore, when they had reached Charrikar, the governor had told him that his filtration point wasn't ready, that his *Tsarandoi*[9] detachment was small and weak, and that he had no KHAT[10] people at all; he then gave passes

---

[9] Afghan government police.

[10] Afghan government secret police.

to the prisoners, and sent them peacefully on their way. Now I knew why people had been shooting at us from behind. The fish had found a hole in the net and had swum away. As I found out later, the same scenario was being repeated in the other battalion sectors.

Our battalion continued to move. A few of our units pressed on to the Gorbant river, where they unexpectedly encountered fierce resistance from a group of about forty people. There was a short-lived battle, during which two machine gunners from the Afghan battalion under my command took positions on the roof of a house commanding the area. With intensive fire they forced the *Dushmani* to withdraw. The battalion forced its way across the river and pressed the attack.

But here, we got an unexpected order. The units that had crossed the Gorbant were to return. I had already crossed the river myself.

On the way, I passed the house from which my machine gunners had fired. In the doorway, I saw the two old men who owned the house. They had their hands tied behind their backs. One of them had a severely bruised ear. Beside them, with a pleased look on his face, Lieutenant Bredikhin was pacing back and forth.

Lieutenant Bredikhin was a remarkable fellow in his own way. He was a chemist by education, and a lion at heart, but judging from certain indicators he must have been a poor student at the academy. My shortage of officers had forced me to place him in command of an Airborne platoon for this operation, and he had already caused me many anxious moments.

First Bredikhin, who had gone into action without a map or compass, got his hills (really mountains) mixed up, turned his unit ninety degrees, passed across the rear of his own battalion, and ended up with his neighbors in the Vitebsk Regiment. They told him what they thought of him and sent him back.

At that moment, a band of thirteen *Dushmani* came upon the left flank of our battalion and set up a well-disguised ambush before a passageway through a *duval*, and a two-man patrol of the 3rd Company walked straight into it. If the *Dushmani* had been patient enough to wait out the patrol, they would have had a good chance of doing serious damage to the 3rd Company, but they rushed things and opened fire too soon. The senior point man was killed, and the junior point man was wounded, but that gave the company enough time to deploy and return fire.

Then Bredikhin, who was still wandering in search of the rest of the battalion, happened to come up behind the *Dushmani* and had the presence of mind to wipe out the entire ambush party in six seconds. That was how we knew exactly how many people there were in the ambush. We captured two machine guns, two carbines, and nine automatic rifles.

Naturally, there was no contact from him during the entire operation, which made me suspicious, so that when he proudly reported his achievements, my estimation of him didn't change much.

The second time his name came up, a group of eight helicopters was targeted on the flank of the battalion where Bredikhin's platoon was located. Again, he dropped out of sight. There were no messages from him, no orange smoke to signal the location of the helicopters. Black thoughts began to fill my head, chief among which was that the helicopters might be shooting, too accurately, at their own men. Thank God, this didn't happen.

Now when I asked him, "Bredikhin, what's going on here?" the lieutenant reported precisely, "*Dushmani*, Comrade Captain. Look at all the 7.62 millimeter cartridge casings!"

And indeed, a lot of cartridge casings were strewn around the walls of the home. But I remembered where our Afghans had been firing from. I untied the two old men, and let them go.

Near evening, an order came down to secure our positions for the night. The battalion staff set itself up in the house where Bredikhin had captured the two *Dushmani*.

The companies reported their readiness. The anxiety of battle gave way to sleep, except for the sentries and patrols. In the courtyard of the house, a fairly spacious shed contained huge amphorae used for storing grain. One of our Afghan platoons spent the night in the shed. No one ever thought to look in the amphorae.

About two o'clock in the morning, there were several bursts of fire and shouts. Apparently, a *Dushman*, the nephew of one of the old men who owned the house, had been hiding in one of the amphorae. As he tried to sneak out, he stepped on somebody's ear. With a little more self-control, he might have been able to get away, but he turned out to be a nervous and ill-bred person. He opened fire.

The Afghan on watch let off several shots. The result was a dead *Dushman* and a dead government soldier. In the amphorae and in other places throughout the home, we found various weapons. So Bredikhin's intuition turned out to be right after all.

Operation "Ring" was a ruble-sized operation which brought in "chump change" results. We returned unsatisfied, in a bad mood, but wars in general, and this Afghan war in particular, do not allow you to maintain any one emotion for long. What the high command may have thought about the whole thing, we don't know, but it can't have been terribly serious. They were occupied with strategy, while we were preoccupied with tactical operations, one or two days in length.

I was lucky. The whole second battalion was sent to Bamian; the intelligence company in Charrikar was making sure that the silly local governor could rest easy. One company of the 3rd Battalion went to guard a textile factory in Gulbakhor. Only my battalion and the 3rd Battalion, minus one company, remained with the regiment.

The 3rd battalion, which was commanded by Major V.A. Vostrotin (a future hero of the Soviet Union), was considered within the regiment to be a seasoned combat unit. The commander of the regiment liked to save it for crucial assignments. And I was given the opportunity to train my battalion to my heart's content.

But add one more problem: the commander of the 108th Motorized Infantry Division, General Mironov, was, in the first place a division commander; in the second place a general; in the third place the commander of the Bagram garrison; and in the fourth place the regional military advisor. In other words, he had the right to give out all military assignments in the region. The 108th Division had two regiments, and the other regiment, again, was kept in reserve for crucial assignments. General Mirnov, therefore, dumped everything else on the 345th Regiment of Lieutenant Colonel Yu. Kuznetsov, and he, in turn, dumped them on me.

PART 4: IN THE BAGRAM VALLEY

It was exhausting work. I flew all over the Bagram valley to no avail; it was a useless exercise. Most of the operations were fruitless. To begin with, the Afghans were born warriors. Second, these were *their* mountains. Third, their intelligence worked. And fourth, even without any intelligence, our old military vehicles made so much noise and threw up so much dust that it was never very hard to figure out where the *Shuravi* (Soviets) were going. Everywhere, we were met with mines, and occasionaly with ambushes, usually near villages.

These ambushes, as a rule, were set up by relatively small forces in the following way. Somewhere behind some half-destroyed little *duval,* with a carefully prepared escape route, two or three people with grenade launchers and their assistants lay in wait.

Two or three figures pop up above the *duval.* Three or four seconds later, a salvo rings out. They duck back down. The assistants, with exact, practiced movements, put new grenades into the launchers. Again, the same figures pop up for the same amount of time. A second salvo. Then, they throw the grenade launchers on their backs and take off like the wind.

The commander of the tank battalion looks around—two or three vehicles are burning, and he drags out the wounded and dead, by which time the birds have flown. Not necessarily all that far away, just into the nearest *kyariz*[11] where it is fruitless to chase after them.

---

[11] A *kyariz* is one of a system of underground tunnels dug out hundreds of years ago; an ancient labyrinth.

You run, nerves on edge, off the roads, along the fields, along dry riverbeds. Intuitively, you either set your men under the armor to protect them from bullets or on top of the armor to protect them from explosions. If they hit a mine, only the driver will get hurt—but that's his job.

You fight with someone over trifles. You return to your regiment, send your vehicles to the park, and unload the unused ammunition. "Well," you think, "at least I have time to go to the bathhouse and scratch off some of these lice."

But no, damn it! You're given a new mission, and in two hours at most, you're kicking up dust in the other direction, and it starts all over again.

Several episodes in this confusing, exhausting period (the end of January to February 1982) deserve mention.

I tried to figure out who was fighting against us and why, and I think I got it right. As far as I could see, they fell into six categories.

First, there were the people who found any occupation troops intolerable. These were proud, independent, and freedom-loving people. Patriots.

The second category was made up of people who, as the result of the kaleidoscope of changes in regime—Zahir Shah—Taraki—Amin—Karmal—had lost some property and hoped to get it back, or acquire new property in the course of the war.

The third category was made up of religious fanatics. Infidels to their land insulted their religious sensibilities. They were waging a holy war—a *jihad*—and were ready to wage it for decades, if necessary, until the last infidel was cut to pieces, swept away, or carried off by the wind. They had the nasty habit of blowing corpses up into little pieces.

The fourth category was made up of mercenaries. They came from various ethnic groups, were brave in all respects, and had a high level of professional training, but they had one Achilles heel. These men sold their ability to fight. To organize an ambush in a letter-perfect way, and then shatter and pillage a passing column—that they could do. But if anyone offered tough resistance, the mercenaries would run, leaving everything behind, including their own dead and wounded.

The fifth category was unique. In Afghanistan, you had to pay for a wife, and it was expensive. A poor man would slave away doing back-breaking work, and, long after he turned thirty, he would still have nothing to show for it: no house, no home, no wife. There are a lot of people like that in Afghanistan. People took advantage of this along the following lines:

"How old are you, Mahmoud?"

"Thirty-six."

"How much money do you need to buy a house and a wife?"

"One hundred thousand Afghani."

"I can give you 200,000, Mahmoud, so you can buy it all, and live like a man. But remember: Allah never gives anybody anything for free. You have to earn it. Or more accurately, you have to fight for it. Just one year, Mahmoud. Before you look around, it will be gone. And then...."

It was an offer he couldn't refuse. Either Mahmoud would get a taste for blood, and then there would be no stopping him; or, after serving out his year honestly, they would settle up: "You fought well, Mahmoud. Thank you, and go in peace."

But nobody, as far as I know, ever went more than a kilometer "in peace."

And to my deep regret, we ourselves were the cause of the sixth category. The *Dushmani* would occupy some peaceful village, shell a Soviet column, and cause it great suffering. The enraged commander, guided by the principle "Let their mothers cry," would turn and let the village have it with everything he had. If he were inventive, he would then call for four to eight helicopters to make a strike on the village.

After the helicopters, an artillery battery would pump two hundred to three hundred shells into the village, and afterwards, they'd find out that out of every ten people killed, one of them might be a *Dushman*, the rest, of course, civilians.

A man, who has absolutely nothing to do with the war and who doesn't want to fight, returns home one day to find that the wife he had is now gone; the children he had are now gone; the mother he had is now gone. And his blood boils. He ceases to be a man; he is now a wolf—ready to kill without stopping. And the longer the war lasts, the more of these wolves you have. And we, with each new shift of replacements, threw a crowd of inexperienced kids into this bloody marketplace. With each passing year, the wolves became more and more hardened, and the kids remained kids.

That's how war goes. But during the war you could still find people stupid enough to say, "Why haven't you won yet?"

In the People's Democratic Party of Afghanistan (PDPA) there were two wings: the Parchunists and the Khalqists. (*Parchun* means "banner," and *Khalq* means "people.") Parchunists made up 30 percent of the party, and the other 70 percent were Khalqists.

Though the minority, the Parchunists, who represented the right-wing of the party, were its foundation. The big property owners, scholars, diplomats, and industrialists—the elite—all went into this wing of the party.

The Khalqists, the left-wing of the party, were a motley assemblage: peasants and workers, low-lifes of all types, extreme left-wing Marxists, extreme right-wing Marxists, Maoists, admirers of the Khmer Rouge; in short, a potpourri of leftists. They made up the formal majority. Ideological blinders, dogmatism, intransigence, and disagreements sometimes reached the point of armed confrontation. It was typical of the Khalqists to solve a party disagreement with the help of a long burst from an automatic rifle. No person, no problem, no more disagreement. It was just like in the well-known song:

> *Yesterday, we buried two Marxists,*
> *We didn't cover them with red calico.*
> *One of them was a left-deviationist,*
> *And the other wouldn't be one for the world.*

Due to their overwhelming intellectual superiority, the Parchunists held all of the leading posts in the Party, and all of the top posts in the army. But from the rank of regimental commander on down, the Khalqists dominated.

The Khalqist wing of the Party hated the Parchunist wing with every fiber of its soul. In the army, this entailed direct disobedience. If the commander of a regiment was a Parchunist, he could give any orders—smart ones, stupid ones, competent ones, timely ones—and it didn't matter. Whatever he said, the exact opposite would be done— because he was a Parchunist.

I learned all this from Mejid, the chief political officer of the 444th "Commandos" Regiment—tall, bearlike, with enormous physical strength. Most of the "Commandos" were small, lean, wiry people, and those whom Allah had blessed with great height were usually so thin they could hide behind a fishing pole.

Mejid had a passionate hatred for the *Dushmani*—who had killed his brother. One evening, as we were resting from our righteous labors, I asked him where he had learned to speak Russian so well. The stern and taciturn Mejid opened up and told me the following story. As a People's Democratic Party of Afghanistan activist, a good orator, and a strong organizer, he was one of those sent to the six-month political officers' courses at the Lenin Academy right after Karmal came to power, or more accurately, was put in power.

"You know, Sasha" (we had become fast friends; it was "Sasha" and "Misha"), "for the first couple of days I went to class, I didn't have any idea what was going on. On the third day, I went into the city. I looked around. Hello, Moscow!"

In short, Mejid plunged into dissipation. They tried to rein him in, to educate him, but nothing helped. The attraction of the beautiful women of Moscow was incomparably greater than any party trumpery.

"When my studies came to an end," Mejid remembered, "they told me that they wouldn't let me graduate. So I made an appointment with the director of the academy and said, 'Comrade General, listen to me talk in the language that the great Lenin spoke.' The general listened—he let me graduate. It was the girls of Moscow who taught me the language."

They weren't able to make much of a political officer out of Mejid, of course. But he was a strong, harsh, and as strange as it may seem, charming man.

Mejid had one way of encouraging his subordinates, and another of punishing them.

If a soldier distinguished himself, Mejid would form up the platoon, company, or squad, whatever he could get together at the time. He would ask the soldier to step forward, and for about ten minutes he would speak eloquently, praising the soldier's real and imaginary good points, not forgetting to mention his parents, brothers, sisters, aunts and uncles, and the village in which he was born, which had produced such a remarkable man. He wished the soldier health, happiness, many children, many donkeys and other livestock, a good home, a good harvest, and much more. Then he would pull several hundred Afghani notes out of his pocket, hand them to the soldier, kiss the soldier three times, Russian-style, and then dismiss him.

All the while, the soldier standing before the formation would be overcome with emotion, as would his comrades-in-arms, who would almost burst with the hope that someday they, too, might do something to make the political officer single them out.

But when a soldier was careless enough to do something bad and found out that Mejid was calling for him, he would start to shake. He walked like a rabbit approaching a boa constrictor, knowing quite well what would happen. It was always the same. As soon as the soldier got within arm's length and stood at attention, he would be hit with a quick, but amazingly strong, jab to the jaw. Nobody flew less than three meters. After that, his brothers-in-arms would carry the unfortunate man off and bring him back to his senses. He would spit out the loose teeth, and remember for a long time that violating military discipline was a bad thing.

Mejid enjoyed unquestioned authority, both among the soldiers and the officers, because he was brave and full of manly self-confidence. No matter what the situation, he would check to see that his soldiers were fed, set up well for the night, and that the lightly wounded were bandaged properly—people with flesh wounds did not get evacuated—and say a few encouraging words to the soldiers manning the posts. He was always the last one to bed and the first up in the morning.

Here, I think it is appropriate to say a few words about stupidity. Stupidity is expensive. I can say with a clear conscience that I did everything I could to protect the lives of my men. I kept it simple: I preached the American "scorched-earth" principle. I used artillery fire, armored vehicles, and helicopters to suppress the fire from enemy emplacements, and never sent my men into foolish attacks. Not many mothers grieved on my account, but there were losses, all the same. No matter how you plan, no matter how you scheme, no matter how you maneuver, you can't fight a war without losses.

But what drove me mad—and the longer I was there, the madder it made me—were the losses attributable to sheer stupidity. After I left Afghanistan, I made a final count: 52 percent of the losses in my battalion fell into the first category—inevitable losses—and 48 percent into the second—stupidity. I gave my men detailed instructions, on the assumption that any system had to be foolproof. Perhaps it helped; most likely, it did. But I never succeeded in completely solving the problem of stupidity.

"Comrade soldiers!" I said. "If you have a tight firing mode selector on your automatic rifle, put it in automatic position, but don't put any bullets in the chamber, and always remember to pull back the slide. If you have a normal firing mode selector, you can put a bullet in the chamber, but put your rifle on safety. If you don't, one false move, and it'll go off. Do you understand?"

"Sir, yes, sir!"

Exactly one day after that, a lieutenant by the name of Shumkov was crawling over a *duval*, with his automatic rifle over his back, barrel pointing down, loaded, with the safety off. He bumped into something—a burst, and one of the bullets hit him in the leg. The lieutenant had to rot for two months in the hospital.

A machine gunner on combat deployment hurried out through the right-side hatch of a fighting vehicle, forgetting to take off his headset. The connector plug got stuck, and he was pulled back by the head. He instinctively stepped down, stuck his foot into the tread, which was moving at five to seven kilometers an hour. The vehicle went another two meters, but that was enough to shred his leg below the knee. A cripple.

There were two inseparable friends in the third company: Nabiev, a machine gunner, and Akhmedov, a sniper. Due to the rocky countryside, and climbing through numerous *duvaly* full of thorny, prickly, spiky bushes and vines, soldiers' uniforms couldn't hold out. Two or three weeks of this and a soldier, no matter how much of a stickler, would look like a tramp.

On one of these operations, Private Nabiev's pants got into absolutely shameful condition. In order to cover his nakedness, he quietly helped himself to an Afghan's pants and went back into action. In the course of the combing operation, the hot-headed Akhmedov saw the bluish-striped ass of a *Dushman* about one hundred meters in front of him. He shot. The bullet went through Nabiev's right thigh, grazing the bone slightly. That day, we established a sort of record. I got a helicopter to pick him up twenty-two minutes after he was wounded. The battalion doctor, Gera Budko, waved his hand dismissingly, and said, "It's nothing! He'll be dancing in a couple of weeks!"

When we came back from the operation three days later, Gera went to the hospital to find out how the wounded were doing.

He came back looking dismayed. "Nabiev died," he said.

"How could he have died? The bullet went through his leg, and the bone was left intact."

"It was a fat embolism. The bullet just barely touched the bone, but it tore off a particle of fat. And that was it. The end of a strong, twenty-year-old man."

I examined other units in the regiment, and even other regiments. And a wild picture took shape. Roughly 50 percent of all losses were the result of carelessness, absent-mindedness, sloppiness, anything other than enemy action. Stupidity is not the absence of thinking; it's a way of thinking. Nothing is counted so cheaply, and nothing costs so much.

Two more events related to this period deserve mention. Mirbachakot is a good-sized village on the slope of a mountain and was a stronghold of the *Dushmani* movement in the Bagram valley. It was combed before me, I combed it, and it was combed after me, but nothing changed. It is etched in my memory for two reasons.

By that time, I had come to a complete understanding with the commandos who had been assigned to me. If you have something that you want to ruin completely, assign that job to the commandos, and you won't even have to check it. They leaked 100 percent of the information—whether through naiveté or stupidity it's hard to say. But no matter how many times you warned them, as soon as you told its officers the mission, the whole battalion would know about it an hour later.

I worked out a tactic that took advantage of this situation. The chief of staff would draw up a decoy plan with plausible-sounding details, which would be given to the commandos as their "mission." Their real mission would be given only to them at night, right before they were to move out. That way there was at least some hope of success.

But the Afghans began to get used to the fact that we were constantly deceiving them. So, I changed my tactics and started giving them the real mission. Mirbachakot! They listened absent-mindedly, and absent-mindedly made some notations on their maps. And in their eyes you could read, "Go on! Go on! It won't be Mirbachakot!"

We planned to move out at 0300. In accordance with established practice, I sent my battalion executive officer, Captain A. V. Popov, to wake the Afghans and clarify the mission for them, and I got busy doing the same for my own battalion.

In half an hour, Popov came back, mad as the devil.

"They're nothing but a bunch of fools! All two hundred of them. Each one has his own tent, and they won't get up. They're playing dumb. No matter how I try, I can't find the battalion commander or the chief of staff; it's no use."

This was something new. Leaving Aleksandr Vasilievich behind to get the battalion ready, I went over to the Afghans myself. I had better luck. As soon as I got there, lighting my way with a lantern, I stumbled on the battalion commander who was stretching and yawning. Soldiers were slowly, sleepily, getting out of their tents. I "unwittingly" turned the lantern on myself. The sleepiness disappeared from the battalion commander's face. He instantly pulled himself together and tried to greet me. I politely knocked him down. The chief of staff appeared from somewhere off to the side, saw what had happened, adopted a servile attitude, and stood off at a safe distance.

Azimov, a wonderful Tajik sergeant, coolly translated everything I said. "The battalion must be ready in fifteen minutes." They were still good soldiers, when they wanted to be. They managed to do it in time, despite each soldier having an individual tent, two blankets, a prayer rug, a teapot, and a bunch of other little necessities.

We moved out. I could see out of the corner of my eye that the Afghan battalion commander was furious, but when I turned to face him, he tried to smile.

The regimental commander, to whom I reported our readiness to start combing, suddenly asked, "Where are you?" I reported our location.

"So you're on the right flank. Wait. Don't start combing yet. Move over to the left flank, where the 26th Afghan Regiment will be waiting for you." He indicated the spot on the map. "Meet up with them, tell them their mission, tighten up their line, and then start combing. Understood?"

"Understood," I answered.

I left my headquarters staff over to the left flank. The outskirts of Mirbachakot were something like our *dacha* or garden plots. One garden was separated from another by a short *duval*, but they were thickly covered with prickly vines. In an hour and a half, climbing, panting, sweating, scratched, and bloody, we got out onto the desired road.

The commander of the left flank company was waiting for me in the appointed place.

"So where's the regiment?" I asked.

"It never came."

I reported to the regimental commander: "I have arrived at the appointed place, but there are no Afghans here."

"Hold on, hold on," he calmed me down. "They'll come."

Meanwhile, the medical instructor, trying to figure out how to repair our scratched hands, found a simple and ingenious solution. With the help of sticks and bandages, he made a makeshift swab and painted our hands, and frequently, our faces as well, with iodine. We all became "half-Moors." Meanwhile, the sun had risen fully, but still no regiment.

To all my questions, Lieutenant Colonel Kuznetsov answered briefly: "Wait!" Finally, a cloud of dust appeared in the distance, which turned out to be two GAZ-66s. A tall man, with a typical Slavic appearance but wearing an Afghan military uniform, hopped out of the first one.

"Hello, guys!"

"Hello," I said, thinking, "This must be an advisor."

After the advisor, a figure literally fell out of the cab, and I burst out laughing. It turned out to be a very old little man, with a wrinkled face that looked like a baked apple. He was all of one meter tall, from his hat to his shoes. God knows where he got it, but his head was graced by a helmet made famous in World War II movies—an SS helmet with little bumps on it that looked like horns. The helmet was far too big for the little old man. He was constantly pushing it up with his finger, but it stubbornly fell back, leaving only his stern gray mustache, big mouth, and little boy's chin visible.

While I was laughing, another advisor jumped out of the other truck and walked up. The little old man finally got his helmet sitting properly, and introduced himself through his interpreter: "Commander of the 26th Infantry Regiment." Other soldiers, just as small, with the same horned helmets, jumped out of the trucks. I stopped laughing.

"What is this, your bodyguard? When will the regiment be coming?"

The tall advisor looked at me sadly. "This is the whole regiment."

"What do you mean, *the whole regiment!*"

Before me stood twenty-six people, formed haphazardly into two lines. To my shame, I was quite wrong about them. These were good men. A regiment which once had about 150 men most of whom had run away due to enemy propaganda, and these little horned men were the only ones to stay. Most of them were just as old as their commander, clearly not able-bodied, with unnaturally heavy, work-callused hands, but I saw this only later. At the time, all I could think of was how I had climbed through those damned *duvaly*, gotten myself and my other people all scratched up, wasting all that time and shoe leather, only to stand here for almost two hours, just to get these... these....

While I raged on, the regimental commander and the military advisors quietly hung their heads. I went off to see Kuznetsov. The regimental commander calmly and reasonably asked:

"Did the regimental commander come?"

"Yes, sir!"

"So that means, you *do* have the regiment. However many there are, they're all yours. If it will make you feel better, make him a platoon commander for the duration of the operation. Now, move out!"

The battalion, with the Afghan "regiment," combed Mirbachakot, but it was a purely formal exercise. When you sit there on a mountain and see that a military formation has been shaping up across from you for five hours, only a complete idiot would sit around waiting for the spring to uncoil and hit him in the head. And the *Dushmani* were no idiots, they were warriors!

Our next operation—Argankheil—was remarkably successful: not a single man was killed or wounded, and there were no explosions. For me, that was the main indicator of success. On top of this, we captured about three dozen guns, a stash of interesting documents, and about ten or so prisoners, a good half of whom, due to the their smooth hands and faces, could not have passed for local peasants.

When I reported the results of the operation to the regimental commander, I heard for the first time: "You've finally learned how to do it right. Congratulations!"

All that was left was a trifle: to cross another six hundred to seven hundred meters and return to the armored group. The first company led the way, followed by the second. The last company, the third, was the rear guard. The armored group stood in three columns, bent a little to the left, due to the configuration of the terrain. My "*khashaemka*" (mobile command vehicle) came after the second company's last vehicle. I walked up to the vehicle and looked around. I could see the head of the third company's column about two hundred and fifty meters away. My driver brought out a canteen with some tea.

Before I could lift it to my lips, I heard a powerful explosion and cries coming from the second company's column in front of us. The canteen flew out of my hands. I dashed off to the site of the explosion. Thoughts came into my head like lightning: "The armor is blocking the road. Some fool must have put a grenade in the barrel of his launcher and forgotten to unload it. Someone else must have squeezed the trigger by mistake and sent the grenade into the turret of the vehicle in front, and. . . ." I imagined what I would see when I got there.

When I reached the company commander's vehicle, my worst fears were confirmed. A dead body lay to the right of the vehicle. The head and left hand were separated from the body. Something had cut out its eyes. You could see through his rib cage. To the left I saw the company commander, Senior Lieutenant Kovalchuk, who was covered in mud, with blood seeping down his right side. On top of the vehicle, his head in his hands, sat a sergeant, swearing. Another two soldiers sitting off to the side had caught some of the shrapnel. What had happened?

Senior Lieutenant Kovalchuk had an orderly, a bodyguard, a cook, and a jack-of-all-trades private named Petrov. He was a Siberian, as big as a house and known for his taciturnity. The soldiers often teased Petrov about whether he even knew how to talk.

While the second company was roaming about Arganheil, one of the soldiers found two Soviet-made PMN anti-personnel mines and presented them to the commander. The company commander was busy, so he didn't look to see if the detonators were in place, and waved them off: "Petrov, put the mines in your pack!"

Petrov dropped the fateful mines in the bottom of his pack. At the end of the operation, Kovalchuk, an experienced company commander, concluding that we were out of harm's way, lightheartedly took off his R-148 radio and gave it to Petrov, too.

"Put it in your pack!"

The soldier put the radio right on top of the mines.

Kovalchuk got the column moving, and stood in the turret's hatch. The sergeant sat down in the left hatch. Petrov, according to eyewitnesses, got up on the vehicle, stood up for a few seconds at full height thinking about something, and then jumped off. He landed in a hole, tried to maintain his balance, stepped back, and hit his back on the side of the vehicle with all his might. The letters PMN stand for "pressure-activated anti-personnel mine."

The two mines exploded. Petrov never wore a bullet-proof vest, which in any case would have been useless. It was his body, with the empty rib cage, that I had seen.

The radio accounted for the shrapnel. Forty-six fragments of that radio hit Kovalchuk, nine hit the sergeant, another soldier caught two of them, and a third, one more.

The doctor and the medics started bandaging the wounded, and the battalion executive officer and two soldiers carefully gathered Petrov's remains. To the right and to the left, the soldiers of the second and third companies sat on their armored vehicles and watched, mournfully munching their dry rations. The sergeant continued to curse. Nobody was surprised, and nobody was shaken, including me. Life goes on. . . .

We had been on the go since midnight. My watch showed 1700 hours, and we were all hungry. Somehow, the captured documents, guns, and all the rest had lost their importance.

When I got to the regiment, another blow hit me. The thirty-piece regimental band greeted us, playing something like "Roll Out the Thunder of Victory!"

"Tell your troubadours to cut it out," I growled to the conductor.

Continuing to wave his baton, the conductor replied, "I can't! The regimental commander ordered me to meet you with the band playing!"

PART 5: THE NIJRAB OPERATION

Starting on February 25, according to plan, the regiment took part in the Nijrab operation. If you look at the map, the Nijrab canyon looks like a big, beautiful tree with lots of branches. From its main, powerful trunk, several tributary canyons branch off to the left and right, thickly settled with villages. I got one of the lower "twigs," about 19.5 kilometers long.

Along the way, one of the motorized infantry's armored personnel carriers fell off a bridge. It was the last APC (armored personnel carrier) in their column, and my 3rd Company, next in line, had to drag the APC and the men out of the river. Out of the six men, two died instantly, three were seriously maimed, and another looked all right, but his mind was affected.

To my mind, the 3rd Company, commanded by Captain Boris Petrov, was unlucky. It was clearly the best company in the battalion, but for some reason—or perhaps because of it—it was the company that had to tread the bloodiest roads. The company always coped with its missions successfully, but for some reason, ambushes, explosions, shellings, raids, and accidents haunted it. So when I heard Petrov's report about the bodies and the crippled victims, the thought flashed into my mind: "The 3rd Company again. What the hell!"

The Nijrab canyon was nine hundred meters wide at its base. The villages began almost immediately. Further on, according to the map, the canyon became narrower and narrower. And somewhere around the seventeenth kilometer was the last lonely little house on the map. A two

"Automatic rifle bursts occasionally penetrated the howling blizzard. Who was shooting at whom, and with what result?"

kilometer "appendix" followed, which ended in a three thousand-meter mountain, covered with snow.

The Afghans marched into the canyon, and we followed. The first kilometer was filled with deathly silence. Not a soul could be seen. A dog, locked in a house, barked somewhere far off.

The Afghans walked calmly and confidently. They were a wonderful barometer of danger. If they walked as they did now, you could breathe easily. If they cocked their heads and took cover, that was it—the shooting would start in five minutes, maximum. How they did it, I don't know. It was either a sixth sense or their knowledge of local conditions. At the second kilometer, the Afghans started looking around, and the enemy opened fire from four places at once. We responded: the Third Battalion firing from the slope, and ours firing from the canyon. The shooting stopped.

We lost a young Afghan boy. He was about sixteen years old, no more, a sort of mascot for the commando battalion. That is probably why he was the only one in the whole battalion to wear a helmet and bullet-proof vest. The boy decided he was as safe as a tank. And he paid dearly for it. The bullet went through the vest and hit him in the heart.

Let me say a few words about bullet-proof vests. I learned not to trust them in Afghanistan, and I do not trust them to this day. The bullet-proof vests that were commonly handed out to the troops could save you from only three things: cold, stones, and blunt or spent bullets. But the vests are heavy, and people get a false sense of security from wearing them.

My good friend and classmate at the academy, Major V.A. Vostrotin, now a Hero of the Soviet Union and a general, but at the time, the commander of the Third Battalion, received a shipment of bullet-proof vests and decided to use them for an agitation and propaganda session. He had the battalion stand in formation, made a speech about how the party and the government were looking out for them, and ordered them to hang a bullet-proof vest one hundred meters away. He shot at it.

"Bring it here," he ordered.

A soldier brought it.

There was a hole through both the chest and back panels.

"Hm.... Hmm.... Let's try from two hundred meters."

They measured it off, hung it up, and he shot at it again. Right through. They hung it at three hundred meters and shot again. Right through.

"When they brought the vest back," he told me, "and I saw the fresh holes, I thought, well, I sure have gotten myself into a mess this time. I wanted to produce one effect, and I had achieved the exact opposite. I had to find some way out, so I said to them: 'Look what good weapons our masters from Tula and Izhevsk make for us! Not one bullet-proof vest in the world can withstand them, not at one hundred meters, not at two hundred meters, not at three hundred meters. With weapons like that, we can't lose. As for bullet-proof vests, I have never worn one and I never will.'"

In the canyon, the temporary silence was broken by the sudden eruption of a real battle. Bullets ricocheted off the *duvaly*, the trees, and the walls of the houses. We used our grenade launchers to suppress their gun emplacements. I moved a tank platoon into position. We fired our mortars. They shot at us from the houses on the neighboring slopes.

The companies of the 3rd Battalion were above these carefully masked burrows and caves and could do virtually nothing to attack them.

It was the tanks that decided the battle. A couple of dozen well-aimed shots shut down several of their emplacements, and the rest fell silent.

A snowstorm also helped. In a matter of minutes, visibility fell to 100 to 120 meters and continued to drop. The battalions crawled through the mountains for three days in this whirlwind.

We knew helicopters wouldn't reach us with our dry rations in this weather.

Automatic rifle bursts and single shots occasionally penetrated the howling blizzard. Who was shooting at whom, and with what result?

The cold, the heavy packs, the constant movement, the tension—all this took a lot of strength and demanded refueling. But our rations quickly ran out. All the cans were licked clean; every crumb and crust of bread was eaten. There was nothing left but the snow and the constant demands to move "Forward! Forward! Forward!"

I will always remember that feeling of helplessness before nature. It didn't matter what you did: you could bang your head against a cliff, howl like a wolf, stamp your feet, fly into hysterics. But nature didn't care about you, a mere pygmy; nature continued biting you with snow, mocking your wind-beaten face with its cracked and swollen lips.

We found nothing, and no one, in the villages except for goats—black, shaggy, looking like devils with bloodshot eyes. The soldiers quickly skinned them. At first, you felt sick because you were so hungry; now you were sick because you were gnawing a piece of goat. The main thing was not to smell it.

In this way, fighting with an unknown enemy, we got almost to the middle of the canyon, to the place where it sharply narrowed and split into two.

Here the damned blizzard finally stopped, and here we verified that no one had been lost in it. The 3rd Battalion, crazy with cold and hunger, came down from the mountains. The long-expected helicopter landed with our dry rations. Then the doctor, Gera, came up:

"Comrade Captain, the helicopter pilots have brought you a package!"

"Who was it? The CO?"

"No, it wasn't the CO."

"Then who?"

"They said something, but over the noise of the rotors, I couldn't make it out."

"All right, thank whoever it is! Divide it up among everyone, in a brotherly way," I said.

Gera was a real paratrooper. He knew two kinds of math: subtraction and division. He divided up and passed around some delicious orange tangerines, some hard-tack, and a piece of sausage among the whole command post. After the goat meat, it was wonderful.

"Oh, Comrade Captain, here on the bottom, it looks like a nice piece of salt pork!"

At those words, "salt pork," the soldiers raised their heads.

"No, no, leave that until evening, " I objected. "Let's not hurry."

Everyone sighed. The last soldier threw away his peel, and wiped his fingers on his pants. Life was beautiful and amazing once again. A paratrooper, armed with his dry ration, is invincible!

The 3rd Battalion, with enough food for three days, lay down in the sun for half an hour or so, and then went off down the canyon. The Afghans split up. Two of their companies and their headquarters went with the 3rd Battalion; one company stayed with me. All in accordance with the previously arranged plan. My 1st and 2nd Companies went up into the mountains.

We didn't get seven hundred meters down our branch of the canyon when a tank hit a land mine, fortunately, with the outer side of the treads: only two wheels and a meter and a half of tread came off.

The explosion was like a signal to open fire. They fired at us with all their "proletarian hatred," from the slopes, from their houses. The units on the slopes gave away their locations by the smoke. The air dispatcher sent a couple of Mi-24 helicopters to take them out. The two surviving tanks, the grenade launchers, and the mortars opened fire simultaneously.

As one of the T-62s opened up, a platoon of Afghans concentrated behind the tank, and in a rather haphazard manner started firing at the slopes.

One of the peculiar features of the T-62 is that it expels spent shell casings through a little hatch in the back of the turret. The tank gunner turns the turret, looking for the target. He finds it. He shoots. The turret spits out a spent shell casing, and it hits an Afghan soldier in the face and chest. Two of his comrades drag him to the rear. The others press even closer behind the tank and open fire, even more energetically. Another shot. The spent shell casing hits another soldier, and two more comrades have to drag him to the rear. I saw one-third of the platoon melt away in the course of a minute. Fools certainly make life interesting.

Finally, through our joint efforts, we were able to suppress the enemy firing points. And the crippled tank crew started to repair their tank. The sappers I had sent ahead found three standard Italian mines and one homemade land mine in ten minutes.

At the same time, the people I had sent out on reconnaissance came back and said that the road was impassable about four hundred meters up the canyon. The hard-working *Dushmani* had diverted a stream down from the mountain. And enormous boulders, which looked as if they weighed a ton-and-a-half each, were blocking the road after the washed-out section. A hot-headed lieutenant, a tank commander, suggested that we blast them away with shaped charges. I cooled his ardor:

"And how many boulders are there? Did you count them?"

"Yes. There are thirty-seven."

"And how many shaped charges do you have?"

"Five."

"So, counting all the tanks, we have fifteen. You shoot all your shaped charges, then all of your high-explosive fragmentation shells, and you still won't make a hole. And even if you do, what the hell good are you to me without any ammunition?"

The lieutenant cooled down.

I decided that we'd have to move forward on foot. We'd leave the vehicles behind—concentrated as much as possible and under guard. The regimental commander approved my decision. We regrouped.

We moved forward about a kilometer and reached a pretty big village, which, strangely, was crammed full of people.

At the entrance to the village, our reconnaissance patrols were met by a group of elders, standing apart from everyone else. They explained that this was a peaceful village, at war with nobody. The people were. They were ready to "let the *Shuravi* through."

I let the elders know that women and children were none of my concern. I had no questions for them but that they were to get all the men together. We needed to find out who had been shooting at us.

They got about seventy people together. Fifty of them were young, strong, healthy—and relaxed. The commander and the chief political officer of my Afghan company said they had an order that every man in the village was to be drafted into the Afghan People's Army. The Afghan officers asked me to let them proceed.

"All right. Everyone else can take a smoking break," I ordered.

The young healthy men were formed into two rows.

The political officer asked, "Are any of you *Dushmani*?"

Everyone in the formation shook his head no.

"Anyone who wants to serve in the People's Army, take two steps forward!"

The entire formation, without hesitation, took two steps forward. Not one of them even had to think about it; everyone had a bright expression on his face; the "enthusiasm" was absolute! The company commander, the chief political officer, and the KHAT officer beamed. The newly recruited government soldiers turned to the right, accompanied by five guards, and trudged off excitedly down the canyon. I never saw or heard from them again.

Usually, such "recruits," even if they joined a unit and got their own uniforms and weapons, turned out to be extremely unreliable troops. The most stupid of them, and there weren't many, ran away in the first days, taking their guns with them. The vigilant KHAT officers ensured that these deserters were caught. They were dealt with in various ways, depending upon the situation. But most of them were smart enough to wait it out for a couple of weeks until they became "part of the team." They wouldn't be fighting today or tomorrow—why not serve for a time in the army? Most of them wanted to leave, but not empty-handed; they wanted to bring their commanding officer's head with them, or better yet, the head of their *Shuravi* military advisor. That would give them instant respect in any band they happened to come across.

Thus delivered of its unexpected burden, the battalion continued moving up the canyon, and by evening, reached its end. My headquarters and the 3rd Company settled down. Above that, there was nothing left in the canyon.

We had finally reached the end. As the poet says, "If the stars are shining, it means that someone needs them." If a battalion is sent down a canyon, that means somebody needed that, too. We had done it, and we felt good about it.

But the 1st and 2nd Companies had to suffer up there on the slopes. And as soon as it turned dark, we heard long bursts of automatic rifle fire directed at our houses.

The 3rd Company reacted instantly, with a lot of noise, but not much effect. Our brother *Dushmani*, it turned out, were shooting by ear in the darkness, and ours were shooting back the same way. We lit the place up.

But you couldn't catch the Afghans with cheap tricks like that. The slopes, the path—everything was empty, not a soul.

Everything quieted down, but not for long. A short burst rang out. After that, a high voice started shouting obscenities in a characteristic accent. Several voices, a little lower in tone, joined in.

It was hard to pick out anything concrete in this chorus of vituper-ation, but the basic sense of it was clear: from the bottom of their dear little Muslim hearts, they wished that we would get the hell out and die. And not only us, but all our nearest and dearest relations as well.

It was understandable. The poor guys were cold, sitting up there in the mountains, and were trying to amuse themselves and get warm in any way they could. They amused us, too.

The 3rd Company answered back lazily. I ordered them to save their ammunition, and to fire back only when the *Dushmani* got too pushy. When dawn came, the people shouting obscenities were smart enough to disappear.

Somewhere around 0730, the commander of the 3rd Company reported that four old men were walking down the path. They were shouting, "Don't shoot!" I ordered them to bring the old men to me. The elders reported sadly that there were many women, children, and old men at the top of the canyon. They had fled there from fright, but they were cold, and many of them were sick. They asked for per-mission to come back to their homes. They said there were no *Dushmani* among them.

I cleared my throat, and then said: "Excuse me, honored fathers, but who was cursing me all night?"

The old men shrugged their shoulders. They knew nothing.

"Honored fathers, I'll tell you what I'm going to do. It took you an hour to get here. I'll give you three hours to collect the people and return. You come last. And when you've reported to me that there's nobody behind you, I'll start combing the empty canyon."

The old men accepted my ultimatum with grumbles and quickly disappeared. Our wait didn't last long. At a little after nine, the regi-mental commander called for me:

"So are you sitting and waiting?"

"Yes."

"Well, drop everything, and get the battalion together. Your mis-sion is to turn the column around, and come here"—he indicated the coordinates—"where you will be at the disposal of the army's chief of staff. The Afghans will remain at the fork. Tell them to report to the commander of the 3rd Battalion."

"But Comrade Colonel, I have told you about my ultimatum. I need more time!"

"I don't care about your ultimatum. I told you to drop everything and go back to the vehicles!"

So we did. I could imagine the look on the old men's faces when they arrived at the appointed time and found nothing but cigarette butts, empty cans of food, cartridge cases, and—nobody. "The *Shuravi* must have been pulling our legs," they would probably conclude.

In a little over two hours the battalion column was formed and ready to move out. We quickly reached the mouth of the canyon. The long and nasty way up the canyon seemed almost offensively short on the way down.

The army's headquarters was in the open. I picked an area for the battalion, and went off to report.

The duty officer asked, "Are you the commander of the 1st Battalion of the 345th? The chief of staff orders you to maintain your vehicles, feed the men, and give them a rest. You'll get your mission later!"

"Later? What do you mean later? Then why did I have to rush here, ahead of the sound of my own voice?"

"Captain! Why are you so upset? If you're told to rest, then go rest. Get yourself a shave. If the chief of staff had been here, he would have given you more than you bargained for. Go, captain, rest and wait."

The colonel stretched and yawned. I left. It was a pleasant command, as commands go. But I was choked with bitterness. I remembered how shamefully and quickly we had rushed down the canyon, and got still angrier. And my battalion would get soft. Indeed, everyone, including the sentries, fell into a deep sleep .

I woke up the battalion's chief of staff and harshly told him what I thought about the battalion's conception of duty. The chief of staff told the company commanders, and they told the platoon commanders. In about thirty minutes, everybody was fast asleep again—but not the sentries.

PART 6: AT MAKHMUDRAKI

We slept a little, serviced the vehicles, cleaned our weapons, and shaved. The more optimistic began to dream of going to the bathhouse.

At 0900 I was called in to see the army chief of staff. Again, he was not there, but a colonel, who had been entrusted to give me my mission, said that the battalion, acting as the army's advance guard, in concert with the movement protection detachment, would be securing the army's withdrawal from the canyon.

"When you get to this sector," the colonel made two marks on the map, which looked to be about four kilometers apart, "the movement protection detachment will cover you, and together you will occupy defensive positions along the road and secure the withdrawal of our main forces plus approximately six hundred Afghan trucks. You will be the last to withdraw."

"Which unit will be the last to withdraw before us," I asked, "and how will I recognize them?"

"What kind of stupid question is that! The rear guard and the mechanized convoy unit, ours or the Afghans', of course! Are all the paratroopers as bright as you are? Who the hell knows which unit will be last! Play it by ear."

But here, I dug in my heels:

"I'm not going to stand by the road counting all the trucks. That's what you guys at headquarters are for, to plan who will go last—us or the Afghans. If you don't, we could be stuck on these four kilometers until the Second Coming!"

The colonel glared up—he was approximately half a head shorter. Our eyes met. I thought, "Caesar, you're angry, and that means you know you're wrong." I put on a calm but arrogant expression. Not able to prevail in the staring contest, the colonel changed his tone:

"So, Captain, are you saying that you refuse to carry out your mission?"

There was an implied threat there.

"No, why should I?" I answered. "I'll carry it out. But I'll wait for the chief of staff, and I'll report to him that I am not satisfied with the way the mission was explained to me, and I will ask him to clarify certain points."

> **"I** *t rained. Vehicles, people, everything began to look like big clods of mud. A bigger clod was a vehicle; a smaller clod, a man.***"**

I could feel the arrogance and self-confidence radiating from me. The colonel broke. He looked at his watch in a businesslike way, and said, "Come back in half an hour."

Half an hour later, I had frequencies, call signs, and even the orders, both ours and the Afghans'. But no matter how hard my radiomen tried to use these frequencies and call signs, they didn't work. Still, the colonel had given in to my "whim."

"Now, is everything clear?"

"Yes, sir!"

"Well, good luck! Move out in an hour."

About seven kilometers from Bagram, there is a village called Makhmudraki. The men who live there are tough and fanatical, and with every means at their disposal, tried to knock out any column—it didn't matter whether it was a tank column or an Afghan infantry company on trucks—that dared to pass through the holy ground of their beloved village. And they did it in some pretty artistic ways.

I met a lieutenant colonel, a sapper, who was the commander of the movement protection detachment. The lieutenant colonel, I found out later, was forty-one years old, but he looked at least sixty. I don't know why, but he looked the very model of a grandpa, and I was dumbfounded that such an old man had gotten into the army.

The lieutenant colonel set the tone:

"So, Captain, you're a paratrooper, are you?"

"Yes, sir!"

"You people are always in a hurry. But no one who really understands what life is all about is ever in a hurry. Do you understand, Captain? . . ."

"Yes, sir!"

"Well, go on, report, and then we'll move out."

I reported, and we started to crawl forward. And I do mean *crawl*. The sappers, led by the lieutenant colonel, proceeded unhurriedly, smoothly, deliberately. It was like watching a film in slow motion. I began to get mad: "At this rate, it'll take until doomsday to get to Makhmudraki!"

But I didn't stay mad for long. At the third kilometer, the lieutenant reported that he had uncovered an Italian mine at a bend in the road. Soon, six more mines were found on the winding mountain road.

One of our drivers, Private Idrisov, fell asleep at the wheel and drove his vehicle seventy meters down between the loops on a sixty-degree slope. By all the laws of physics, the vehicle should have flipped and become a coffin for Idrisov and the other three people inside.

Somehow—Idrisov was so shocked, he couldn't remember how—he eased the vehicle down onto the lower loop of the road.

When I arrived at the scene, Idrisov was standing next to his vehicle, looking with crazed eyes at the tracks he had left behind. Then he sank limply to his knees and started banging his head against a rock. He was brought around, his forehead was bandaged, and I solemnly proclaimed him to be the best driver in the Airborne troops. The column moved on.

But soon we did lose a vehicle. One of our trucks found a mine with its right rear wheel. An improvised commission pronounced the truck dead: it could not be repaired. The pale, shaken driver and the men unloaded the truck, poured out all the diesel fuel, and pushed it over the edge. There's never a dull moment when you drive with us!

It started to rain, just a drizzle at first, but it got stronger and stronger. A road which seemed like solid concrete began to dissolve before our eyes. The liquid mud covered the soles of our boots, then the toes, and in two hours we were wading in mud up to the ankle. Vehicles, people, everything began to look like big clods of mud. A bigger clod was a vehicle; a smaller clod was a man.

From the end of February to the beginning of April were the nastiest months in Afghanistan. The hard ground began dissolving at a monstrous rate. Dirt roads became impassable to any kind of wheeled transport—even tanks and BMPs. After walking thirty meters, you could no longer see your shoes, and no one could tell what you were wearing on your feet.

The lucky people who had managed to procure rubber boots were envied and resented. Mud was everywhere: liquid, sticky, clinging.

The mine-sniffing dogs refused to continue their work and just looked at us guiltily, with their tails tucked between their legs. The sappers slowed down even more.

We moved forward like this for another kilometer and a half. The rain had become a solid wall, and the road became indistinguishable from the surrounding countryside. In some places, it was covered with water for up to 150 meters. Even the stubborn lieutenant colonel began to lose heart. We decided to stop for the night.

We were all soaked clear through to the skin: there was no way to warm up or dry off. We didn't even try to pitch tents. It would have been useless. We posted guards, and manned the nearest high ground. The men were ordered to rest in their vehicles. It was cold, wet, damp, and uncomfortable. But what could you do?

The battalion's material-supply platoon brightened things up a bit. Led by the powerful hand of Chief Warrant Officer Kostenko, the cooks got the tea boiling in record time, and while the battalion's shivering men gnawed at their husks of bread and drank their hot tea, they cooked up a double portion of tasty buckwheat *kasha* with meat for everybody. Neither before nor since have I tasted *kasha* like that. And it even seemed as if the weather had gotten better. It doesn't take much to make a man happy!

By morning, the rain had died down to a drizzle, but it had done its work. The column barely crawled along: two kilometers an hour, no more.

I pondered gloomily about how long I'd have to sit in Makhmudraki waiting for all the troops to withdraw from the Nijrab canyon. Thinking about the Afghans especially irritated me. They had "first-class" vehicles, all of it wheeled, mostly GAZ-53s. The only way I could imagine them sifting through this mess was being towed by a heavy tracked vehicle.

We were shot at, almost lazily, on the approaches to Makhmudraki, and we shot back. The shooting livened things up a bit, but we passed through Makhmudraki without any special problems.

The drenched, partially destroyed village seemed as if it were dead.

A reinforced motorized infantry company in BMPs was there waiting for us in the appointed place. I turned the movement protection detachment over to their care, and we said a warm good-bye to the lieutenant colonel and his sappers.

It was strange: while we were working together, my relations with the lieutenant colonel had been dry and correct, but when we parted, we suddenly discovered that we liked each other very much. It seemed that a tear even came to his eye, but perhaps not; it was hard to tell in the rain. Vladimir Semenovich Vysotsky was a thousand times right when he wrote:

> *If he frowns, and he's glum, but still comes,*
> *If he's mad and won't talk, but still walks....*[12]

---

[12] This comes from a song about mountain climbers, who may not be outwardly friendly, but whom you can trust with your life on a difficult climb.

I started establishing control over my sector of the road. I have to say that four kilometers of road for a battalion of a little over two hundred people is an awful lot. We set up zones and sectors of responsibility, the sectors of fire for the armored vehicles, the grenade launchers, the mortars, and the machine-gunners. I reported that we were ready for the column to pass through.

I received a laconic response: "Wait."

By evening, the wind picked up, blew away the clouds, and the rain stopped. The weather became penetratingly clear, and significantly colder. It was March 8 (International Women's Day), and the officers joked that our wives remembered us and wished us well, and that their collective request had been heard in the offices of Heaven; hence, the good weather.

But Makhmudraki's reputation gave me no peace. I didn't understand why it had been so easy to enter the village. A battalion stretched along a road, one vehicle for every 120 to 150 meters, squeezed up against *duvaly*, and the side of the road (because the road itself had to be left free for the columns to pass through) presented a tempting target for attack. Yet as I was reconnoitering the area, over and over, criss-crossing the various zones and sectors, I didn't see a living soul. Still, we all sensed we were in a dangerous position. I could read the alarm on the faces of the officers and men. Jokes hung in the air. It's unpleasant when you think you've told a funny joke and get nothing but tense faces and anxious eyes.

Night came. I checked the guards myself, and then sent my chief of staff to do it again. I listened to the company commanders' reports. Everything was quiet. An hour passed quietly, two, three. . . .

Night. Darkness. The soldiers were exhausted. The officers were even more exhausted. Eyes drooped. People began to feel that everything was all right, and would continue to be all right. But the *Dushmani* from Makhmudraki had acted simply and wisely: they had slept quietly while we were awake, and at dawn, when it seemed as if the danger had passed, they crept up on us as only these brave mountain warriors could—silently, like a cat walking on a thick carpet. The salvo exploded the darkness. Cannons roared in response, and machine guns and automatic rifles started rat-a-tat-tatting. Along all four kilometers, a wild bacchanalia broke out. It lasted about five minutes. I led the battle myself, but the thought kept gnawing away: "Boy, did we screw up!"

The last burst of automatic rifle fire rang out.

"Company commanders, report the situation and your losses," I ordered.

First Company: situation normal, no losses.

Second Company: a gunner in an APC was killed by a direct hit from a grenade, the driver was wounded.

Third Company: normal, no losses.

I had expected the worst. So, I couldn't believe this report.

"Check and report again."

After a few minutes, the 1st and 3rd Companies confirmed their reports, and the 2nd Company clarified theirs: the wounded driver had been hit with grenade fragments in the back of the leg. Nothing bad—he'd live until his wedding. He was lucky.

A strange feeling came over me. On the one hand, a pity for the gunner. I had known him well, a big and brave soldier. But on the other hand, I felt an enormous sense of relief.

I stood in the hatch of my vehicle, holding an automatic rifle. The cold dawn had only just arrived, enveloping the earth in a patchy fog. In front, to the left, to the rear, everything was quiet; there was no movement. On the other side of a *duval*, a field spread out for about one hundred meters, ending in some sort of structures. And in that field, near those structures, I saw the silhouette of a man. To the right of him I saw two more silhouettes, standing practically next to each other. A wave of anger swept over me. We had just beaten back an attack from an unfavorable static position, and now, to lose men through someone's stupidity—idiots!

"Hey, you!" I sputtered in rage, sharply turning the hatch to the right.

The single silhouette sent a burst of automatic rifle fire that hit the antenna and fuel tank of my vehicle. Soon, three automatic rifles were blasting at me. The automatic rifle flew up to my shoulder. I shot the first man with a long burst of tracer bullets, and got him. The other two hit the ground. My brain accurately, coldly registered the precise hills where the two had dropped to the ground. I emptied the rest of my clip on that place. I quickly put in a new clip and shot off another thirty rounds. The driver and two radiomen joined in. They hadn't seen what had happened, but they shot by guesswork, following my tracer bullets.

"Cease firing," I said.

Everything died down. I ordered one of the radiomen and the driver to keep a watch on those structures, jumped down to the ground, and lit a cigarette:

"Volodya, go look and see whether they hit anything."

The battalion's chief communications officer, Lieutenant Volodya Galaburdov, inspected the antenna, the tarpaulin, and looked quickly at the fuel tank. It had an amazing number of bullet holes in it; there was nothing left to patch.

While Volodya was looking at the fuel tank, I stood and smoked, relaxed, and thought about what an idiot I had been, how I was a fool to shout at the figures, how childish it was to shoot at the lone *Dushman* who started it all rather than the two together who would have been easier to hit, how one bullet is enough for any mortal while dozens had buzzed around me.

I have always been a fatalist, subconsciously. But on that morning, on the dawn of March 9, 1982, that fatalism was transformed into something resembling a religion.

"Forget about it, Volodya! If you can't patch it up, we'll just get rid of it. Or you can keep it as a souvenir if you want."

Volodya burst out laughing. The driver and the radiomen joined in.

And with that, we resumed our progress. Tanks and BMPs began towing all sorts of wheeled vehicles—both ours and the Afghans'—

along the softened and monstrously damaged road. Everything was covered with mud; engines roared at their highest capacity; commanders swore artistically at their men—but everything kept on moving, moving, moving.

Toward evening on the second day, a well-formed column of several tanks and tank tractors approached the command post. Each of the three tractors was pulling a wheeled vehicle; a motorized infantry company in five BMPs covered the column. The column stopped, and a gray-green, unshaven, dirty colonel jumped out of the first tractor. He introduced himself as the acting head of the army's tank service and said, in a simple, everyday tone: "There's no one left behind me. After me, you may go. Good luck, Captain."

The column pulled out. I waited another half hour and gave the command for us to move out as well. The Nijrab operation was over.

PART 7: GARRISON DAYS

Due to the persistently bad weather, things were relatively quiet. Within a week, the battalion had itself back in order. Everyone finally scraped off all the lice, got enough sleep and enough to eat, and serviced the equipment and the weapons.

Knowing the bad influence of idleness on a soldier's soul, I got the regimental commander to approve a combat training plan for the battalion, and started implementing it. All of the battalion's specialists competed. The winner's reward was a banner, with several cans of stewed meat and condensed milk, and a bag of candies attached to it. Only a trifle, but a pleasant one.

And combat training is not like the world championship; if you lose this year, you don't have to wait until next year. The losing teams, urged on by their commanders' pride, corrected their mistakes, improved their coordination, practiced, and frequently were able to get their own back in a couple of days, to the general delight of the unit. The victors tried to hold their positions, and the training turned into a pleasant sporting event. Everything went well, and everyone was happy.

But things don't always go well. Sometime around the end of March, two events occurred, which, if they had gone "right," could have changed my life.

One day, it was the turn of my 3rd Company—a deserving, fighting unit, which had won all possible laurels, including more prize-awarded stewed meat than anyone else—to guard the base.

One of the posts, manned by a squad which was headed by the battalion's best sergeant, was directly adjacent to the 108th Motorized Infantry Division's material supply battalion (OBMO). That battalion had a bakery, which was run by a warrant officer, a true artist. Everyone, from soldier all the way up to marshal, loved the bread.

The "world's best sergeant" decided to honor the bakers by sampling their unequaled product. For this purpose, he sent two absolutely incompetent "diplomats."

If the "diplomats" had shown the slightest amount of courtesy, gallantry, or politeness, they would have returned with the bread, but their Airborne chauvinism did them in. They arrived at the bakery with an enormous bag, and in a haughty tone, demanded that they fill the bag with freshly baked bread immediately.

The bakers had respect for their work, and were big, strong men with characters to match. Without so much as a disrespectful word, they gave the "diplomats" black eyes, bloodied their noses, knocked out a few of their teeth, and kicked them out of their territory.

The ambassadors appeared, pitifully, before the man who had sent them. The sergeant could not bear to see his subordinates humiliated this way, and "sounded the alarm." A BMD descended upon the bakery from its main position. The team assumed its designated positions, wiping bloodied noses, and the infantry was deployed. All of these actions were accompanied by loud threats.

The bakers, who had their own pride and dignity, took up the challenge, and from their side, a KamAZ, which had a ZU-23-2 anti-aircraft gun system attached to the back, moved into fighting position. Anyone who had anything jumped into the back of the KamAZ. The *"Zushka's"* gun pivoted around in a threatening way.

I arrived just as the duelists had reached the point of hesitation. If some soul with weak nerves had fired a shot, this childish farce would have turned into tragedy. And I wouldn't be here to write about this now.

I remember the *"Zushka's"* gunner: he was wearing a white apron, with a towel around his waist, and a helmet. It's hard to say who would have won this duel. The vehicles were about 120 meters apart in an open field. But there is a general principle that goes like this: he who shoots first, laughs last.

I roared like a bear. Both sides ran away, but, to their credit, without leaving their weapons behind. The "world's best sergeant" became the "world's best private."

Later, at the end of May, the sergeant, who had been restored to his position and had been discharged into the reserve, admitted honestly that my arrival had been like manna from heaven for him. The boys had driven themselves into a corner; they could see no dignified way out of this foolish situation. They couldn't just shout: "Bakers! We give up!" They couldn't! Their Airborne pride wouldn't let them.

The second little misunderstanding took place two days afterward. At 0610 that morning, everyone had been present for morning PT, but at 0815, at roll call, the first company was one soldier short.

That soldier had served a year already. He was an ethnic Gagauz, and people thought highly of him. But there was still reason to be uneasy. I reported it to the regimental commander.

Yuri Viktorovich Kuznetsov, a renowned hothead, instantly ordered: "Drop everything and go find him!" So we started searching. At 0900—nothing. At 1000—nothing. At 1100—still nothing. At 1130, the regimental commander ordered that the search be broadened, that we should bring Captain Serikov's 2nd Battalion into it.

Until two days before, the second battalion had been stationed in Bamian for several months. Due to the bad weather, the battalion had not received its food deliveries for the past two weeks. Thanks to that, everyone, from the battalion commander to the soldiers, was so thin that they could model the structure of the human skeleton.

Caught unaware by this command, the "starving battalion" started deploying. But the search soon ended, although, as it soon became clear, the situation had only begun to heat up. An UAZik[13] stopped near regimental headquarters, and the regimental supply officer, Lieutenant Colonel Slava Zhukov, jumped out, dragging the lost soldier by the collar. The soldier stood there, downcast. Zhukov ordered: "Call off the search! Everyone into the commander's office!"

The battalion's chief of staff, Major V. I. Livensky, and I went into the regimental commander's office. Vladimir Ilyich Livensky had arrived in Afghanistan in June 1979. This was his third year in the country. He had all sorts of good qualities, but his directness and his short temper had held back his rise in the service. Vladimir Ilyich did not know how to bootlick.

The office was small. There was a T-shaped table in the middle, a few chairs around the wall, a map, a portrait, and a safe. Just a normal office.

Lieutenant Colonel Zhukov sat at the table, and the soldier, looking completely broken, stood by the door. The commander himself wasn't there. Livensky and I hadn't had time to open our mouths before the command rang out: "Attention!" and the commander burst into the room.

Yuri Viktorovich was extremely upset, although, in my view, that was his normal condition. He began bluntly:

"You! You're supposed to be commanders! And yet your soldiers run away like rabbits!"

"Comrade Lieutenant Colonel, let's investigate this from the beginning. The soldier...," I began.

"What? Investigate? No! I'll be doing the investigating from now on. And you can go to°°°°"

---

[13] A four-wheel drive vehicle which looks somewhat like a Jeep Wrangler.

Vladimir Ilyich and I reacted to this crude expression in different ways. Livensky turned white as a sheet. As for me, the blood went straight to my head. I sputtered: "Go where?"

"What's the matter? Are you deaf? I said go to****," Kuznetsov roared.

Zhukov's mustache started twitching nervously. The soldier in the corner shrunk back, and he seemed to stop breathing.

It was a small office; only one step to the door. The first thing I did was to get Livensky out of there. Then I stopped at the door. Looking straight in his eyes, I asked the commander once again: "Go where?"

He answered: "Go to****"

With all the strength that nature had given me, which was doubled by my rage, I slammed the door shut behind me. The partitions in the headquarters were made of plywood and lightly puttied; the blow had a lot of noisy consequences. The door itself slanted in a strange way, the putty came out of many of the cracks, and the duty roster came banging down from the wall. A glass-and-tin kerosene lamp fell off its stand and crashed onto the floor. The duty officer and his assistant were numbstruck. I stood and waited.

But the commander did not emerge from his office. For him, we no longer existed. Taking the arm of my chief of staff, who was numb with rage, I went back to my quarters.

As it turned out, it had been much ado about nothing. The night before, the soldier had had a stomach ache. This was very common in Afghanistan. Everybody got them. I do not know a single person who served in Afghanistan who had not experienced the charms of such a stomach ache at least once.

After having the runs all night, and being the disciplined soldier that he was, suffering through morning PT, he checked in at the regimental dispensary. In response to his complaint, the normal military doctor said, "Suck it up and get back to work, and don't forget to sign the guestbook on the way out."

Undone by this boorish behavior, the soldier remembered a hospital about two kilometers away. His stomach got worse, and the soldier, running and squatting in spurts, set off for the hospital. When he finally made it, another no-less-military doctor dealt a final blow to his faith in the medical profession: "After lunch, go report to your duty doctor!"

After assessing his strength and concluding that his health would not permit him to go back, the soldier made the correct decision: await the duty doctor and try finally to get some medical attention. He found a bathroom in the hospital's backyard and dug in beside it.

A group searched the hospital. They conscientiously questioned the duty doctor (by that time, a different doctor), the nurses, the sick, and the wounded. They walked around the hospital's grounds. It did no good. Nobody had seen or heard of him. Nobody looked in the backyard. The regimental supply officer, conducting his own search, happened to go into the backyard at the very moment when the soldier had started running hell for leather to the bathroom. He ordered: "Stop! What's your name!"

The soldier, stood at attention, not without difficulty, and reported. As the result of this incident, my chief and I were sent to °°°° by our commander.

This was the first time that such a thing had happened to me in my military career, and to Livensky as well. Slamming the door didn't really help. Since we weren't used to such treatment, it was hard to take, and we sat in my quarters, gloomily looking at each other.

But soon my ability to think clearly and coolly returned:

"Ilyich, did he just send us to °°°°?"

"Yes," the chief of staff confirmed.

"Far away?"

"Far away!"

"So what are we going to do about it? Just sit here swinging our legs?"

"What should we do?"

"Duty officer!"

"Here!"

"Tell the technical supply officer to report to me."

"Yes, sir!"

He appeared.

I briefly explained the situation to him. "We have been sent to ****. We're sitting here waiting for the commander to put us back to work! So, Vyacheslav Vasilievich, until then, you will be in command of the battalion! Any questions?"

I knew the idea shocked and frightened him, but he simply said, "No, sir!" and asked for permission to leave.

Why did the choice fall on the technical supply officer? Because at the time I had neither an executive officer nor a chief political officer. We had only three senior officers left in the battalion.

Nobody bothered us. The next morning, the soldiers went to PT, washed up, and had their breakfast. That day, there was a regimental roll call. Out the window we heard: "Attention! Eyes left!"

We heard the soldiers snapping to attention, and then, a knock at the door. Vyacheslav Vasilievich appeared on the doorstep:

"Comrade Captain, the battalion is formed up and ready for roll call. Everyone is present! Technical Supply Officer, Major...."

Depressed by the burden of command which had suddenly descended upon his shoulders, knowing full well that if he led the battalion to regimental roll call he would be blamed for something that was not his fault, Vyacheslav Vasilievich decided to pretend that nothing had happened. I could understand and even sympathize, but there was nothing else to do. I took the official position:

"Vyacheslav Vasilievich, I entrusted the command of the battalion to you, and even explained the reasons why. So, Comrade Major, go on and command it!"

The technical supply officer shifted from foot to foot a few times, sighed deeply, waved his hand, and left.

From outside, his tenor voice could be heard: "At ease! To the regimental column, Forward MARCH!"

Outside the window, my battalion marched off in the direction of the parade ground. Livensky and I exchanged glances; we both thought, "We've gone too far to turn back now!" There was nothing left to say.

Then Vladimir Ilyich found an unexpected way out:

"Commander, let's play dominoes."

In the corner of my little room stood a little table with long legs, covered with thick polished glass, given me by my attentive chief political officer, Major Golubev. I had had virtually no free time, so I hadn't used that box, but now. . . . We set up the table and started playing. What Vyacheslav Vasilievich told the regimental commander remains a mystery. But within fifteen minutes, he came into the room without knocking, sweaty and panting:

"Comrade Captain, the regimental commander is calling for you!"

"Report to the regimental commander that the chief of staff and I are still going in the direction he sent us, and are waiting for him to call us back. Go on, Comrade Major!"

"Comrade Captain, Aleksandr Ivanovich. . . ."

"Do it, Comrade Major!"

We resumed the game.

A few minutes later, the door opened, again without knocking, and the chief of the regiment's political department, Lieutenant Colonel S. M. Kudinov, stood on the doorstep. He looked frail, but he was smart, authoritative, and brave. We stood up. Sergei Mikhailovich looked up at us attentively with his intelligent eyes, and with a broad but forced smile, said, "Boys, is there something I don't understand, or are you engaging in some sort of rebellion? The commander of the regiment summoned you, and you didn't show up. Your technical supply officer fed us a line of bull. Let me remind you that, although it doesn't say so in the newspapers, we are at war. This situation can come to no good. Aren't you afraid of what might happen?"

Without even glancing at each other, we both smiled, broadly and joyfully, and said, "What kind of rebellion can this be? The commander of the regiment publicly sent us, officers of the Soviet army, to. . . uh. . . how can I put this politely? Well, let's just say that he needs to bring us back from where he sent us. We're sitting here patiently. We're ready to carry out any order of the Party or the government—no problem."

"You both know full well that the commander is a hothead, but that he doesn't hold grudges. If you come back, he won't say anything to you, believe me! Is it worth it to get into such trouble over something this trivial?"

"It's not trivial, no matter what you might think," I objected. "And therefore, it *is* worth it."

"And do you think that the commander will come here and apologize to you?"

"That's what we're hoping!"

"Well, don't say that I didn't warn you."

Sergei Mikhailovich's mustache twitched for a little longer, and then he smiled and walked away.

We returned to our dominoes. Dominoes, in my view, is a game which is on an intellectual level only slightly above tug-of-war. We both hated playing it, but, having chosen this form of demonstrating our nonrebellion, we were doomed to play until the bitter end. So we shuffled the dominoes once again.

But we never had the chance to finish the game. A shadow rushed past the window, and Yuri Viktorovich Kuznetsov appeared on the doorstep, looking like an enraged bison. Anger had almost deprived him of the ability to speak, so he shouted in bursts that sounded like automatic rifle fire:

"You!... In wartime!... A flagrant demonstration of disobedience. ... You'll be court-martialed...."

I picked up the table and sent it crashing onto the floor at the commander's feet. Glass, table legs, and dominoes went flying in various directions. Something, either a table leg or the tabletop, hit the commander in the shin.

Yuri Viktorovich wasn't a bad guy, I was sure of that, but nine out of every ten words coming from his mouth were obscenities. Then, he would cool down and be sorry about what he had done, but the train, as they say, had already left the station. He had the reputation of being a rude, foul-mouthed man. But there was nothing he could do about it.

Everyone in the regiment knew about in the commander's character, and if someone simply gave in, Yuri Viktorovich would keep on abusing him forever. Any resistance, as strange as it may seem, had a soothing and restraining effect on him. As happened now: rubbing his leg, meeting unexpected and extremely stiff resistance, the regimental commander instantly changed his tone:

"Sanya, Ilyich! What's going on, fellows? I just lost my temper. You know what a hothead I am! You know I'm a psycho. Why did you have to do this?"

And with that move, Ilyich and I felt guilty.

"Come on! Let's go!"

So picking up our hats, we trudged off after the limping commander.

We all got up onto the platform. Kuznetsov commanded: "Attention!" The regiment froze.

"I lost my head and sent the commander of the first battalion and his chief of staff to ****. I hereby take those words back. Comrade Captain, Comrade Major, get back in formation, and command your battalion!"

"Yes, sir, Comrade Lieutenant Colonel!"

We took our positions on the right flank, accompanied by the smiles of the officers standing in formation. And the biggest smile of all was on the face of Vyacheslav Vasilievich, who had suffered so much for the truth.

PART 8: THE APRIL OPERATION

Life and the service went on. At the beginning of April, the regimental commander summoned his executive officer, Lieutenant Colonel Pavel Sergeevich Grachev, the commander of the third battalion, Major Valery Aleksandrovich Vostrotin, and me, and defined the mission as follows:

"The *dukhi*[14] have gotten too big for their britches. Soon they'll be sitting on our heads. It's time to do something about it. But if we come rattling after them in our vehicles, nothing will come of it. So let's try feeling them out a little differently this time, more quietly, on foot. The operation"—the commander pointed out an area three kilometers from our regiment's base on the map—"will be carried out by the 3rd Battalion. Pavel Sergeevich, you will be in charge of the operation as a whole. And you"—the commander poked me in the chest—"will get together a reinforced company in armored vehicles and take personal command of it, and if something goes wrong, you will secure their withdrawal. The operation will start early in the morning. You have a day to prepare. Report your solution in three hours."

We worked it out, coordinated our plans, and reported back. We got his blessing. Vostrotin's boys equipped themselves carefully. They jumped about like rabbits to make sure that nothing rattled or squeaked too loudly.

The next day, at 0400, the 3rd Battalion set out noiselessly for the area of the proposed operation. The 3rd Company, with a mortar platoon, a platoon of AGS-17s, and a self-propelled artillery platoon, waited in the regiment's depot. I was to head this part of the operation.

Time went by agonizingly slowly, and various versions of the upcoming operation would play out, over and over again, in the imagination. There was nothing but the silence of the morning before dawn. Dawn came slowly. The sky turned red, and became brighter and brighter. The silence was soothing, and I decided that nothing would happen: Valery Aleksandrovich would have an easy time of it and return safely.

The quiet exploded. A grenade launcher went off, and the characteristic thud of the DShK machine gun could be heard above the rattling of the automatic rifle fire. The battle was catching fire and spreading. I got in touch with the regimental commander, hinting that

[14] Literally: "ghosts," a slang term for the Afghan resistance forces.

perhaps it was time for us to move out. The commander growled at me: "Don't shove your nose in where it doesn't belong. Wait until I give the order!"

I don't know what was on the commander's mind, but I knew it was time. I could feel it in my bones.

"Start your engines!" I ordered.

The vehicles roared and became wreathed in smoke, and at almost the same time I could hear in my headset: "'Hunter,' this is 'Duck.' Move out, 'Hunter.' Move out!"

The column went about three kilometers,

> *In any military action, there is always a first and a last man killed. There's nothing you can do about it; it is Fate.*

plunged into a labyrinth of villages, and emerged on the bank of a narrow canal about eight meters wide, with a concrete bed. I could hear the blast and rattle of guns. We opened fire, but that was just to clear our consciences. The battle was virtually over.

The Afghan *Dushmani* were warriors of the first order. In addition to their other positive qualities, they were pragmatists. Why stay and fight armored vehicles, which can crush you into the wall of a *duval*? The moment they heard the roar of our engines, they turned and ran.

A couple of Mi-26s passed overhead, firing several NURs, and one helicopter dropped a bomb. I have a strong suspicion that this was also to clear their conscience.

Again there was relative quiet, but this time it was completely different.

Grachev and Vostrotin sat under a *duval*, smoking gloomily. About ten meters away, a soldier lay dead, with his hands stretched out wide. There was a black hole where his right eye was supposed to be. Two soldiers were bent over, dragging Senior Lieutenant Astakhin to an APC. With each step, Astakhin's head rocked back and forth unnaturally. He was dead.

Five minutes later, the soldiers carried away Senior Lieutenant Popov, who was seriously wounded. Popov had not been wearing his helmet, and there was a long wound which bared the skull on his close-cropped head. Bone fragments, straw, and other trash stuck out of the wound. There was almost no blood near the wound, but it pulsated out of his mouth in spurts.

A little later, they carried out still another dead man and several wounded men. It was all too typical: no matter how carefully, quietly, and competently the 3rd Battalion had gone into the indicated region, it had been followed, and the enemy had taken appropriate measures. When the battalion began to send reconnaissance patrols across the canal, the enemy suddenly opened fire from several directions.

I had always envied Vostrotin's good training. It explained how they were able to survive a bad ambush with only three dead and seven wounded. Astakhin's death gave everyone another pretext for discussing fate.

Astakhin had served out his time honorably in Afghanistan, and had been awarded with the Order of the Red Star and the medal "For Bravery." His replacement had already arrived, and he had turned over his position, but then this operation came up, and he said:

"Boys, I'll go on this last operation with you, and then I'll go back home to the Soviet Union."

When Vostrotin found out about his decision, he ordered: "Tell the fool to shut up and get ready to go home." But Astakhin argued so passionately, insisting that he was an officer and had given his word, that Vostrotin finally gave in:

"The hell with you! Go on, then!"

When the shooting started, Astakhin was standing on the bank of the canal, next to the steel bar framework of some hydro-technical equipment. All that was left was the framework of steel bars. A bullet hit Astakhin in the right shoulder, knocking him down; he hit his right temple on the metal framework, and his body slipped into the water. It wasn't the bullet that killed him. It was the blow to the head that knocked him unconscious and allowed him to drown.

Another of the dead was "Shurik" Popov, who had been one of my cadets. He was short and neat, a smiling, well-built young man. He had come as a replacement two or three weeks before the operation. It was his first and last one, because, three days later, Senior Lieutenant Aleksandr Popov died in the hospital, without regaining consciousness.

That quiet morning had put the final period on the lives of two senior lieutenants, one of whom had served impeccably for almost three years, and the other, who had never been in action before.

In any military action, like in any war, there is always a first and a last man killed. There's nothing you can do about it; it is Fate.

With the dead, it didn't matter, but it was urgent that the wounded be evacuated. The column had jumped along a rut next to the canal, and had lost all maneuverability. Not even the most adroit driver could turn his vehicle around. It would have been stupid to backtrack, it would have taken too much time. The canal stretched forward on the map another three kilometers or so before disappearing in the thicket of villages.

But the column had to turn around somewhere. Taking two riflemen and a sapper, I walked forward along the canal hoping to find a weak *duval* and a field behind it. The plan was simple: we would knock down or blow up the *duval*, pull the column into the field, and pull back out through the hole. In 250 meters, my face broke out in a blinding smile. There was a short *duval*, and behind it, a big, flat field.

We found a nice crack in the wall, put our crowbars in, rocked back and forth, and a huge piece of the *duval*, and then another, shook loose, fell off, and rolled into the canal. The company commander pulled up the column, and the first APC, growling, crawled onto the field.

But it had been too easy. Some clever soul had seen before me that if the column were to turn around, it could do so only here. The APC roared, shifting gears, lurched forward, and the air resounded with an earsplitting explosion.

Standing about ten meters away, I was hit by something, and when I came to a few seconds later, I found myself sitting in a muddy field with sharp pains in both legs below the knee. The top of my boots had deep dirt marks from the clumps of clay that had hit it. I mechanically rubbed my hands over them, looking for a shrapnel hole. But there were no holes.

I stood up. The APC had hit a mine with its right tread. Three wheels had come off, and large chunks of tread. I looked for dead or wounded soldiers.

The driver stood beside his APC, sucking in air like a fish out of water, wiping the blood off his injured nose in hesitant, sad motions. A sergeant wearing a headset stood in the hatch senselessly shaking his head.

I walked all around the APC. I heard a ringing in my ears. For a few moments, everything around me seemed touchingly dear to me. Then this idiotic feeling passed, but the ringing remained. No one had been killed; no one had been wounded. The only casualty was the driver with his bloody nose.

The mistake had been mine; I should have sent the sappers to check the field for mines. But still, I had every reason to roar at them: "Sappers! Goddammit, get over here!"

But the sappers, without waiting, had already started to check the field. They found two more Italian mines, and then reported: "That's all!"

"Check it again! I have no intention of putting my damaged APCs up for a fire sale!" I ordered.

They checked it once again. It was clean. We towed away the damaged APC, and moved on without further adventures.

PART 9: COMING HOME

By that evening, I had to switch to shoes. Both of my shins hurt unbearably. It was a rather foolish situation. That there was not a single piece of metal in the clods of dirt that had hit me was, unquestionably, a plus. But my legs were killing me, and I imagined myself going to a doctor and having him say, "What's the matter, did you get dirt in your boots?"

The battalion's doctor, Gera Budko, did rub them with something and the pain went away for a while. But in the middle of the night, the pain came back. By morning, amazingly painful sores that looked like pine cones had appeared on my legs; three on my right leg, and two on my left. I decided to swallow my pride and went looking for the regiment's chief medical officer.

Captain Aleksandr Vasilievich Sukhorukov was a remarkable doctor and a very nice guy. In short order, we set off together for the hospital.

It seemed that I had severely injured the periosteum in both legs, and I was to wipe something on them, and drink something. I wiped the stuff on my legs, drank what they told me to

> **"When I landed in Moscow, I saw the Russian birches.... With a lump in my throat, I turned away, pretending to look for something."**

drink, but the damned pine cones did not disappear, and the pain did not go away. By morning, the cones had moved ten centimeters to the side.

Some sort of unexplained infection was wandering through my body. The doctors got mad and looked at me suspiciously: "Why, this guy's nothing but a malingerer!" I, in turn, looked at them suspiciously: "Why, they're nothing but quacks!"

I continued to perform my service duties. I walked painfully, unlacing my shoes whenever I could, but nothing helped.

The matter ended when Sukhorukov, unbeknownst to me, reported to the regimental commander. Yuri Viktorovich appeared at the dispensary, looked at me, and expressed himself in his typical manner:

"What a sissy! Gets his bones grazed a little bit, and he's already got some sort of high-falutin' illness. You're on furlough, starting tomorrow. A month from now, I want you back here, healthy as an ox."

I went to the Fergana hospital and the hospital in Ryazan. They took a quick look at my legs and instantly diagnosed an inflammation of the lymph nodes, and told me there was nothing to be done.

So I returned to my native Novocherkassk, but with serious doubts as to whether I would be able to return and carry out my army duties.

In Novocherkassk my mother, who knew nothing about medicine, fixed up a bucket of hot water with aloe in it, and I stuck my legs in. I kept them there because I didn't have anything better to do, not because I believed that anything would come of it. But after my first treatment, the pain, to which I had grown accustomed, began to disappear. I brightened up and spent three days sitting on the front porch with my legs in a pail of hot water.

The result exceeded all my expectations: everything cleared up and never returned. I slept for fourteen hours straight, and when I woke, I was as healthy as an ox.

I don't know what it was. A nervous ailment? I'm not a nervous person, and nothing like that ever happened again.

One thing stands out from this furlough: when I touched down at the Moscow airport and saw Russian birch trees again after the naked cliffs and deserts of Afghanistan, I got such a lump in my throat that I had to spend about five minutes looking away, pretending that I had lost something.

I returned to Afghanistan sometime in mid-May. In my absence, the regiment had taken an active part in the Panjshir operation and when I got back on deck, it turned out that there was no longer any "deck" at all.

My battalion had been torn apart: one company, headed by the battalion's executive officer, was in Anava, and made up the regimental commander's reserve; another, led by the battalion's chief of staff, in compliance with the order to broaden the airport's security perimeter, was manning a control point near Makhmudraki; another company, less one platoon, had been given to the 3rd Battalion. The other platoon of that company was on constant guard duty at regimental headquarters, and had not been relieved for seventeen days straight when I returned.

I lost my head. My battalion, my mailed fist, which I had lovingly nurtured, had been split apart into individual fingers, and these fingers had been spread far apart. I asked the regimental supply officer, who was on duty at the time, "So where will I go in this situation?" I received an honest answer:

"Hell if I know! Probably to Anava. The CO and Grachev are there. The 3rd Battalion with your company is there, and your reserve company is there."

So I packed up and got out onto the heliport to catch the next flight in that direction. About ten minutes later, a helicopter touched down and Yuri Viktorovich Kuznetsov jumped out. I reported to him.

"Are you healthy now?"

"Healthy as an ox!"

"Good boy! But where do you think you're going?" Kuznetsov asked.

"To Anava!"

"No! We've got enough goldbricks there without you. What do you think you're going to do there? Drink vodka and goof off?"

"What do you mean, drink vodka? I've got two companies there."

"I've got Pavel Sergeevich there, and from all indications, I won't be getting him back for a while. So you, buddy, will be my regimental executive officer. Turn around and go back to headquarters! Forward, MARCH!"

Yuri Viktorovich was right. For those first three weeks that I served as acting regimental executive officer, I was morally exhausted. There were dangerously few people left in the regiment, and problems kept piling up. And there was no one to serve as replacements. Soldiers and officers were dead tired and learned how to sleep standing up. No amount of shouting or goading helped—you had to force yourself to do it.

We had to change the service rotation, and increase the rations. The sick and wounded gradually returned, all from different units. We organized composite squads and platoons and put them to work.

The cold storage unit broke down. We had to kick an Afghan anti-aircraft battery out and set up a makeshift cold storage unit in their cold barracks.

The 108th Motorized Infantry Division battalion's bakery burned down, and we had to start our own, turning yesterday's riflemen into bakers. The bread problem was solved.

Another dozen or so problems arose. In short, it was a madhouse!

But gradually, everything was more or less settled. I became a battalion commander again, but without relinquishing my newly acquired duties as acting regimental executive officer.

Then a wave of orders came through, cutting the commanders of various units to shreds for slovenliness, short-sightedness, and poor combat preparation of their subordinates. They demanded heightening some things, shaping up others, finishing off others, and achieving still others. A cycle of demonstration exercises was ordered.

The regimental commander entrusted this to me, explaining:

"You served in the academy for eight years! That means you're a specialist on these things. That academic 'hole' of yours has almost disappeared, but there's something left; after you finish, you can be my deputy again."

I immersed myself in the demonstration exercises—how to march, how to deploy, how to undeploy, how to carry off the wounded, how to storm a village, how to clear a minefield.

I baked plans like pancakes, and the regimental commander approved them without reading them. As a rule, it took me a day to prepare an exercise, and then we demonstrated, demonstrated, demonstrated.

Somewhere near the beginning of June, I was sitting with my back to the door, laboring over the plan for my next demonstration exercise.

The door squeaked, and someone walked in. Without turning around, I rumbled, "Go back out and come back like you're supposed to!"

"Is that any way to talk to your regimental commander?"

I jumped up. Yuri Viktorovich had graced my little kennel with his presence. Judging from his appearance, he was in a wonderful mood. He reminded me of a happy cat, waiting for a second helping of cream.

"What are you doing?"

"Drawing up plans for the next exercise."

"Put them away. Come with me."

That meant there was something he wanted to drink to. I had no time to drink, and besides, I didn't want to. I declined politely: "Thanks, but I don't have time. I need to. . . ."

Yuri Viktorovich blew up. There was not a trace left of the purring cat.

"Captain—attenTION! I am ordering you to come with me!"

This was something new.

"Yes, sir, Comrade Lieutenant Colonel!"

In the commander's spacious air-conditioned room, a table was spread out. It was luxurious by Afghan standards. The regimental executive officer and the most respected chiefs of the arms and services were already sitting there, whispering and looking at each other. What sort of holiday was this—"thank God it's Wednesday," perhaps?

The commander took his place at the head of the table. The chairman of the political department stood up. He unfolded a sheet of paper, and, in a solemn voice, he began to intone:

"By order of the Presidium of the Supreme Soviet of the USSR, the commander of the 345th Detached Airborne Regiment, Yuri Viktorovich Kuznetsov, is to be awarded the title of Hero of the Soviet Union."

All was clear. The commander was beaming, and we all relaxed. We recalled various wartime episodes, stressing their humorous side, made toasts, and gave congratulations. There was a lot of drinking with good food to chase it down. Somewhere around 2330, the head of the political department, Lieutenant Colonel Kudinov, made a purely rhetorical remark: "We're celebrating in here, but the regiment doesn't know anything about this."

Which put the proverbial spoon of tar into the commander's barrel of honey. Yuri Viktorovich reacted instantly: "Deputy, go form up the regiment!"

I demurred: "What do you mean, 'form them up'? Taps was an hour-and-a-half ago. We can tell them in the morning."

The whole party turned to attack me.

"What's the matter with you! A Hero of the Soviet Union is giving you an order, and you dare...."

Yuri Viktorovich was so upset that he temporarily lost the ability to speak.

I went to form up the regiment.

As I was walking, I got more and more annoyed. I was more than a little tipsy, and I had always been opposed to anyone commanding troops while in that condition. But there was nothing I could do. I had a direct order from my regimental commander, and a Hero of the Soviet Union to boot!

I got the regimental duty officer and the operations duty officer together and gave them their orders:

"Without any undue fuss, quietly, wake up the whole regiment and form them up on the parade ground in columns by company, *without weapons*, to hear an extremely important message. Turn on all the searchlights."

They set to work. They informed all the units, but things got mixed up. The soldiers, especially the officers, had learned from painful experience: "If they're getting us up in the middle of the night, and if they're going to be giving us a message, then there's got to be more to it! If we run over there without our weapons, they'll say, 'You fools! Go back and get them!'"

So the companies and platoons rushed to the parade ground in full gear, armed to the teeth, flame-throwers and all.

During the hubbub, I sobered up completely, but the people in the commander's room had crossed over that certain line, to put it mildly.

What does it mean to be drunk? It's when you've had more than you should, but less than you want to. When I went off to report, everyone was in such a good mood!

Kudinov said that perhaps I had been right, and we could tell the troops in the morning.

I lost it: "The regiment is formed up now. Just try and tell them that we were just joking, that they should just put their weapons away and go back to bed. 'Good night, children!'"

That had some effect. The regimental commander and the chief of the political department marched off to the parade ground. It was hard, but they courageously set a course for the platform and climbed up onto it.

I gave the command: "Attention!" Kudinov, despite his slight build, could hold his liquor. He managed to keep from slurring his words by enunciating them clearly and with intervals in between. While he was reading, Yuri Viktorovich stood quietly at the corner of the platform, tears glistening in his eyes. From time to time, he bowed from the waist.

The regiment understood, and forgave the condition of its commander and his deputies. In the light of the searchlights, the faces of the officers and men were serious and solemn. And in them, you could also see pride in their regiment—a regiment which had a difficult lot, which had been split up by the will of the authorities, but had flowed back together and gathered into a single fist. And it understood correctly that their own collective work as soldiers, their courage, their valor, their will, had materialized in that title of Hero of the Soviet Union which had been awarded to their commander.

After the reading was over, the regiment shouted "Hurrah!" three times, and that shout, from the lips of the whole regiment, was warm and heartfelt.

A few more days were spent doing the exercises. And then, one morning, on the 13th of June, a sergeant from the regiment's communications section came up to me:

"Comrade Captain, if you please, I have something to tell you! But I have to whisper it to you, Comrade Captain!"

> **"T**he mine exploded. The soldier's helmet and his head inside were intact. But from the head down, there was nothing but a bloody cage and rags.**"**

At another time, I would not have tolerated anyone talking to me like that, but something mysterious shone in the soldier's eyes.

"Well, tell me!"

"Comrade Captain, you have been awarded the rank of major ahead of schedule. The order is dated yesterday and came by telegram. But if the commander knew that I spilled the beans, boy, oh boy!" and the sergeant held a finger to his lips.

To be honest, I had been waiting for that order. I even had a guest list of twenty-four people ready. So I assured the sergeant that I wouldn't give him away, and gave him ten checks[15] for the good news.

In approximately one hour, the regimental commander called me in and ceremonially read me the order, gave me my new shoulderboards, and congratulated me.

"I serve the Soviet Union, sir!"

Afterward, I said, "A major who hasn't washed the news down yet is not a real major. So permit me, Comrade Lieutenant Colonel, to invite you to a celebration at 1900 this evening."

"Will you have time to set it up?"

"I'll have time. It's not the kind of thing I'd screw up."

"How many guests are you planning on?"

"Twenty-four, twenty-five people."

---

[15] Soviet troops in Afghanistan were paid in scrip called "checks."

"Where?"

"In the bar."

"Give up that idea! You won't be able to fit that many people in that little bar. See if you can make a deal with the artillery people."

"Yes, sir, Comrade Lieutenant Colonel."

The artillerists were the envy of the battalion. They had a dormitory with fifteen square meters of living space *per soldier*. So I paid my respects to the artillerists. The artillerists congratulated me and consented to let me use their mansion for my celebration.

Everything was ready on time. All the guests had shown up. There was only one thing missing: the regimental commander. But an event like this could not start without the "father," so everyone waited patiently. After about fifteen minutes, I sent my executive officer off to find him. He reappeared about five minutes later:

"The commander is talking with General Mironov. They're drinking a few shots to the Hero. He says he'll be here soon!"

Another fifteen minutes passed. I had already decided to go myself, when a soldier appeared, the commander's orderly:

"The commander and General Mironov are coming to congratulate the battalion commander!"

"Understood!"

Two spaces were freed at the center of the table. We placed the best vodka there. Five, ten, fifteen, seventeen minutes passed. At the eighteenth minute, a furious regimental commander burst in.

The sound, the fury, the cursing—I didn't know what was going on! The tale later unwound: intending to congratulate me on my promotion, the commander of the 108th Motorized Infantry Division, Major General V. I. Mironov, accompanied by the regimental commander, set off for the ceremony. What the CO was thinking of, I don't know, but he took the general to the bathhouse. The bathhouse manager, spotting the regimental commander and his VIP guest, and knowing the CO's temper, locked himself in the bathhouse from the inside.

Yuri Viktorovich pulled the handle. The door did not open. Struck by this lack of hospitality, which looked like mockery, Yuri Viktorovich went crazy. He started pounding on the door, but it didn't budge. The general exploded: "I've had enough of your Airborne hospitality. You invite me, and we're met with a locked door. I'll never set foot in this nest of boors again!" After that, he turned sharply away, walked as fast as he could to his UAZik, and without another word, flew off to division headquarters.

Now the commander, seeking a scapegoat for his bathhouse misadventure, sent a squall of abuse down on our heads.

After this torrent of vitriol, many of the officers decided they had urgent business elsewhere.

In due course, the commander cooled down and made a heartfelt speech about how you could make a real man out of any unfinished cadet commander if you really wanted to.

Early that summer, the battalion and I conducted a few insignificant operations. Major V. I. Livensky was in command of the reinforced company near Makhmudraki. This company was the best in the battalion: it was the most cohesive, the best trained, and my best fighters. But they were frustrated. After listening to increasingly irritated reports about adverse conditions and how Afghan donkeys were wandering into and exploding the company's minefields, I appealed to the regimental commander to let me relieve the company. My prayer reached God's ears. Sometime near the beginning of July, the regimental commander gave me the following mission: "Get your troops together, and go get your favorite company!"

By the next morning, I set off at the head of a reinforced Airborne company. Livensky had been informed and was supposed to be waiting at the head of his column, which was to be ready to move out.

His reports had been pessimistic. It was unbearably hot. The men's clothes rotted away in a matter of days. Soldiers were reporting for duty in underwear, helmet, and bullet-proof vest. The scrupulous Major Livensky was sickened by the company's deterioration.

We took the scenic route to avoid mines, which were the bane of life in Afghanistan. It was five kilometers longer than the straight route, but we almost never touched a road and we didn't hit a single mine. The sappers went ahead of us on tank tractors. When we were only six hundred meters from the meeting place, the sappers laid a path along the gentle slope of a hill. Nearby was a shattered road, with a village tucked behind the foothill.

In ten minutes, we met Livensky. It took another ten minutes to form up into a single column.

The observers reported that all was quiet around us. Moreover, even though it was still morning, it was already terribly hot. I gave the command:

"Get up on top of the vehicles. Report your readiness to move out."

"Ready! Ready! Ready! Ready!" I heard in my headset.

"Move out!"

The tank tractors, and behind them, the whole column, pulled into the path we had just come through, thinking it safe. We approached the hill. The tank tractors passed along the slope, and the APC with the sappers in it. I came fourth, and the chief of staff fifth. The company commander's vehicle came sixth. I had almost finished rounding the hill, when I heard an explosion and saw a column of smoke and dust fly into the air.

"Stop! Prepare for action!"

But there was no battle. The explosion had struck our sixth vehicle and thrown Senior Lieutenant V. M. Pinchuk and the command squad in various directions. According to the chief of staff, who had seen the explosion, in spite of their shell shock, they did not forget to pull the slides of their automatic rifles and were ready, in firing position, when they landed. They acted as good soldiers should.

The driver had been severely bruised, but was not otherwise wounded. One other soldier had been inside the vehicle instead of marching alongside, because he had felt sick. The mine exploded under him. He had been wearing a helmet. The helmet and the head inside were intact. But from the head down, there was nothing but a bloody cage and rags.

The sappers cleared the way. We got out of that damned path, and went back into the roadless expanse. That was my last operation in Afghanistan.

On July 10, the regiment movingly and warmly said good-bye to its "academics." Many of us were going to various academies—eleven in all.

There was a party that evening. Everything went well. A chief warrant officer from the sapper company, a man about forty-five years old, who was deeply respected in the regiment, joined us. Like any normal Russian, he suffered from an excessive devotion to alcohol and was soon pretty well plastered.

Someone decided to play a joke on him by pouring him half a mug of straight alcohol and half a mug of water and then switching the mugs on him so he was given the water first, and then the alcohol. The idea was that the drunken warrant officer wouldn't be able to tell the difference. Chasing the water down with the alcohol, he'd choke, cough, wheeze, and we'd all have a good laugh.

He drank the water carefully, wiped his mustaches, and just as carefully, without even moving a muscle, drank the alcohol. He politely poked his fork at something on the table. He directed a quiet, contemptuous glance at us. The warrant officer had clearly demonstrated his moral superiority. Nobody laughed. We all felt like cattle. Thank God we had the sense to apologize.

The old man was merciful; he said, "All right, I forgive you. You are all too young to know any better anyway!"

The next morning, the airplane set its course for Fergana. The spiderweb of *duvaly*, the tightly packed houses in the villages, built according to the principle "my house is my castle, and my village is also my castle," flashed under the wing for the last time. They grew smaller and smaller, and then, finally, disappeared. Under the airplane's wing, mountains, mountains, and still more mountains floated by.

We sat, closely packed together in the cabin. Theoretically, we should have been happy, but for some reason, there was no joy.

Everyone's face was gloomy and introspective. Everyone was deep in his own thoughts. All attempts to strike up a conversation just hung there in midair. That flight, as I recall, was filled with unexplainable grief, unexplainable dissatisfaction, and the faces around me were just as dry and severe as the mountains we were passing over.

In Fergana I spent a week settling accounts with the regiment. I sent no letters or telegrams home—I hadn't seen any point in it: I'd be flying home soon enough anyway. But that, it turned out, was a mistake.

God knows what the regimental clerk had been thinking, but when he typed the order for the new battalion commander, he typed, "to replace *the late* Major A. I. Lebed." The regimental commander had obviously signed the order without reading it. And the "soldiers' telegraph" quickly carried this phrase to faraway Ryazan.

A conscientious fool is more dangerous than an enemy. There was just such a fool in the Ryazan Airborne School, who brought this news to my wife.

She didn't believe it. She had only begun to receive the money which I had sent her faithfully from my first arrival at Bagram. She had written to me that everything was fine, that she had enough money, that everyone had enough to eat. And now she had steeled herself to await the official news.

My former battalion commander, Lieutenant Colonel Vladimir Ivanovich Stepanov, a man with wonderful spiritual qualities, paced in circles, unsure of what to do: on one hand, I had been killed (he had seen the official order!) and he had to tell her the news; but on the other hand, a smiling woman was walking with her children, walking to the store—how could he deal her such a blow? And then I arrived—arrived to see my wife turning gray at thirty years of age. It had cost her much to maintain her shell of inexhaustible faith. How happy Vladimir Ivanovich was! I'm not sure which one of us was happier: he, for me that I was alive, or I for him, that he had kept that heavy boulder to himself, and had not dropped it on the mother of three children. She would have believed him.

The transition from war to peace was a two-hour flight, but it wasn't that easy. Peace is the normal human condition: smiling women, laughing children, stores doing business, men, in no hurry, not afraid of anything. Two hours ago, I saw flaming vehicles, charred bodies, entrails on the *duval* walls, and a head in a helmet—the remains of someone's son, brother, or grandson.

You can't wipe war out of your memory. In peace, hypocrisy is an easy mask to wear, but war makes us indecently naked: either you're a man and a warrior, or you're a man in name only.

We brought Afghanistan home with us—in our hearts, our souls, our memories, our habits, in everything. This incompetent political adventure, this attempt to export our revolution, which had not justified itself, spelled the beginning of the end. In 1986 Alma-Ata caught fire, and then Karabakh, Fergana, Georgia, Tajikista. . . and on it spread. The number of those killed and wounded on Soviet Union territory has long since outstripped the number killed on Afghan soil.

Who failed us? A corrupt bureaucracy. Today, these same people have simply exchanged their Party cards for democratic banners. We must understand that, or nothing will change. It will only get worse.

CHAPTER 5:
THE ACADEMY

NAROFOMINSK. THE TRAINING CENTER for the M. V. Frunze
Military Academy. It was the end of July 1982. From every city and
town, from all the ends of our vast country, motorized infantry officers,
Airborne officers, intelligence officers, border guards, chiefs of staff,
battalion commanders, regimental executive officers—all of those
whose military service had earned them the right to continue their
military education in the academy, found their way here.

Nobody took your Party card. Nobody turned you in if you told a
political joke. Most of us had served in Afghanistan. In the first hours
and days, we were on the way to forming fast friendships. Our motto
was "let the best man win." Two groups of Airborne officers passed the
entrance exams. I was the commander of one of them. When I arrived
and reported to Colonel Aleksei Petrovich Lushnikov, he shook my
hand, and without letting go said, "Ah, the group commander has
finally arrived." I don't know what prompted him; I had never seen
him before. But that's how I became a commander.

But I was depressed. It was the atmosphere. The atmosphere was
saturated with humiliation. I was a battalion commander with thirteen
years of service behind me. I had been responsible for the course and
the outcome of military operations, for the lives of my soldiers. I was

accustomed to respecting myself and to having people respect me. And suddenly, I again felt like a young floppy-eared puppy in basic training, reporting to his first sergeant. The transition from one world to another was too drastic.

Every morning, we had to clean up the campus: our job was to pick up cigarette butts and scrap paper. So, where were the brooms, the rakes?

"Any idiot can do it with a broom. Use your hands." We made ourselves brooms and bought rakes in the store. We cleaned up the campus in a civilized way. After all, we were paratroopers.

Or, they'd say: "Your group's job is to mow that field over there. You've got until morning to do it!"

"What about scythes?"

"Any idiot can do it with a scythe. . . ."

The store didn't have any scythes. Heroic battalion commanders, veterans of the Afghan War with medals on their chests, cut themselves wooden swords with penknives, and joked angrily: "At least we get to relive our childhood!" The field was cut by the appointed time. And who gave the commands? As a rule, an idle, rude supply corporal or warrant officer. They could report any of us if we complained, and a black mark would go in our personnel file.

Then it came time to take the exams. To pass them, you had to follow two principles: 1. Never say, "I don't know." The most outrageous guess, if arrived at by racking your brain, would at least earn you a C. 2. Never bring a crib sheet. The penalty for violating these principles: expulsion.

You could also get kicked out—if you lost a classified book. That meant the "heave-ho" for the group commander, the person in charge of keeping classified information, and the person who actually lost it. As a rule, there wasn't anything really secret in such books. But that didn't matter. The book had the stamp on it, so off you go!

There were other ways you could get kicked out, but for us, everything went normally. We passed. After each exam, only about two or three people would fall away.

I remember two of the five exams: the one on military vehicles, and the language exam. Some genius decided that for the test on military vehicles, you had to memorize 18,500 numbers.

You had to remember these numbers in the time allotted to prepare for these exams. It all turned to mush in your head, especially since most of these figures referred to tanks, armored personnel carriers, and other "infantry" vehicles. In Afghanistan I had been assigned tank platoons and tank companies. I had given them missions, they accomplished them. Sometimes, they hit mines and blew up. In order to avoid giving them ridiculous, impossible missions, I knew their fighting characteristics, what kind of weapons they carried, things like that. But what need did I have to know how their engines or suspensions were built? I had a "guitar" (a mechanical gear in a box shaped like a guitar) of a T-62 tank. Luckily, some thoughtful person had written in tiny letters in pencil on the "guitar" what it was and what purpose it served. With that and a little improvisation I got a B.

On my English test, it was even more ridiculous. The day before the exam, the teacher took a sample set of questions and explained in great detail what the answers were. Sitting in the first row, I listened carefully to everything, and the next day I got that very set of questions.

Our group finished first in the exams. The rest of the class took another two days. Wouldn't it be great, we thought, if after all this tension and humiliation, we could just take it easy? But "social justice" triumphed.

"Since you're so smart, we've got a storage shed and a pile of slate. While the other working stiffs are still taking their exams, make us a roof and be quick about it."

The work hummed along. The shed next to us was being roofed by the correspondence students. We were captains and majors, they were majors and lieutenant colonels. We made a ladder, a big firm one, to work from. The lieutenant colonels had to climb up a rickety old tree to get to their roof. They quickly got sick of it. They came over and started talking about how, since they were older, more experienced, and higher ranking, the ladder, by rights, should belong to them! To which I explained that while we were sitting on these roofs, age and experience didn't matter—we were all equals.

One lieutenant colonel tried to solve the problem in amazingly crude fashion. He took the ladder and dragged it over to their shed. But we were paratroopers! At once, four of us quickly jumped down from our roof and restored the status quo. In polite terms that would have been fit for the floor of a parliament, we explained that to steal a ladder that had been built by the sweat and toil of others was simply sinful.

Then some wise man said philosophically, "The fact that we're sitting here on these roofs is only a temporary phenomenon. The fact that we are officers, that is permanent! Why don't we use that as a starting point?"

Everyone laughed, and that was the end of the conflict. The ladder was shared.

For the rest of our three years, nobody had to pick up cigarette butts, dig ditches, mow, or paint anything. To this day, I can't say whether this month of humiliation was a planned part of the system or an exploitation of those who would do anything to get into the academy.

Whatever it was, I am sure of one thing: it was absolutely unacceptable. An officer must always remain an officer. To allow a subordinate to shove an officer into a pile of crap for a month or two does inestimable moral harm to an officer's dignity. An officer digging a trench, yes! An officer pulling a cannon, along with his soldiers, yes! Any soldier's work, even the most back-breaking, can be noble. But cigarette butts, or mowing a field with sticks?

As soon as we got down from the roof, we were read the order that officially made us students. We were given five days to put our personal affairs in order and ordered to report by 1000 hours on August 31.

At the appointed time, the class assembled in the corridor on the seventh floor of the academy. A gray-haired, simple-looking colonel appeared, and ordered: "At ease!"

He introduced himself: "I am your class commander. My last name is Romanov, the same as the last Russian czar. And my name is the same as Suvorov's, Aleksandr Vasilievich." "Papa" Romanov was always able to defuse a situation with a smile, with an apt sharp word. He was omnipresent and omniscient. He always appeared where he was least expected and was as methodical as a German. He loved the military order as a whole, and was

> **"R**eeking of alcohol, the artillery instructor told us ancient jokes and stories about parachutes and paratroopers, guns and artillery—and UFOs.**"**

able to develop in us a taste for it as well. In his hands, the class worked like a well-built watch. In my (and not only my) view, Aleksandr Vasilievich was the model of an officer and an educator.

If "Papa" decided to chew someone out (and he never chewed anyone out for no reason) he did so in polite, literary language. But in spite of this everyone agreed that it was best not to be on the receiving end of one of "Papa's" tongue-lashings.

In addition to all that, Aleksandr Vasilievich was a great diplomat, and he protected us from all political organs. We lived and studied, as they say, in the bosom of Christ. All of us remember and love him for what he instilled in us—that always, everywhere, no matter how high you rise or how low you fall, you must remain a man, and preserve your honor.

At first, as always, the academic process was difficult. There were both objective and subjective reasons for this. The main objective reason, in my view, was that the academy was founded in 1918, at a time when cavalry, infantry, and a rather antediluvian artillery ruled the army. Armor and aviation were in their embryonic stage. Nobody had even thought of missile forces, space forces, or airborne troops. Time passed, and new arms and services were created; tactics, operations, and strategy were perfected and raised to a qualitatively new level.

Military study, which had paid great attention to Hannibal's attack plans, now had to make room for other subjects. The number of subjects grew, as did the number of departments, but the academy failed to create adequate relationships between the disciplines, and the curriculum still lagged behind real life in the army. I stress that this is only my view.

God save me from saying anything bad about the past and present directors of the academy, who have remained at their posts or had brilliant careers. But every director is, above all, a man, with certain sympathies and antipathies. One may be partial to tanks, a second to artillery, a third to the missile forces. And this is reflected in the curriculum.

Everyone in the army has his "ceiling." Not everyone feels it, but everybody has one. Someone can be a good battalion commander, can go to the academy, and come out a fine regimental executive officer. Good for him. They make him a regimental commander, and he finds that damned ceiling. The two hardest jobs in the army are company commander and regimental commander. An officer can try hard, can work like a dog, come in early, go home late—and still not know what's going on. Things in the regiment get worse and worse. The worse things get, the more he shouts and curses. The more he shouts and curses, the worse things get. You don't have to shout, you have to lead, and leading is just what he can't do.

The wise old bosses take a good look at him. . . and they make him a teacher. It's the old vicious circle: he who can, does, he who can't, teaches. And those who can't teach, teach the teachers.

The teachers who were "teachers by the grace of God" at the academy could be counted on one's fingers. They were Colonels Nikolai Nikolaevich Kuznetsov, Aleksei Petrovich Lushnikov, and Viktor Grigorievich Barulin. Among these titans—whose influence stayed with students their entire lives—Colonel Kuznetsov stood out. He was a huge, bear-like military intelligence officer from World War II days, with a head that still quivered slightly from shell shock. He was fanatically devoted to his subject, which was tactics. The most complicated tactical operations gave up their hidden meaning when he explained them, and became simple to understand and easy to carry out. Nikolai Nikolaevich taught us to think. He allowed our own opinions, and rewarded creative thinking. Sometimes he got carried away, like a boy, sometimes he got sarcastic, but he never forgot himself. People always saw the Master in front of them.

Others—who will remain anonymous—stood out for other reasons. There was the Artillerist who taught a four-hour class on the artillery of an airborne division. Reeking of alcohol, he would tell us ancient jokes and stories about parachutes and paratroopers, guns and artillerists, and even about UFOs. About five minutes before the end of the period, he'd ask, "Is there anyone here who doesn't already know all about airborne artillery?" We grunted that we knew.

"All right then. Carry on."

And then there was the Pilot. He came to the first class, drew a circle on the blackboard, a stick on either side—a cross-section of an airplane. To the right of that circle, he drew another circle, another set of sticks, and a crooked ellipse on top of the circle—a cross-section of a helicopter. And then for two hours, without pausing for breath, he proceeded to tell us which bombs and missiles could be stuck on the one and the other, and what you could do with them. At the second class, he did the same thing. When he showed up for the third class, someone had already drawn the circles and the sticks on the blackboard and had written down everything about the bombs and the missiles. His face betrayed his thoughts—"Why can't they just let a guy earn his living?" He canceled class, "for health reasons," and left.

There was the Communications Officer. He'd come in: "How are you doing, guys! When I served under the banner of the unforgettable Vassili Filippovich Margelov..." and on and on, without stopping, for two hours, about anything but communications.

Most of our teachers tried their best. And it was not their fault, but their misfortune that, in the final analysis, the academy was dominated by routine. It needs a breath of fresh air, new blood, new thoughts from top to bottom. The academy should be the bearer of the most advanced military thinking, and for that to happen, it has to work closely with the military-industrial complex, the general staff, and the main staff of all the arms and branches of the armed forces.

> **"W**ithout using anesthetic, the doctor set my bones and put my arm in a cast. I will remember those forty minutes for the rest of my life.**"**

An influx of new blood could be guaranteed by a systematic exchange of officers. Officers from, say, the rank of regimental executive officer to division executive officer could be sent to the corresponding academy for six months, and for the same period, teachers could take their place in the ranks. Teachers would come back, enriched by their experience among the troops. Their temporary replacements would come back, having learned the academic method. It's something to think about here.

I am thinking from the point of view of a rank-and-file major, a battalion commander, who was a cog in the machine. If anyone sees these reflections as an attempt to besmirch the academy, he's wrong. If anyone sees this as an attempt to denigrate the teaching staff, he's also wrong. The army is a deeply conservative institution, and for the most part, that's a good thing. But it is also possibly to drown in dogmatism, and in the army that can lead to catastrophic consequences.

September 1982. We had finished our lecture courses and had begun practical exercises. One day, I was asked to distribute the reading list for the next day's lesson—twenty-two different titles! Some students returned from the library toting an enormous stack of books. But it was too much even to skim by class time.

Most of us decided there was no point in even trying. So we were filled with dire thoughts of Ds, Party investigations, and other troubles. The exercise began—and it went off without a hitch. The teacher didn't bring up the twenty books at all.

When the class ended and the teacher left, everyone rushed over to me demanding to know where I'd gotten "that stupid list." It took me a while to convince them that I hadn't just made it up. But from that day on, we read only what we thought we had to.

We also had physical training. I remember one day in June 1983 our class went out in full force to the academy's training center. I don't know why, but I have always liked gymnastics. Being more than six feet tall, I knew I could never be much good, but I liked it. So, after doing some setting-up exercises, I jumped up onto the horizontal bar. I swung around the bar, did a kip, a crossover, and another swing with a 180-degree turn and... when I picked my nose out of the sawdust, I saw my left hand. My palm was lying unnaturally flat against my forearm. I had a sharp pain in my right leg. My first conscious thought was: "You idiot! You've managed to break your left hand and your right leg." Everything turned out all right with my leg—a bad tear of the periosteum—but two bones in my hand were broken.

Two of my comrades used handkerchiefs to tie my arm to a dirty board—a makeshift splint. They took me to the dispensary, but it was closed. So I was taken to a private car and driven to the Narofominsk hospital. The doctor on duty was halfway drunk. After looking fastidiously at the dirty board, he took me in to have my hand X-rayed. Taking the still-wet picture and looking at it carefully, he made his diagnosis: "Both of them, in the usual place!"

"You've lucked out," he said. "I'm a surgeon, and not just a surgeon, but..." he lifted a finger, "but never mind that. If I put you under anesthetic, you've got a 50 percent chance; if we do it without anesthetic, you've got a 100 percent chance. Take your choice!"

"I want the 100 percent, of course!"

"All right. But don't say that I didn't warn you."

He rather unceremoniously untied the board and the handkerchiefs, threw them in the wastebasket and dropped my hand—which somehow seemed separate from the rest of my body—on the table. I was convulsed with pain. He took a long time washing his hands carefully. He wiped them off and lit a cigarette.

"Give me one, too!"

We both lit up. While we smoked, I looked at him, trying to judge how drunk he was and weighing over the possible consequences for my hand, which was in enough trouble as it was.

He squinted at my hand like a sculptor, intending to cut everything superfluous away from the raw stone to reveal his masterpiece to the world.

He put out his cigarette. I put out mine.

"Ready?"

"Ready!"

He set my bones and put my arm in a cast. The whole thing took about forty minutes. I will remember those forty minutes for the rest of my life. He had an original way of doing things. He judged how well he was setting the bones by the reaction on my face. As soon as he had put the fragments back together, and a spasm of pain went through me, the major muttered in satisfaction: "Good, good. . . ." He wasn't the one who needed the anesthetic.

For the first ten minutes I kept quiet and was covered with a cold sweat. For the next ten minutes, I moaned. Then I alternated between growling and muttering indistinct curses. By about the thirtieth minute, I began to have a near irresistible desire to punch him. An inner voice told me that that wouldn't be the right thing to do. But I wanted to so badly! I thought of how I would hit him, how far he would roll, and decided to count to ten before making my wish come true.

"Masha," I heard him say. "Come here and grab his right arm. He's about ready to hit me with it."

He said this quietly, but the nurse (a big, elderly woman) instantly rushed over and grabbed hold of my right arm. I relaxed. He had charmed me. It even hurt a little less. The doctor knew his psychology. But he gave the order just in time.

I smoked another cigarette with him, and while we were smoking I told him that he was a sadistic swine. Well, that's a bit of a fib. I actually told him much more than that, and in much more colorful language.

He didn't get mad. He took a drink of the alcohol the nurse had measured out for him, sighed, took a deep drag on his cigarette, blew out the smoke, then spread his hands theatrically: "Well, what can I say. I guess I'm a swine at that. It's all part of the job."

I went back to camp, got my things together, and after being dismissed by "Papa," caught the bus to Moscow.

As always happens in such cases, the road was remarkably bumpy. My fingers ballooned before my eyes. By the time I arrived, they looked like reddish-bluish-greenish sausages.

The doctor on duty at the academy's dispensary looked at my hand in fright. She said she was a therapist, but didn't know what to do with a hand like this. She recommended that I go to the trauma center.

"Where's the trauma center?"

"I don't know."

"At least, point me in the general direction."

"I don't know."

It was already dark and getting late. Mad as a hornet, I asked passers-by in the street if they knew the way to the trauma center. Someone remembered that if you got on such-and-such a bus, and went four stops, you would see the trauma center. I went, scaring passengers with my glowing face and bulbous hand. I found the trauma center, but it was just for children.

"Could you do something for me anyway?" I asked.

"No. Our center is a children's center, and you. . . . Sorry, but we can't."

"So where's the trauma center for adults?"

They told me, thank goodness, in detail. When I got there I found a doctor just as drunk as the one at the hospital. And probably for that reason, he was stingy with his words.

"Take off your sling!"

I took it off. He took a pair of scissors, and with a beautiful sweeping motion, cut through the bandages. He grunted, moved the cast back a little bit, and then squeezed it back together.

"Better now?"

Pins and needles flew through my fingers. "Better now," I affirmed.

He rebandaged my hand. "Well, take care!"

"Thanks."

The hand healed just fine.

Now, all I had left to do was to go back to the "sadistic swine" who had set it, and give him my sincere, albeit belated, apologies for having insulted him.

I would like to report one more story, which I witnessed thanks to my wife, who worked as a typist in the department of CPSU history and Party political work.

In 1982 the department, at its Party meeting, issued an order that every teacher had to have the degree of Candidate of Science in some field or other. There was a colonel named Mikhail Vasilievich who had taught in that department for many long years. I don't want to reveal his last name. He was a nice, cordial man, well respected, and a very good teacher... but he was no scholar! Mikhail Vasilievich was forty-seven years old and had three years to go before retirement. And here he was hit with this decision from the Party organization! If he hadn't complied, he would have been left out on the street.

So Mikhail Vasilievich began to write. And when he was finished, he gave my wife his dissertation to type on the condition that she type it at home and not show it to anyone.

His "scientific work" was a big, thick notebook filled with a hodgepodge of long quotations clipped from the works of Leonid Ilyich Brezhnev, the department's textbooks, the magazine *Kommunist*, and other such publications. These printed quotations were loosely tied together with two or three of his own handwritten sentences. The ratio of clippings to handwritten text was about nine to one.

As my dear wife was typing all this, she would from time to time burst out laughing and call my attention to the especially funny parts. There was only one name for it: nonsense. Its scientific value was limited to whatever you could get for recycling it. But to my amazement, Mikhail Vasilievich received a good review, and walked around proud as could be. But then Fate dealt him a terrible blow—Brezhnev died. His dissertation instantly lost all its value.

Mikhail Vasilievich grew thin in the face, but he did not give up. Out of the scanty material by and about Yuri Andropov, Mikhail Vasilievich gave birth to a new opus. The method of composition was the same, but the work was only one-fifth the size of his Brezhnev effort.

Mikhail Vasilievich must have known the true worth of his dissertation, given the conspiratorial way he had turned it over to my wife to type. Certainly he had no reason to fear that his dissertation would fall into the hands of the CIA, although it certainly could have endangered American intelligence. Had the CIA gotten their hands on it, half of them would have died laughing. His dissertation once again received a favorable review—but again fate struck. Andropov died! This was nearly too much for Mikhail Vasilievich. But he had nothing to fear. The department's initiative quietly died out.

Our last year of study at the academy was marked by the renowned decision of the Politburo that we sinners, who had all drunk like fish before May 15, 1985, would all go on the wagon by the morning of the sixteenth.

The dolts who enforced this edict screamed with glee as they chopped down all the grapevines, smashed all the bottles at all the distilleries, and hurried back to report that they had done their job. Party organizations reported that they had won a decisive and irrevocable victory over the "green snake of alcohol abuse." The general secretary was naturally the first to declare his sobriety. Top officials, at any appropriate occasion, heaved deep sighs and said, "We never touch the stuff. Not a drop." Bosses of all sizes, ranks, and calibres, in short, everyone at the top did the same thing.

And below? Below, the Soviet people, who had a deeply rooted sense of contradiction, quietly started drinking themselves to death.

Even people who had been teetotalers all their lives started drinking. Earlier, vodka was there in the stores: if you wanted to, you could buy it; if you didn't, you didn't. Now you received ration cards—two bottles a month. Who could resist standing in a long line to trade in those cards for a bottle? It became a holy cause! The more they tried to limit per-capita alcohol consumption, the more the Soviet people went crazy. They began to drink anything they could get their hands on: eau de cologne, rubbing alcohol, varnish.... They figured out which medicines included alcohol and ordered them all. They started home-brewing with a vengeance. Anything, and everything, became raw material for brewing liquor.

Listen, Comrade Bosses, that's the wrong way to go about it! You have to understand the mentality of the population you control. Use reverse psychology! Erect monuments to alcoholics who died before their time from too many binges. Organize "socialist drinking competitions" between shifts, shops, and entire enterprises, under a banner: "Whose boozers will die first?" Make a sport of it. Hold "drink-offs," preferably with a lethal outcome. Bury the victors as national heroes. Create the title "Honored Wino of the USSR," and so on. And before you know it, peasants will rise up and destroy the wine shops and rush madly out to cut down their own grapevines.

Officers, of course, are part of "the people." So when we graduated in June 1985, we were all seized with a terrible thirst. Our group, truth be told, had never abused alcohol, but we unanimously decided that we would spit on the ridiculous regulations and off we went to the very center of Moscow to get absolutely wasted, along with our much-esteemed and respected teachers, Colonels Nikolai Nikolaevich Kuznetsov and Aleksei Petrovich Lushnikov. And when we got out of the restaurant, we had to go to Red Square and sing something warm, something with feeling, in short, something Russian....

"Good evening, comrade officers!" A police sergeant, tall and dapper in his uniform, stood before us.

"Singing is forbidden here in Red Square!" But he politely moved aside, to let us pass. And you could read in his eyes: "I warn you, guys.

You're all higher-ranking than I am, and there are a lot of you, but think it over!"

If he hadn't moved aside, we would of course have pushed him out of our way. But he was polite, he acted like a real man and a gentleman. And without talking it over, we turned around and decided not to sing in Red Square. Perhaps it was for the best.

CHAPTER 6:
PARADES AND ORDINARY DAYS

IN THE SUMMER OF 1985, I successfully completed my studies at the Frunze Academy. The eighth group, which I had the honor to command, graduated with brilliant colors. For the first time in the academy's history, at least according to the dean of the class, a single group of sixteen people had two valedictorians—Major Popov and Major Gaidukevich—and another five people graduated from the academy with honors. Nor were their good grades doctored or phony. Today, six of the seven honor students are generals. They are: Major Generals Kolmakov, Popov, Babichev, and Gaidukevich; and Lieutenant Generals Vostrotin and Lebed (me). Three of the six are division commanders, and the other three are: a student at the General Staff Academy, an army commander, and a deputy defense minister responsible for emergency situations. I am proud of my group. The three years that I spent as a deputy platoon commander were not in vain.

Just like all graduation ceremonies, ours was full of excitement and bustle, especially because of our success. After a long absence, the well-trained officers were eager to get back to the troops. The festive mood was not spoiled either by the Central Committee's decree on drunkenness, or by the unkept promise that I would be promoted to lieutenant colonel ahead of schedule.

But something else did sour my mood: the total confusion in personnel policy, and the uncertainty which inevitably accompanies it. I will illustrate it by my own experience. At a meeting with the director of the personnel section of the Airborne troops, I found that I would be a regimental executive officer in Pskov. But the first deputy commander of the Airborne troops, Lieutenant General V.N. Kostylev, categorically rejected Pskov and announced that I would be the chief of staff of a regiment stationed in the city of Alitus. Then the commander of the Airborne troops, General of the Army D.S. Sukhorukov, in his typically tactful manner, let me know that I would go to the city of Tula as a regimental executive officer. When I finally got my orders the day before graduation, I found out that I would indeed be a regimental executive officer, but in Ryazan.

The way of job placement did not allow us to get our minds set on one particular region and prepare for the move. Going to Afghanistan, or to Gyandja, or to the Baltics, are all different things; they all require different kinds of preparatory work. An officer must have a chance to settle his family affairs, so that when he arrives at his new unit he can occupy himself with the service and not have to worry about his hastily abandoned wife and children.

But all things come to an end, and everything eventually gets settled. Before leaving for vacation, Ivan Babichev, who was assigned to the same regiment as a battalion commander, and I decided to stop by our future unit and introduce ourselves to the regiment commander.

The regiment commander was away, but a pleasant surprise awaited us. The first person we bumped into was the regimental executive officer, Lieutenant Colonel Viktor Ivanovich Mironov. Apparently there were now two regimental executive officers there, with only one job between them. And, according to Mironov, the commander of the 2nd Battalion, who was supposed to be replaced by Ivan, had no intention of going anywhere. We gave up and left for vacation.

When we returned, almost nothing had changed, and I did not feel good about it. On my first day of service, I arrived at 0500 in the morning to observe reveille, PT, and morning inspection, and to get a sense of the organization of which I was now a part.

But I was in for a surprise. In the middle of the night, a high-level commission from the headquarters of the Airborne troops had arrived unexpectedly to inspect the regiment. I hurried to report to the regiment's commander and plunged into action. Nobody cared that I had been on the job for just two hours, and nobody gave a damn that I was "regimental executive officer number 2." From every direction I could hear, "Regimental executive officer, why is this podium scratched? Why is it covered with leaves? Why is the marching ground unskillfully and improperly marked? Line up your officers for PT!"

There was no point in trying to explain—I just smiled and said, "Yes, sir!" I ordered people to scrape and sweep. I lined them up and told them what to do. I personally presented every inspected item.

On the third day of the inspection, after the regiment command had parachuted for an exercise involving commanding staff officers, I spoke with the division commander, Colonel F. I. Serdechny. My personal performance had been evaluated by the inspection as good or even higher. Obviously, the division commander liked it and he started asking me about my career. He was not impressed by my service record, so within two months he appointed me commander of the 331st Airborne regiment, stationed in the city of Kostroma. On September 11, 1985, I flew with the division commander to Kostroma.

Kostroma welcomed us with penetrating wind and drizzling rain. The regiment was lined up on a small and poorly paved courtyard that, for some reason, they called a parade ground. The division commander introduced me and said, "You have ten seconds to comprehend the fact that you are now the commander of this regiment." And then... he left!

I knew the regiment was performing badly in all respects. I was assigned to fix it, and to sink or swim in the process.

Lieutenant Colonel N.V. Vashkevich returned with me to head-quarters. He pointed his finger: "Here are the barracks of the 1st and 2nd Battalions and those over there belong to the 3rd Battalion and the Special Forces Battalion. This is the depot, and over there—you can't see it from here—are the warehouses. Well, take care!" He got in a car and left.

So, I went on to inspect my new domain. It was colorless and wretched. The newest building was at least forty years old, and the base was a trash heap without a single visible trash can or dumpster. In the depot, metal hangars were crammed together without any plan or system. Their gates were dented and beaten up. The awnings tilted, and the vehicles were covered with dirt. The ground was infested with weeds.

The wretched condition of the barracks was especially striking. There were only two barracks on the base. The astonishing concentration of people fostered a total disregard for cleanliness. The toilets and sinks were broken, and three-fourths of the faucets were twisted off. The walls were covered with slime and mildew. Everything was overflowing, leaking, and smelled terrible. In the sleeping facilities, the side tables and stools were broken, and the entire hall had only two or three light bulbs, which were coated with dust.

The senior enlisted personnel had adequate bedding, but the rest had to scavenge. Some of them had to use a second mattress instead of a blanket, while others had blankets but no sheets. There were no floor mats, no slippers, and not a single bright spot on the wall that you could rest your eyes on. Everything was bland, poor, and depressing. Boredom, hopelessness, and the desire to do something nasty, mean, and cruel to your neighbor hung in the air.

These barracks all but compelled a man to do something criminal. It is no wonder that of the fifty-five crimes and accidents that had taken place within the division, twenty-seven had taken place in the miserable Kostroma regiment. In general, as Dmitri Semyonovich Sukhorukov once put it, the regiment was like an old village cemetery with lopsided crosses.

It was especially painful because this was supposed to be a model regiment. They specifically selected soldiers who were good-looking, tall, and well built. And what could and should have been the model of the Airborne troops, and actually was, on the parade ground, in everyday life had to live under the most inhuman and shameful conditions. The eyes of soldiers were gloomy and distrustful, without any spark.

I returned to the headquarters depressed, to put it mildly. I sat in my office and pondered. I knew that I would not put up with the squalor, that I would have to break everything down, tear it to bits, and then reassemble it. But how and where to start?

From somewhere nearby, I heard drunken voices singing a little out of tune. I came down from the second floor and went out to the porch. Down there, about twenty officers and warrant officers stood. They were singing "Stenka Razin" while giving me defiant looks.

I thought, "What do they expect from me? Are they waiting for me to start swinging my fists in rage?"

With a happy expression on my face, I came down from the porch and got in their midst. "You sing badly and out of tune," I said, "Now, sing along with me!"

His black brows came together
In a thunderclap of wrath.
The Ataman's eyes turned red with blood,
None dared to cross his path.

This last stanza, with its ominous message, was purely coincidental, but the last two lines I sang alone.

"Come on," I urged, "let's keep going!"

Somehow, they didn't feel like singing any more. Their quickly sobering looks were a mix of astonishment and confusion.

Taking advantage of the moment, I accompanied them to the checkpoint and through the gate, giving them a little talk along the way: "Well, you overdid it. But these things happen. Go home now. Tomorrow, we'll start working for real."

I went back to the office and placed a phone call to the commander of the Airborne troops himself. I said, "Comrade Commander, my personal inspection of the base has revealed that the 331st Airborne Regiment, which has been entrusted to me, is a disgraceful excuse for an Airborne unit. To whip it back into shape, I need you to give me exclusive authority to make whatever personnel assignments I see fit, and additional funding."

Here, I must interject that for the entire existence of the Airborne Corps there were only two real commanders: the great, inaccessible Vassili Margelov, and the profound and wise Dmitri Sukhorukov. I am deeply thankful to Sukhorukov for his wisdom in understanding immediately why a regimental commander, on his first day on the job, would call him directly, bypassing all intermediary levels. First I got the authority, and later the money.

The conclusion that I drew from my conversation with the commander? It can be summed up in the Marxist cliché: "Existence determines consciousness." First you have to restructure people's "existence," create normal human living conditions, make them feel like people again, and not baboons. Then you can use this factor to elevate their "consciousness." If a man lives like a man, he will act like a man; if he lives like a pig, he will act like a pig.

Everything on the base made my eyes sore. But our hands are there to take care of what our eyes fear.

The regiment was stationed in the boondocks, six hundred kilometers from division headquarters. According to the old-timers, only two types of people were sent here: people who hunted more than they drank, and people who drank more than they hunted. Under such wise management, the regiment was deteriorating rapidly. Only one commander, Ivan Andreevich Khimich, seriously tried to improve the situation, and he managed to do quite a bit, but unfortunately he wasn't here long.

Extensive construction work was begun. Three-story additions to all the barracks were to house bathrooms in accordance with regulations. The old bathrooms were ripped out, and the vacated space was dried up and refurbished for lounges and clothes-drying facilities. The barracks were painted white, the chandeliers were hung, and all the light bulbs were screwed in. They put paintings on the walls and flowers on the columns. Everyone got his own set of bedsheets. Everyone got clothes and footwear. Trash cans and dumpsters were placed throughout the base. Order was restored in the cafeteria. The combat training became organized, and the soldiers' eyes finally began to shine again.

But for the mood to change completely, they needed a major success.

At about that time, I attended the Oblast Party conference. Yuri Nikolaevich Balandin, the first secretary of the Kostroma Oblast Party Committee, had held that position for twenty-four years. It was like the old joke: "Is it hard to be a platoon commander?" "Only for the first seventeen years—then you get used to it." That was Yuri Nikolaevich's guiding principle. For the past seventeen years nobody had asked him any questions. The blasphemous thought of doing so never even entered their minds. How can you question the Sun?

Everything was just as it was supposed to be: the speech, the "prolonged applause," the important speakers, the approval of the resolution in principle, the approval of the resolution as a whole, and the final "prolonged applause."

But this time, while Yuri Nikolaevich was reading his speech, a regiment commander, Major Lebed, wrote him indicating that, in violation of such-and-such a decree of the Central Committee of the Communist Party of the Soviet Union dated such-and-such, the Kostroma City Executive Committee had failed to provide the regiment with a large number of apartments. The note was taken to the presidium. When the speech was over, the members of the presidium started passing around my note, shaking their heads in disapproval.

When the note reached Yuri Nikolaevich, his face expressed boundless surprise.

He picked it up—like a bomb.
He picked it up—like a porcupine,
Like a double-edged razorblade.
He picked it up—like a huge snake:
Twenty stingers strong, and two meters long.

Yuri Nikolaevich unfolded the note awkwardly and scanned it. Something about a Major Lebed and some apartments. He turned his anguished face toward the presidium and gestured nervously with his hand: "Well... give it to him!" The next day I got seventeen apartments.

It was a success, but only a partial one. Eighty people were in need of apartments; the new housing could accommodate only about 20 percent of them. But plots of land were at my disposal. All I had to do was to relocate twelve families from the huts located on those plots, demolish the huts, and build new housing. So we started relocating families from those hateful huts to comfortable apartments.

Then, one day, a commander of the nearby missile division came to the base and sneered at me: "Major, I am the title holder here. I have my own civil engineering unit and a property management unit. Your weaklings won't be able to build anything. You did the relocation—good for you and thank you very much. Give me the plots to develop, and stop jerking around."

I dug in my heels: "These are my plots, and I'm the one who's going to develop them!"

"Well, well," he mocked.

An hour later, the director-colonel of his civil-engineering unit was in my office with an ultimatum: either I demolish the huts in ten days, and transfer the clean plot to him for development under my plan, or he would demolish them himself and develop the plot according to the division commander's plan. I said, "All right!"

The colonel gave me a grin and left. I started thinking. Two of the huts were sturdy, thick-walled buildings that could pose a serious problem to dismantle. It was November. There was not much snow, but it was cold. Clawing at those huts with crowbars and picks wouldn't do the trick.

Suddenly, it dawned on me: I had two tanks. I ordered my technical supply officer to bring the tanks to the base. Two beaten up but reliable T-55 tanks arrived.

The operation began: it was tanks against huts. The crews turned their turrets around, took aim, and the first tank delivered a powerful blow to the corner of the hut. The building quaked, the bricks fell, and the tank backed up. The infantry quickly cleared the visors and the hatch. Another blow, and a crack started running along the wall. The tanks trampled over the huts, turning them into huge heaps of broken brick, stucco and gravel. The entire neighborhood ran down to watch the spectacle, and posed an additional challenge.

The next problem was to remove several dozen tons of construction debris. But by now I had fortune by the tail. While I was pondering what to do about it, I was told that a chairman of a garage co-op was eager to see me. A short, and confident figure appeared. "Commander, how much do you want for that garbage outside?"

Inside, I was almost screaming with joy at the quick solution to a difficult problem. But I had to gamble. I took a stretch and yawned: "Nothing, but I'm a betting man."

"What do you mean, 'a betting man,' Commander?"

"This is what I mean: if you remove the construction debris within three days, I won't charge you a thing, but if you miss the deadline even by an hour, you'll have to pay double."

The eyes of the chairman sparkled. As it turned out, he was also a betting man. Out of respect for me or because he was feeling superior, he changed the way he addressed me:

"Chief, you've got yourself a deal! Let's talk deadlines."

"Stop right there, buddy. Spoken words fly away, but written words stay."

So we drew up a little contract, and the co-op chairman took his bet seriously. He got right to work.

I rushed to the director of the Civil Engineering Unit. "Let's go inspect the construction site and make an official record of it," I said.

The director thought I must be joking, but he came to the site, walked around it, and made grunting noises. "All right, Major, I'll build it for you." He was as good as his word.

Some of my experiences were less successful. On October 1, the division commander, F. I. Serdechny, came to inspect the regiment. It was a cruel inspection but, I have to confess, not unreasonable. The regiment shot quickly, but not accurately. Not many could make it through the obstacle course at the tank testing range. Vehicles broke down constantly. Weapons malfunctioned. Legs did not reach the horizontal bar, and on and on. I was stunned with humiliation when the division commander finally gave the regiment a C after pointing out such mitigating circumstances as the young age of the regiment commander and his proletarian ancestry.

On October 10 the regiment left for a parade. It was my first parade. I've been in five parades, two of them as a commander of an Airborne infantry regiment, and another three as a division commander. But I'll remember this one for a long time. A rear support unit was dispatched to set up tents for the regiment's accommodation, as well as a cafeteria and other facilities.

The parade ground had a concentration of ten thousand troops of different arms and branches of the armed forces and several hundred units of various combat machinery. There were dormitories, depots, warehouses, parking lots, and cafeterias. Only a powerful, strong-willed, and strict individual could keep such a motley crew in check. The chief of the parade ground garrison, Major General Beltiukov, was just such a man. He was short and stocky, and wore a Beria-style pince-nez. He was the embodiment of energy, efficiency, and strictness, which sometimes bordered on cruelty.

At daily meetings, General Beltiukov could give any faulty unit commander a complete, unexpurgated dressing-down. But if any high military official were to show up, he would say, "They are all great officers, without exception." That was why, even though he could give you hell, you would forgive him anything.

A parade, or rather, preparing for a parade, is hard work. There was an entire system of little tricks and incentives designed to encourage the soldiers to work conscientiously. These included: handing out chocolate or movie tickets to the best performing units; putting heat on master sergeants to train poor performers in their off hours; assigning the worst units to clean-up duty; and sponsoring numerous competitions for best marching song, best weapons storage room, and so forth.

> **"F**or twenty-four hours, the Russian bumpkin we enlisted removed snow with his old tractor—fueling himself entirely with regimental alcohol. He was a good man."

But, despite the strenuous preparation, the dominating atmosphere was businesslike and even festive on occasion. There were peak moments of high stress—the two nighttime training sessions on Red Square and the general dress rehearsal, attended by the defense minister, his deputies, the commanders of every branch of the armed forces, the commander of the Airborne troops, and other important officials. Each of them was proud of his "boys," and wanted them to outshine the others. They would be caught up in the spirit of feverish competition. And this was passed on to the troops.

Finally, parade day arrived. We got up at 0400 and by 0600 were in position, close to Red Square. My regiment and I would have to spend four hours standing in the autumn-winter cold. Here, I should point out that only two units—the Airborne regiment and the Marine regiment—traditionally march without heavy coats. But we knew a few tricks. The most popular one was to stick hot pepper patches to the soles of your feet. My favorite was to go up to officers wearing greatcoats and say, "Wouldn't it be great, guys, right now to drink a glass of ice-cold beer?" They would instinctively shiver, "You and your beer can go straight to...."

At 0900 commanders showed their passes and led their columns out onto Red Square. We had only one more torturous hour to wait. On the one hand, I could not let the soldiers freeze, but on the other hand, it would be indecent to hop around on the nation's most important square. We stuck it out. We walked decorously back and forth.

Something unexpected happened. In the neighboring column, two officers passed out. They were replaced with back-ups. I thought, "God save me from such disgrace." So, I forgot about being decent and made my subordinates warm up and tell each other funny or irrelevant stories, to ease the pressure.

Finally they gave the command to begin, the defense minister reviewed the troops, read his speech, gave commands, and we set out. Turning left at the Historical Museum, I pushed the button of my stop-watch. Feeling amazingly light, I goose-stepped past the podium of the mausoleum and heard the ringing sound of boots stomping in unison with metronome-like precision behind me. I felt with my back that we were going confidently and beautifully. I shifted to the right and pushed the stop button. Then, after showing my pass, I came to the evaluation point in front of the mausoleum.

The endless stream of combat machinery was flowing majestically past the podium. After the last four jeeps had disappeared, the defense minister started his short evaluation, and then it was over. In a matter of hours, we had to hand in four hundred units of firearms, our dress uniforms, sets of insignia, quilted vests, bed sheets, and so on. Meanwhile, each soldier was scrounging around looking for some kind of memento of the parade. What looked like a disciplined machine just a few hours ago, turned into a crowd of small-time thieves, but I came to realize that this was just a way of letting off steam.

At midnight, Moscow time, the regiment got off the train at the Kostroma railway station and, in column formations, set out for the base, accompanied by a brass band.

The holiday was over, and regular workdays began. "Existence" was improving rapidly, and "consciousness" was following in its train.

In March the regiment was going to participate in a divisional exercise that included parachuting. In my youth and inexperience, I thought I had more than enough time to prepare for it, but I had only a superficial understanding of how to train my men properly.

On January 21 the regiment was placed on drill alert for a maneuver to pre-planned locations and, afterwards, to newly designated areas in full kit. That alert was part of the division commander's plan to prepare the division for the upcoming exercises. I managed to accomplish the first part of the mission well enough—getting our supplies out of the depots and warehouses and forming up the columns outside the perimeter of the base—but when the march began, I bitterly regretted our lack of proper training. Columns slipped into disarray; vehicles overheated and stalled; and communications broke down, as did my leadership.

Our regimental vehicles to clear the snow from our path broke down almost immediately. So we had to enlist a typical Russian country bumpkin in a hat with one flap up and the other down, wearing a padded jacket revealing a shirt with ripped collar and a small crucifix. He drove his antiquated tractor with a snowplow attached for twenty-four hours, fueling himself entirely with regimental alcohol, waving off any food to chase it down. It is thanks to just such nameless, conscientious, and abused country hicks that Russia has won all its wars. He was a good man.

I finally gathered the regiment at the designated area. For the first time for many hours I was able to sit down for three minutes and drink a mug of tea. And that of course was when the division commander descended. If he had found me in some other place, the impact may not have been so hard. But I received an incredibly harsh tongue-lashing. I thought I had gotten used to the injustices in the army. But I had never been evaluated so low and with such contempt. Tears of frustration came to my eyes for the first and last time in my life. To Colonel Serdechny's credit, he instantly backed off.

I learned my lesson and set out to eliminate our deficiencies. Only my subordinates and I knew what a hell of a job that was and what kind of training we went through.

The most important thing was the result. At the next exercise, my officers at every level demonstrated exemplary leadership skills and the regiment was the only one to get a good grade, given personally by the commander of the Airborne troops, General of the Army D.S. Sukhorukov.

The 331st Kostroma Airborne Regiment became my pride and joy. We made it through together. We got up on our feet. And today, it is still glorious and standing tall.

The regiment easily passed the spring inspection with a good grade. On July 30, 1986, the commander called and congratulated me on my promotion to the rank of lieutenant colonel. My promotion led to a new assignment. An order dated December 10, 1986, appointed me executive officer of the 76th Airborne Division in Pskov. The regiment bade me a heartfelt farewell. And I might as well admit, I felt a nagging pain where, as some believe, my soul is supposed to be.

On January 20, 1987, I introduced myself to my division commander, Colonel V.S. Khalilov. He was the embodiment of explosive energy and inexhaustible organizational talent. He commanded his division beautifully.

On August 1, 1987, the division commander went on a month's leave, and in accordance with regulations, I became the acting commander. Colonel Khalilov abided by the principle that a deputy acting commander should be ordered to do in one month everything that the commander hadn't had time to do in eleven months: the deputy won't know how hard it is and may actually do it. So, energetically, I got down to business.

But on August 7, nature threw a monkey wrench into my frenzied activity—a hurricane passed through Pskov. The wind reached speeds of fifty-five to sixty miles per hour. The hurricane was accompanied by pouring rain. The storm continued for almost two days.

More than four hundred poplar trees were struck down throughout the division's base, and falling trees cut power lines, broke windows, and damaged roofs. Other roofs were torn off by the wind, and the entire place was flooded with water. I had to drop everything and deal with the consequences of the storm.

For the whole month we were busy cutting trees, removing debris, and rebuilding what had been damaged.

By the commander's arrival, the status quo had been restored, but nothing else had been done. The commander knew what had happened on the base, and I knew that he knew. Nevertheless, he feigned surprise: "So, what have you been doing here all month?"

Serious changes in the Airborne Corps took place in November 1987. General of the Army Sukhorukov became the chief of the Main Department of Human Resources and a deputy defense minister. Colonel General Nikolai Kalinin was appointed as a commander of the Airborne Corps. He informed me directly that I was "nominated for the post of a division commander. Get ready by January!"

On January 10, 1988, I was promoted to the rank of colonel before I was due. In a few days I was summoned to Moscow for an interview. I interviewed briefly with Colonel General Kalinin and then with several officers at the Main Department of Human Resources. The next day, I had an interview with the Central Committee of the Communist Party.

I arrived at the Party's Central Committee and showed my Party membership card. They let me in, and I found the right office and introduced myself. I was asked to wait.

I waited for three-and-a-half hours. Then I was offered a polite apology—there would be no interview that day. When I wondered when it would be, I was told that the date would be confirmed later.

I went back to Pskov.

Then I received a call: "The day after tomorrow you have an interview at the Central Committee." In an hour they called and canceled it. Two weeks later, I got another call, "Please come for an interview!"

I came, showed my Party membership card, and found the designated office.

During my first visit to that office, everything had been quiet, but this time it was different. I do not remember all the details, but somewhere a tank from the Western Group of the Armed Forces had lost its way, gotten onto the railway tracks, and collided with a train, causing many casualties and injuries among the passengers. A big investigation was going on. It was terribly noisy, and I found myself surrounded by sweaty, red-faced generals and officers. "Wrong time, wrong place," I thought.

While I was reckoning how I might be able to distance myself, someone touched my elbow. I looked back, then down. This someone was knee-high to a grasshopper, balding, and pot-bellied; his eyes behind the glasses pierced me: "Are you Colonel Lebed?"

"I am Colonel Lebed."

"I was assigned to interview you."

We went to the opposite end of the corridor, came to an office, sat at the T-shaped desk, and the interview started. The desk was totally clean—no desktop set, no pens, no papers. For the entire forty minutes, he did all the talking, his manner of speaking similar to Mikhail Gorbachev's—after three minutes you would lose his train of thought and forget what he had said just two minutes before. Usually, I never get confused by anyone, but no matter how hard I tried I couldn't remember what he had been talking about. He possessed a special higher art of talking bull, something like: "That, perhaps, I guess, a sure thing, but concerning its relativity, maybe that should be done, since, in case some sort of things happen, it would be readily available!" All I had to do was say, "Yes," "No," and "Yes, sir!"

Eventually, he concluded the conversation, "That'll be it, you may go. You'll be informed about the results of your interview." I left shaking from angered humiliation. For forty minutes, that piglet had gotten drunk on his loquaciousness and hadn't asked me a thing. *He* held my destiny in his hands. My fury was only partly abated by the order of the defense minister that as of March 18, 1988, I was appointed a commander of Tula Airborne Division. I did not suspect that my new assignment coincided with the beginning of a new era. For in February and March of 1988, a new page—unpredictable and unexpected, absurd and bloody, and at times extremely dirty—was opened in the history of the Airborne Corps, in the history of the Motherland, and in my life.

CHAPTER 7:
THE AGONY BEGINS

IT IS HARD FOR ME to write about the next few years, because the consequences of our cowardice, baseness, and opportunism are evident. So much blood has been spilled, so many lives have been ruined. How many more will there have to be?

In March 1988 I received a division at a moment when one of its regiments, the 137th Ryazan, had already been in Sumgait for more than a month trying to localize the Armenian-Azerbaijani conflict.

While familiarizing myself with the state of affairs, I naturally had no chance to go to Sumgait. The job I inherited was tough: first of all, the division was divided up geographically into five garrisons. The Kostroma regiment was 600 kilometers away from division headquarters, and the Yefremovsky, 150 kilometers away. Second, my predecessor, F. I. Serdechny, was an excessively stern and harsh man. Many in the division hated him, and as a result the main links of the chain of command were substantially weakened. Morale also left much to be desired. Being too hard is no less harmful than being too soft.

I got to Sumgait a little later. And there, for the first time since Afghanistan, I saw burned-out trucks and buses, charred houses, and people's hair, naturally black, turned white from the horrors they had seen. And the eyes... the eyes.... All this, in *my* country—as it was at the time!

I visited my far-flung regiments, beginning with the Kostroma regiment which I had previously commanded myself and which was the farthest away.

I was appalled by the regiment's air of gloom and suspicion. I also discovered that many soldiers were lacking belts, boots, and belt buckles. I also noticed that some soldiers had dirty pieces of cardboard sewn onto the right breasts of their jackets. On them, written in colored pen was the word: "guard." This they wore instead of the traditional guard pins. Why?

It turned out that before my arrival, the regiment's political officer, Major Zakharik, assembled the regiment, inspected them to see if there were any violations of the regulation uniform, and ordered everyone to take off all the belts, boots, and belt buckles that did not pass inspection and put them in a pile. They brought out a block, an axe, and smashed them to smithereens. There were no belts, boots, or pins in stock.

"Where are the guard pins?" asked Zakharik.

"We don't have any pins, Comrade Major, there aren't enough to go around," answered the soldiers.

"Cut them out of cardboard, out of wood, out of anything you like, write on them, and stick them on!"

And so they did.

The political officer was satisfied. He thought he was being tough and would impress me. Toward evening, Major Zakharik presented himself.

"Sit down, Comrade Major!" I said. "Tell me how you, a senior officer, the political officer of a regiment, a man who has to answer for the men's education and their moral condition, can mock the guards' pin in this way and so massively violate regulations?" To my surprise, he didn't explain, but put up a vigorous counterattack.

"Comrade Colonel," he said, jumping to attention. "I do not have to explain anything to you. Yes, I am responsible for the education and the moral condition of these men, and I will do my duty! The Party put me in this post!"

"Comrade Major, stop blowing smoke out your nose and get to the point! The Party also made me the commander of this division; in fact, I was cleared by the Central Committee. To the point! To the point, Comrade Major!"

Zakharik shifted his eyes to a point somewhere above my left ear, the picture of insulted innocence. The conversation wasn't going well.

"Well, if you don't want to tell me, Comrade Major," I said, "you don't have to. But based on what you've done so far, I'm going to give you an unsatisfactory fitness report, and I am warning you personally that if you ever do this again, I will have you relieved. You may go. We'll take this up again later."

"Yes, sir!"

I called in the commander of the regiment.

"Yevgeny Yurievich, where did you dig up this relic? If he had been born a little earlier, he would have made a good deputy for Beria."

It was, of course, no fault of the commander's that he had been given such a political officer, but educating him was the regimental commander's job, so the commander smiled guiltily.

In a few minutes, the phone rang. It was Lieutenant General S.M. Smirnov, a member of the Military Council of the Airborne troops. Without even saying hello, he went after me with both barrels: "I voted for you! But you! The political officer! A bad fitness report!" There was more sputtering indignation before the receiver was slammed down. Three minutes later, he rang again. He'd caught his breath.

"How could you? How dare you!"

He started sputtering again, and the line went dead. I rang the switchboard:

"If General Smirnov calls again, tell him I went off to the training ground."

After waiting a few minutes, I called Major Zakharik back in. Open curiosity shone in his normally expressionless eyes. Not finding the desired effect, Zakharik extinguished it. Again, he stood at attention, eyes expressionless. Anger bubbled up inside me. But I quickly suppressed it.

> **"What kind of "democracy" can there be in the army when one has the right to send another to his death?"**

All my experience in the service told me that the worse the swine who stands before you, the more even-tempered and restrained you have to be. If you talk to him, always use the polite form. Whatever happens, don't raise your voice. And always have no fewer than two witnesses.

So I was cold as ice:

"Comrade Major, tell me: who is your commanding officer, and who are your direct superiors?"

An anxious thought disturbed his poker face. Zakharik responded, tentatively: "My commanding officer is the regimental commander. My direct superiors are the division political office...."

I interrupted him: "That's enough! Did you tell the division political officer about your bad fitness report?"

The anxious look intensified. "No, I didn't report it to him!"

"On what basis did you go over the head of your direct superiors and tell the member of the Military Council the story, in distorted form?" Silence. There was nowhere to hide.

"Comrade Major, your hot-headed actions have made it clear to me that I was right in giving you that bad fitness report. Let's take a walk around the regiment, and you can tell me, or better yet, show me what you've done as the regiment's political officer to make the living conditions of the men better and create healthy morale."

So we went. On the porch, I gave Zakharik the first question: "Here are two barracks. Tell me at which entrance, on which floor, each unit lives." This used to be my regiment, and I knew quite well who lived where. He couldn't put anything over on me. His answer was confused, contradictory, and wrong.

We went to the tea-room—a foul, dark place. You could see the tracks of the soldiers' boots on the floor. The tables were filthy. About half the chairs were missing. The dishes were dirty.

"Why is the tea-room in this condition?"

"That's the quartermaster's responsibility."

"The quartermaster's job is to make sure that the necessary materials are there. But whose job is it to organize the work, to make this place comfortable and pleasant to look at?"

The answer again was precise: "That's the regimental commander's responsibility."

"So what's your job?"

Silence.

We went to the park. In the park, I asked Zakharik to tell me where each unit's vehicles were stored. He stood there, as haughty and silent as a camel.

"I see, Comrade Major. And now, the last question: take me to the battery maintenance shop and there, you can tell me whether the battery maintenance workers are getting enough milk[1], and whether they have enough protective clothing. I'll follow you."

Zakharik walked in exactly the opposite direction from the battery maintenance shop. He walked so confidently that I started to have doubts: had the regimental commander moved the battery maintenance shop to another place? But as we walked, my doubts vanished, and I tried to guess how he would get out of this one. Zakharik stopped and peered into the sheds.

---

[1] Battery maintenance workers received a glass of milk in their daily food ration to compensate for the health hazards in their work—breathing sulfuric acid vapors.

"Comrade Major, I asked you to take me to the battery maintenance shop."

"It used to be here!"

I burst out laughing.

What next? I got a call from the commander of the Airborne troops, Colonel General Kalinin, gently recommending that I be more careful with political officers. To which I retorted that, so far as I knew, no one had abolished the principle of unitary command, and that he was just another deputy regimental commander like all the rest. And an empty-headed, malicious deputy at that, whose work, or more accurately lack of work, had brought incomparably more harm than good. General Kalinin declined to discuss the subject further.

Then Lieutenant General Smirnov, member of the Military Council, paid us a visit and heads rolled. Two warrant officers were discharged and everyone was penalized, except, of course, Zakharik, who, due to his position, *had* to be right—after all, the Party had put him in his job!

Times were changing.

That summer was spent working, bustling, training, and shooting; autumn came, and with it, preparations for the parade. Now, as division commander, I headed the Kostroma Infantry Regiment, the Ryazan Mechanized Regiment, and part of the artillery regiment. The technical part of the parade preparation did not differ substantially from previous years. But a "democratic wave" was passing through the country, and magazines like *Ogonyok* and *Yunost* were stirring up hatred against the army, especially against soldiers and the low-ranking officers. As a consequence, when our columns passed through the streets of Moscow it was not uncommon for apple cores, eggs, and stones to be thrown at our vehicles.

Fortunately, no one was hurt, but it was hard on morale. A soldier, an officer, is a public man, an official of the state. What he does isn't his own decision; he has to follow orders. It's ridiculous when clever people talk about "democratizing the army." For God's sake, what kind of "democracy" can there be when one man has the right to send another to his death? Should they have a meeting and count the votes first? In battle, it is the primary and most sacred duty of a commander of any rank to shoot on the spot, like a mad dog, without any investigation or trial, anyone who even contemplates such a discussion. Yes, relations in the army can, and must, be reformed. The officer and the soldier can, and must, be brought closer together. The working day can, and must, be regulated. Any serviceman can, and must, be compensated for additional work. Much can, and will, be done to make things better, more humane, and more reasonable, but there is not, and cannot be, such a thing as a "democratic army." If there were such a thing, you could call such an organization anything you like, but not an army. An army without the principle of unitary command, an army where orders have no force, an army without discipline—such an army is nothing more than a mob. In any armed confrontation, half of them would run away and the other half would be mowed down. And as we would soon discover, our days in a peacetime army were numbered.

CHAPTER 8:
TO AZERBAIJAN

ON NOVEMBER 21, 1988, the division was put on alert. We marched to the airports and landed in Baku. Gorbachev was away—later, it became clear that it was Gorbachev's style to get out of town whenever it looked as if a conflict would break out somewhere—and the division's mission was put in extremely vague terms. If you cut through all the verbiage, the verbal order sounded something like this: "Fly down there. It's a big mess. It isn't clear who's beating whom. When you get there find out and put a stop to it. Your fists are bigger than theirs. But for God's sake don't shoot! Try to talk them out of it."

We took off from the Chkalovsk airport, dusted by the first snowfall and lashed with biting winds, and landed in the warm, even hot by our standards, Baku autumn.

All was quiet. The *Stavka* (General Headquarters) staff officers who met us reported that a meeting of several thousand people was going on in the city's main square, Lenin Square, on the usual subject—Karabakh. The situation in the city was relatively calm, but there were local clashes between Armenians and Azeris.

We went to *Stavka*. Along the way, we could see that on the whole the city was living its normal life. The stores were open, and public transportation was running. Most of the people looked well and even happy. We met several small groups of youths, about thirteen to seventeen years of age, who waved flags with crescents on long poles screaming, "Ka-ra-bakh! Ka-ra-bakh! . . ."

The operations group of the Ground Forces Command was already there. We coordinated our actions. I received my mission: take whichever regiment arrives first and move it to Lenin Square from the west along Prospekt Neftyanikov, locate the command post of the Interior Ministry troops on the square, and, together with the senior Interior Ministry officer, organize joint measures. I was told neither the name nor the rank of this senior officer, nor the exact location of his command post. But that wasn't the worst of it. I set off for the Nasosnaya airport, thirty kilometers from Baku, where the first airplanes, with the Tula Airborne Regiment on them, had already landed.

At about 1000 on November 24, at the head of the regiment's column in an UAZik, I reached the approaches to Lenin Square. Only that far because the number of people kept growing and growing, and the column's speed kept slowing and slowing. About four hundred meters from the square, the column came to a complete stop. The avenue was dammed by people "from building to building."

I had no idea what I was supposed to do in the square, and especially what an airborne regiment in BMD-1's[1] and full combat gear, with well-prepared soldiers should be doing. I got out of the truck, and people instantly gathered around me. There was no hostility on their faces, only anxiety:

"Why have you come here?"

I told them honestly: "Hell if I know! There's supposed to be some kind of disorder here."

They told me heatedly that this was not the case. This was an organized political meeting. There were many people, yes, but representatives of the Popular Front were keeping order. No violence was breaking out, and God willing, it wouldn't.

---

[1] An airborne infantry fighting vehicle.

I told them that if they were really no threat to anyone, then I was no threat to them. The column would stay where it was and, if they didn't object, I would walk around the square.

I took with me the regiment's commander, Lieutenant Colonel V.I. Orlov, and two men with automatic rifles and set off.

When I got to the square, I could see why there was such a traffic jam on the Prospekt Neftyanikov. The entrance directly to the square was blocked by armored personnel carriers belonging to the Dzerzhinsky division of Interior Ministry troops. In front of the armored personnel carriers stood a bunch of soldiers wearing helmets and bullet-proof vests, with automatic rifles behind their backs, holding billy clubs and shields. The crowd raged, demanding to be let into the square. The soldiers (whose exhausted appearance told that they had stood there for at least a few days) answered that they had no orders to let them through; if they had, they would. I found the senior officer on the "barricade," briefly explained who I was, where I was going, and why. A big, strong figure moved aside, leaving a narrow slit between the armored personnel carriers, and we squeezed through to the square.

The square was large. It adjoined the House of Soviets and was previously used for ceremonial occasions. All this immense space, and the little squares that adjoined it, was filled with people; how many, I couldn't tell exactly. I also couldn't tell what point there was in posting barricades to block off the approaches to the square. The Interior Ministry troops were virtually surrounded, with a crowd in front of them and another crowd behind them. I got the impression that the main purpose of the barricades was to irritate people.

I walked all around the square, trying to find a command post. It was a strange spectacle. Some people squinted at us suspiciously, others cursed under their breath, most watched us, surprised. Some people tried to stop us and told us what lousy people the Armenians were. An intellectual-looking youth waved a placard with the inscription: "You're a slave, you're a crook, you're an Armenian," with the signature A.S. Pushkin underneath it. A great number of tents had been set up underneath the trees, which were strewn with banners bearing slogans in Russian, Azeri, and God knows how many other languages. People were slaughtering sheep, broiling *shashlik*, and cooking a soup called either *"shulen"* or *"shurpa,"* I don't remember which. Entrails, skins, stench. Having no other place for it, the people answered nature's call in the bushes.

A crowd of about four hundred people were on the steps of the House of Soviets, chanting the name of Vizirov, the first secretary of the Azerbaijani Communist Party's Central Committee. But to make it sound more Armenian, they changed his name slightly: "Vi-zir-yan! Come out! Vi-zir-yan! Come out! ..."

I finally realized what was going on. It seemed that the crowd had been here for three days, demanding that Comrade Vizirov show his face to the people, and he, for whatever reason, had not appeared. In various places stood lonely chains of overworked Interior Ministry troops. The citizens of Baku gave the soldiers cigarettes and fruit.

A little to the side, I found the command post I was looking for, which resembled an LAZ bus. There I found Major General Safonov, the representative of the Interior Ministry troops. When I introduced myself he greeted me joyfully:

"So, I'm not the only fool here! You've found me. Now you don't have to hang around this square anymore. But I warn you, you won't find any Party or government leaders here. Here I'm God, czar, and commander-in-chief! And I don't know how the hell I got here, what I'm doing here, or how long I'll have to stay here!"

"Are you in communication with anyone?" I asked.

"With everyone below me."

"What about above you?"

"Above me!" the general shrugged his shoulders.

"How long have you been here?"

"Two days."

"What's your mission?"

"The usual. Maintain public order. Don't permit bloodshed. But nobody's disturbing the public order. You can see for yourself."

"So why did they send me to you, and what actions am I supposed to 'coordinate' with you?"

"Who the hell knows? Sit down, have a cup of tea. . . ."

With this gloomy turn of events, I was in no mood for tea. I said good-bye politely and walked back across the square to my column. Despite my vague orders, one limitation was clear: "Don't communicate by radio." So, like a true commander, I walked to the nearest pay phone, put in my two kopecks, and dialed the number I was told to call if I needed help. I introduced myself: "Colonel Lebed, Airborne division commander. To whom am I speaking?"

"Major General. . ." and he mumbled his last name.

I briefly reported the situation: "I am with an Airborne regiment on the approaches to Lenin Square. The head of the column is four hundred meters west of the square. I have established contact with the MVD representative, but do not consider it possible to coordinate actions with him. He does not know what his mission is. I am asking you to clarify the purpose of the mission!"

Unexpectedly, he answered hysterically, "Attack immediately! Break through to the square! Surround the House of Soviets!"

I was taken aback. I had just finished walking around the square. It was full of people who, for the most part, were behaving decently enough. They had given fruit to my soldiers, who were sitting on their armored vehicles. There had been a small incident, true: a schizophrenic had come out of the crowd and punched a warrant officer in the lip, but the crowd hit the schizophrenic on the head and carried him away, expressing their sincere apologies.

The warrant officer, who was twice as big as the schizophrenic and ten times as strong, was dumbstruck at first, and then burst out laughing. That made the soldiers burst out laughing, and then the people. What kind of "attack" could there be in a situation like this?

I tried to explain this to the general, but he started screeching, "Colonel! I repeat, you are to attack! Immediately!"

I was still a young colonel and a young division commander, and I considered myself to be polite, at least polite enough not to tell unknown generals to go to hell. But this made me mad. I was sick of this hysterical ass, giving orders in I don't know whose name. If I had obeyed his senseless order, I could have provoked colossal bloodshed. The scenario for such an attack—with the crowd standing like a wall—could only have been for everyone to get into their armored vehicles, stick their guns out the peepholes, machine guns blazing, and then walk over the corpses. And these were *peaceful* people. I briefly, and, as it seemed to me at the time, eloquently told him what I thought of his mental capabilities—and hung up.

Nobody saw or heard anything more from that general. But his voice still rings in my ears—the voice of a fanatical half-wit, the voice of a moral monster, able to sacrifice hundreds if not thousands of lives to the altar of God knows what. And by whose hands? By the hands of the army, whose first and most sacred duty it is to defend the people from an external enemy. It didn't make any difference what ethnic group they came from, these were *our* people!

I went back to the column. Lieutenant General Kostylev, a wise, experienced man, was already there. He immediately found a way out of the situation: he ordered everybody to do what they usually did—service their vehicles, put their uniforms in order, clean their weapons. But he arranged for additional patrols.

I told him about the conversation I'd just had.

"What was that fool's name?"

"I couldn't make it out."

"You're not lying?"

"No, I really couldn't make it out."

"So what did you tell him?"

"I gave him an evasive answer—I told him to go to hell."

"Good boy! Don't make any attacks! Listen, Sanya, no attacks! Wait for me. I'll be back soon."

General Kostylev left. An hour, two hours passed. The number of people around the column kept growing. People continued to give the soldiers fruits and vegetables. They even tried to give them money. The soldiers refused the money, but accepted the fruit gratefully.

A permanent "discussion club" formed around me. They cited countless historical examples of how the Armenians had arrogantly seized land which had been Azerbaijani from time immemorial—Karabakh, to be exact. They told various stories to show the perfidy and baseness of the Armenian people. For my part, I tried to tell them that I did not know of a single ethnic group made up exclusively of scoundrels, and that they must not look on all Armenians as enemies—that every nation had the right to have its own geniuses and scoundrels, wise men and fools, teetotalers and drunks. They looked at me condescendingly. They asked the same question over and over:

"Have you ever been in Azerbaijan before?"

"No, I haven't."

"Then you simply don't know what kind of people the Armenians are. Live here a while, and you'll find out."

And then they'd hit me with another stream of cases, facts, and parallels.

Finally, General Kostylev arrived, disheveled and angry.

"Turn the column around, and take it to the brigade's territory. The devil only knows what's going on here!"

We politely said good-bye to the crowd, wished each other success, health, and long life, and the column turned carefully around and went back to brigade headquarters.

Immediately upon arrival, I was called to a meeting with the commandant of the special region of the city of Baku, Colonel General Tyagunov. Tyagunov, sixty-eight, with more than one war behind him, was wise and good—a tall, thin man who looked like Don Quixote. He began the meeting by getting acquainted, and then read the orders appointing various generals and officers as commandants of individual regions of Baku. (I became the commandant of the Nasiminsky *raion* of Baku, with a population of 240,000 people.) General Tyagunov concluded by saying something on the order of: "Comrade Generals and Officers! We are embarking on a mission which is completely new to us. There is no basis in law for such a mission. I can't give you a list of your rights and duties. But I ask you to be deliberate, patient, and carefully weigh every step you take. I ask you to remember why we are here on this earth. These are our people. A conflict has arisen between them, and they will sort it out. Our job is to prevent bloodshed. We have to lead the situation toward political negotiation. We must not defile our banners and our honor by making war against our own people. Remember that. God be with you!"

When everyone had left, he kept me behind:

"Lebed, you probably have the toughest sector. There are two regions in it which are compactly settled by Armenians: Armenikend and Armyansky Khutor. There will be constant provocations, scuffles, fights. In addition, the Nasiminsky *raion* borders the twenty-six Commissars *raion*, which, as you know, contains Lenin Square. Try to do all you can, son, to make sure that people stay alive. When they come to their senses, they will thank you. This will pass. It has to pass."

I went to take charge of the territory, which was a thickly settled sector of the city. The fourth floor of the *raion* Party committee headquarters was set aside as my headquarters.

I put an airborne battalion in each of the Armenian areas, defined where the command posts would be, and created a triple reserve. I defined each regiment's zone of responsibility.

There were a few surprises. Our sector, which looked flat on paper, was actually full of ravines. It also turned out that these people were not accustomed to martial law and curfews. Nobody paid any attention to them; curfew violations were rampant. On the third day, a patrol tried to stop a *Zhiguli*, a small car, in which there were two couples—an Azeri couple and an Armenian couple. The Azeri man was at the wheel. The soldier raised his rifle and tried to stop the car. The driver, who was drunk, tried to run the soldier down. The soldier did a "fish roll" to the side. The second soldier, a lieutenant, was the patrol commander, a conscientious, hard-working officer. The car tried to run him down, too. The lieutenant dodged the car, pulled back the slide on his weapon, and fired a burst of seven rounds at the fleeing car. The little *Zhiguli* swerved and crashed into a lamp-post.

Soldiers pulled out the passengers, who were drunk and scared but alive and healthy.

At the expense and with the materials of local businesses, we made a mass of barriers and signs, saying "Stop! Command Post," and "Stop or I'll Shoot!" and constructed boards with long nails protruding to puncture the car tires of drivers we didn't stop. We also used one of the *raion's* movie theaters as a detention center for curfew violators—an exercise in futility. The soldiers caught the curfew violators and brought them to the movie theater, where they were guarded by local policemen who thought it was all a game. Anyone who could pay could get out within the hour.

There were other problems. The Azeri, we found out, were systematically refusing to supply the Armenian regions with bread and other food products, so we had to organize a "food" commission. Then there was the doctor, a gung-ho Azeri nationalist, who wrote his prescriptions not in Latin, as was common practice, but in Azeri. This doctor was one of the leaders of the local medical profession, so all the drugstores of the region were filled with prescriptions in Azeri, complete with grammatical mistakes. The pharmacists, most of whom were not ethnic Azeris, were confused. We had to put out this outbreak of foolishness by creating a "medical commission."

Then we had the problem of unauthorized construction. A good quarter of the *raion* was made up of nice little houses built by so-called *"samostroi,"* literally "self-building." This meant that people, through, got the tacit blessing of the authorities to build a house, but without any documents giving them the right to use the land, or any agreements by the architectural department. These homes existed in fact, but legally they were "dangling in the air." Moreover, many Armenian families were trying to sell their houses and apartments, exchange them, or rent them. But they were repeatedly told by Azuri neighbors to "Leave everything where it is, pack your bags, and get out of here, swine, while you're still alive!"

The commandant's office was hit with a squall of phone calls. We had to create an evacuation commission to accompany the people who were fleeing with an armed escort. We tried to count the cars, but the count ran into the thousands before we lost track. I remember that the longest column we escorted was five hundred cars long.

And there were accidents. The sewer system has to run, no matter what regime is in power. It's there, it flows, sometimes it overflows. A foul-smelling puddle formed on the square in front of the *raion* executive committee building. The puddle grew at a threatening pace. Vehicles drove through the square, picking up traces of it on their wheels and tracking the puddle's contents into the nearby streets. Hepatitis, dysentery, and other infectious diseases were in the air. The *raion* executive committee officials, headed by the chairman, shrugged their shoulders: "The plumbers are on strike!" I was sick of it, so I gave an order: "Give me their addresses. Operations groups, forward!"

The operations groups caught and dragged in three plumbers, who were scared half to death. Death is easy to face when you're part of a crowd, but when the government pulls an individual out of the crowd, few are brave.

I put the plumbers under administrative arrest for thirty days and sent them off under guard to clean up the mess. The plumbers had the mess cleaned up in less than two hours, and the fire trucks I had summoned hosed away what remained of the puddle of sewage. The plumbers were immediately "amnestied" and sent home, happy.

On the third day many enterprises in the region were working at only half capacity, or less, because workers were being stopped and threatened by thugs on their way to work. We had to patrol the area, and increase the guards at the enterprises.

We were astonished at the position the local law enforcement agencies were taking. Armenians, whether suspects or victims, would be subjected to insults, humiliations, and beatings. There was no question of justice, at least not for Armenians.

The head of the *raion's* KGB section, whom I had summoned, came to me dressed like a stereotypical detective: big leather jacket, oversize hat, long black scarf that covered the bottom half of his face, and dark glasses. He sat there for an hour, listening. At the end, he croaked hoarsely, "It shall be done, Chief!" and disappeared. I never saw him again. I was told he had gone somewhere on business.

He didn't, of course, do anything at all. Violence—wild, primordial, and bestial—hovered in the air. Nobody trusted anyone. Not each other, not the government, not the Party, not the Soviet power. The meetings in the square continued. Vizirov still did not come out and speak to his people. Bewilderment and suspicion of him soon turned to contempt and hatred. The number of people on the square ebbed and flowed in waves. They slaughtered sheep, cooked *shashlik*, and left the entrails. The stench got worse and worse, and sanitation specialists warned us that 100,000 people can produce in short order 30 tons of urine. These tons settled around the bushes and trees surrounding the square. The bushes and trees withered away.

The tension significantly increased when Azeri refugees began arriving from Armenia. Ragged, beaten, hysterical, without a kopeck to their name or even a crust of bread, they were scary, because of the fever of their rage, their thirst for revenge. They were unfortunate first because they had fled for their lives from violence and cruelty, deprived of everything—a roof over their heads, cattle, furniture, clothing, money—in the course of an hour. And secondly because they were far from welcomed in their "historical homeland." After living for centuries in Armenia, they had lost much of their language, customs, and habits, and were immediately given the contemptuous nickname of *"Yerazy"*—Yerevan Azeris—and were treated as "untouchables." They were held in contempt, or with squeamish compassion. The Azerbaijani authorities limited themselves to giving each refugee fifty rubles.

When a cat is driven into a corner, he becomes a tiger. If the state doesn't take appropriate measures and leaves its citizens on the edge of survival, these citizens will take measures themselves. The Azeri refugees began to seize Armenian apartments and houses. Inhabitants were told: "They drove us out of our homes, from our land, so we'll drive you out! 'An eye for an eye, and a tooth for a tooth!' Get out!"

(The same thing happened in Armenia with Armenians who had fled from Azerbaijan.)

And again, violence, violence, violence.... After one outbreak of "forcible resettlement" I went out looking for the chief of police and found him in a house where lay the still-warm corpse of a man, about thirty years old. His head had been crushed by a powerful blow, and a twisted steel rod smeared with traces of blood and hair was nearby. With the chief of police was a police colonel, a doctor, and various other officials. I had come in just as the colonel, standing with his back to me, was dictating to the sergeant: "Cause of death: myocardial infarction."

I went nuts: "Whose death are you writing that about? His?"

"Yes, sir!"

"How can you call that a 'myocardial infarction'? There's the steel rod he was killed with!

> **"Can you fly?" I asked. The man began to stutter.... "If I threw you off that balcony—" I demanded again. He began to sweat."**

He didn't even have a chance to meow for help!"

With his dark, lusterless eyes, the colonel said, "Comrade Colonel, you don't understand. He was hit in the head, he had a heart attack as the result of the blow, and he died as a result of the heart attack. The doctor confirms this."

The doctor nodded.

I had the barely controllable urge to take a automatic rifle and mow down these police "cattle" and the "knowing" medico in one good burst. I turned and stalked out.

These police, I knew, were deep in the spirit of "socialist competition" for the title of best policeman, best police precinct, and so on. If the colonel had reported a violent death, the police would have had to open a criminal case, conduct an investigation, and look for the murderer, and, with so many crimes being committed, they had little chance of finding him. That meant they would lose the "socialist competition."

Two incidents that happened at about this time characterize the reigning atmosphere in Baku better than any analysis. On late November night, the power went out in Armyansky Khutor, a region densely populated by Armenians. Now the people instantly remembered back in February in Sumgait, it started like this—the electricity was cut off, and in twenty minutes, the bloodbath began. The neighborhood was on hair trigger alert—men with axes, sharpened stakes, shotguns, women howling in inhuman voices, and children crying hysterically.

Everyone demanded that at least two soldiers, or better yet, a whole squad, or a tank, guard his house. They asked, "Do you know how to shoot? How many rounds do you have?" And no matter how many there were, they would say, "That's not enough!"

I put the whole battalion and the reserves on alert, and went off to see the *raikom*[2] first secretary, Afiyatdin Dzhalilovich Dzhalilov. Everyone who visited him made a respectful bow of 30 degrees, and went out backwards. When I asked him why people came in to see him the same way they would come to see a sultan, he shrugged and explained that it was tradition.

I got a lot of satisfaction out of my visit to him. I opened first door and let it bang shut, said hello to him and, without being asked, sat down across from his desk. He was terribly angry. The moment I walked in, the healthy ruddiness disappeared from his cheeks, but he didn't say a word. I may have been a usual boor, but I had a force at my back!

I began: "Afiyatdin Dzhalilovich, the power is out in Armyansky Khutor! Everyone is in a panic. Let's do what needs to be done and get the power back on."

---

[2] An acronym for *Raion* Party Committee.

"Aleksandr Ivanovich! That's nothing to worry about. We've got to save electricity."

A cold rage rolled over me, and I drew my pistol and put it in front of me. I couldn't hold it in my hands; it somehow burned my fingers.

"Can you fly?" I asked.

He began to stutter: "W-w-what?"

"If I threw you off the balcony right now, would you fly up or down?"

He broke out in a sweat.

"If you can't fly, take a telephone and start dialing. I want the lights back on in an hour. And not a word of Azeri. At the first word of warning, I'll knock you in the teeth with the butt of this pistol. There won't be a second one."

It was something to behold! Speaking nothing but Russian, in a matter of minutes, he had given out dozens of instructions. In forty-two minutes, electricity was restored, the tension fell away, and the people calmly returned to their homes.

The second episode took place at the same time. It was reported to me that a man and a woman wished to see the commandant on urgent business.

"Well, send them in," I ordered.

A man with the marks of a recent beating on his face and a bandaged right hand walked in, accompanied by a woman, who was weeping bitterly.

"Sit down," I said. "Last name?"

He told me his name.

"You're not an Armenian, are you?"

"No. I'm Ossetian."

"So what happened? I didn't think they had it in for Ossetians these days."

After waiting for almost twenty years, this man had finally been given an apartment. His family consisted of himself, his wife, two toddlers, and his mother, who was paralyzed.

Before that, he had lived in a small prefabricated duplex housing two families, but the apartment which he was told he had to move into immediately, had neither electricity nor heat nor gas. He went to the Department of Housing to complain: how could he move into such an apartment with two little children and a mother who was paralyzed? The head of the Property Management Department had planned to make the Ossetian's half of the house into some sort of warehouse or storage room, so he was curt: you have a day to move out, and no more back talk!

The Ossetian refused to move out. The head promptly arrived at the Ossetian's house with his "troops" (seven mechanics) and his "military vehicles" (a crane with a half-ton wrecking ball). The Ossetian, being a proud hot-blooded son of the Caucasus, barricaded himself in his pitiful little dwelling, with his wife, his children, and their grandmother.

"Ossetian, come out!" they shouted, threateningly.

In response, they heard nothing.

The mechanics broke down the fence and smashed the windows. Nothing.

They brought up the heavy artillery. With cries of "Ossetian, come out!" they put the wrecking ball into action and smashed in the roof of his house. After the third blow, the Ossetian, wounded by glass fragments and realizing the futility of further resistance, flung himself on the mercy of the victors.

But the triumphant victors did not show any mercy: they blackened both his eyes and broke his nose, and they terrified his family. They then smashed all the tiles of the roof—and also, incidentally, wrecked the neighbor's apartment.

"Now you know who's boss around here!"

I dispatched men to bring me the chairman of the *raion* executive committee, the chairman of the construction department, and the head of the Property Management Department. Dzhalilov, the *Raikom* first secretary, appeared on his own. When everyone was assembled—with the deputy chairman of the executive committee asking the place of the chairman who had wisely gone missing—Dzhalilov tried to take the reins in his own hands: "I'll take care of it. We'll get to the bottom of this right away!"

"No! Now *I'll* get to the bottom of this!" I answered. "Put all three of them into an office with a city telephone. Under guard. Don't let them out until the Ossetian and his unfortunate neighbor show me the order for their apartments and report back that they are satisfied. And thank you, Comrade Dzhalilov, for your help."

During the first hour there was much shouting in Azeri, which neither I nor my soldiers could understand. In eighteen hours, the happy Ossetian and his neighbor appeared. They showed me their orders, and reported that they had both received apartments in a nice building and had already moved in. They said a lot of warm words about the friendly workers of the *raion* executive committee. I did not wish to grieve them with the news that their main "benefactors" were under guard in a nearby office. I congratulated them on their new apartments and said good-bye.

The situation in and around Lenin Square continued to heat up. And the unsanitary conditions worsened at a catastrophic pace. On the night of December 3-4, the decision was made to use the Dzherzhinsky Division to clean the square by force. The order was given to let anyone out but not to let anyone into the square. The operation was planned by some of the MVD people, and I didn't look too closely at the details.

I thought at the time, and continue to think, that it is not the army's business to be involved in putting down internal disorders. Not because the army's not strong enough to do it, but precisely because it's *too* strong. Giving police functions to the army in general, and to the Airborne troops in particular, is a great humiliation. The army is not prepared psychologically to undertake actions of this type, and if it is forced to do it, it will lead only to fierce resentment by the army, and severe loss of respect from the people.

The people in the blockaded square were repeatedly ordered to leave within an hour. They were promised safe conduct and told which routes to take. The thick ranks of tall, strapping soldiers of the Dzherzhinsky Division, dressed in bullet-proof vests and helmets, with shields and billy clubs, acted as a sobering influence, and the overwhelming majority of the people did as they were told.

But about eight hundred people remained in the square. The Interior Ministry soldiers, banging their billy clubs against their shields, marched in and arrested them. No one was killed, but some were spanked with billy clubs.

The plan was to put everyone who was arrested on buses, take them off to a "corrective-labor colony," about twenty kilometers from the city, and sort everything out there. By 0500, everyone was on the buses, and the column moved out. Three blocks from the square, five buses turned left from the established route, went another couple of blocks, stopped, and swung wide their doors:

"You're free, boys!"

By 0700, leaflets were strewn all over the city: "The soldiers killed more than one hundred people on the square! The Fatherland is in danger! Rise up, people!" And the people rose. The streets filled with an excited, angry mob. The vast majority of them were honest, decent people, whose sincere indignation had been aroused by a lie.

Any sharp movements could have turned the situation into bloody chaos. I gave everyone the order: "Do not use force unless absolutely necessary! Talk to them. Explain things to them. Invite those who shout the loudest to come out of the crowd and take them to the square. Show them that there are no bodies, no blood, no traces of mass murder."

I went out onto the street myself. Here and there, hysterical screaming and sobbing broke out. In the crowd, "eyewitnesses" rushed around, doing their destructive work.

I got up on some kind of pedestal and, shouting down the crowd, declared that the rumors of mass murders were lies. I asked them to show some restraint, and proposed that they choose a delegation that I would take to the square personally to show them the truth.

As always in such cases, there were many honest, principled people in the crowd. Five of them got into the back seat of my UAZik. Taking shortcuts and back alleys, I took them to the square. We saw about three dozen pairs of shoes, an umbrella, buttons, cigarette butts, some old rags, but that was all. The dust settled. I took them back, demanding harshly that they tell everyone, loudly and persuasively, what they had seen. They did and the crowd began to calm down. By early afternoon, the situation in my *raion* (I can't speak for the entire city) had returned almost to normal.

The troublemakers decided to change their tactics—they sent youngsters out to fight. Stuffing their pockets with "pieces of silver," gangs of young men in their mid to late teens, drunk or high on drugs, tried to spark mass disorder in Armenian neighborhoods. But our battalions stopped them. The riffraff then scattered throughout the *raion*. They waylaid and tried to beat to death any Armenians, Jews, Ossetians, or Georgians they could get their hands on. They vandalized and looted their apartments, stores, and little market stalls. In a matter of minutes, phones were ringing off the hook, and the victims, bloody, beaten, and robbed, were reporting in droves. The howling, moaning, and crying went on nonstop.

I gave the order: "Prevent and put a stop to this hooliganism by force, armed force, if necessary. Take everyone arrested at the scene of the crime to the commandant's office, with brief descriptions of their deeds and the names of any witnesses."

My soldiers and officers set to work. But I had underestimated the scale of what was going on, and in the course of one hour, fifty-seven people were brought to the commandant's office. They had been caught in the act, and all of them were high one way or another. Having nothing to lose, they had put up a fierce resistance.

To this day, I look back on my soldiers with pride. What fine soldiers they were! They were true "Airborne wolves" for whom no mis-

sions were impossible. In the toughest situations, they contemptuously rejected using their guns except to parry a crowbar, a piece of
pipe, a stake, or a knife. They were professionals, highly trained, and
confident that their work was necessary.

The losses on our side were insignificant, seven or eight people
slightly wounded. But the other side was a sad, pitiful sight. Stood up
against the walls, bloodied, drunk, and mean, they wailed, moaned,
and cursed. There was blood on the floor, blood on the walls, blood on
their faces.

"Doctor, go get as many doctors as you can. Have each one,
guarded by two soldiers, start sewing and bandaging these people," I
ordered. I told my chief of staff to sort everything out and to make
sure that these beauties were delivered to the nearest jail, and then
to clean up the place.

The doctor took off, and soon all the doctors and medical instructors he could find set to work.

Confident that things were on the mend, I went to my office to
hear the reports of the regimental commanders and the heads of arms
and services. They all reported that the situation had stabilized. The
very difficult, taxing day was behind us, and I walked out into the hall.
The cosmetic repair job on the hooligans was winding up.

The division's chief medical officer was treating his fifth patient,
an enormous, wild-eyed man about thirty years old. Judging from his
unintelligible mumbling, he was high on some sort of narcotic. His
head, beaten in many places, and his face, which was one big bruise,
showed how much resistance he had put up, and how hard it had been
to subdue him. When the doctor finished bandaging him, the man was
encased in an enormous cocoon of bandages, with two little holes for
his right eye and his mouth.

The doctor sighed with relief: "That's it! Next!"

The bandaged giant suddenly jumped to his feet, and, with a low,
deafening roar, shaking his huge hairy fists, rushed at the doctor. The
soldier standing next to him struck the giant with a fast, powerful blow

with the butt of his automatic rifle, just above the left ear. The giant howled and crashed to the floor. A bloody spot appeared in the cocoon.

The scene ended tragicomically. The doctor, who had been in danger just a few seconds before, balled up his fists and rushed at... the soldier! I was barely able to pull him back by the collar. From his disjointed, furious explanation, I found out that the doctor had just spent half an hour washing, sewing up, and bandaging the countless holes in that druggie's head... it was hard work, skilled work, and he, that is, the soldier, had ruined it.

And suddenly the soldier burst out laughing. Then the doctor, who had cooled down, also burst out laughing. And after that, the medical instructors and people in the commandant's office, who had come running at the sound, broke out laughing, followed shortly by the freshly bandaged criminals standing up against the walls. It was a weird and terrifying laughter, the laughter of people who, just a few hours before, had been ready to kill one another. Yet it somehow defused the situation. They picked up the giant, sat him down, unbandaged him, and the touchy doctor sewed up his freshly acquired wound, and bandaged him up again.

Representatives of the appropriate agencies finally arrived, with the appropriate vehicles—Black Marias. They formed up the bandaged hooligans, read them an order stating that they were under administrative arrest for thirty days, and led them out.

A little over two weeks later, I checked on them and found that not a single criminal case had been filed.

But now, convinced that it was a bad idea to mess around in the *raion* controlled by the Airborne troops, the hooligans didn't try anything on that scale again. Only low-down, cowardly things like throwing a stone at a window or someone's head, pulling a woman's hair, or punching an elderly man, leaving the veteran with a bloody nose dripping onto his Order of the Great Patriotic War, Second Class.

Things were relatively quiet until December 7. On the evening of the 7th, on the *Vremya* television news program, it was announced that there had been a huge earthquake in Armenia. The cities of Spitak and Leninakan had been completely destroyed, and a great number of other towns had suffered damage to varying degrees. The exact number of victims was unknown, but even from preliminary figures, it was enormous, numbering in the tens of thousands.

Our only television stood in the entrance hall of our improvised commandant's office, and everyone watched it—staff officers, soldiers in the operations groups, workers of the *raion* executive committee. The anchorman started talking about something else, but no one listened to him, and soon, the television was turned off. An oppressive silence hung over the office.

Then suddenly, a sound broke into that silence, or more accurately, a number of sounds, blending into one common, triumphal shout of glee. Trying to figure out what sort of sound it was, five or six other officers and I walked out onto that balcony. And all became clear.

On the other side of the street sat a big, nine-story apartment building. The lights were on in all the windows, and on all the balconies, people were standing, shouting, screaming, and laughing wildly. Empty bottles, burning pieces of paper, and other objects flew down.

The cannibalistic glee could be seen in all the adjacent buildings. Everyone was howling triumphantly. People who considered themselves civilized and educated, many of whom, I would venture to guess, believed in God and followed the commandments of the Koran, all these people were indecently and barbarically celebrating another people's colossal grief. I had the intense desire to take an automatic rifle and criss-cross that damned nine-story building with one long burst to force these people who had descended to the level of baboons to return to the human race.

I had met so many good, happy, reasonable, cordial people among the Azeris! I had heard so many persuasive speeches from many of them! Where had they gone? It takes only one step back, just one, from any stage of civilization to return us to the apes.

I went back to my office and gave the order to reinforce all posts and to put all reserve units on alert. The night went by quietly.

Morally, the earthquake was the last straw for the Armenians living in Baku. It proved to them that normalcy would never return. A mass exodus began. No amount of entreaties did any good. People listened, nodded, but we were outsiders. We had flown in and would fly back home, but they had to live here or leave! And the overwhelming majority left.

> **"Few people in my life have been foolish enough to insult me personally, and they all have paid for it dearly."**

Work increased for our units who had to accompany the columns of departing cars and guard the airport and train station. The train station was in the area which was entrusted to me. I first had to double, and then triple, the number of patrols.

Conflicts at the station were numerous but short-lived. Groups of young men roamed the station. They didn't look as if they were trying to start any trouble, but as soon as the patrol would turn its back, there would be a lightning-quick raid on a departing Armenian family, a couple of punches in the face—a man's or a woman's, it didn't matter—and the hooligans would disappear into the crowd, leaving behind screaming, terrified children, and bloodied, bitter adults. The patrols had more than they could handle.

We had to increase our efforts by using the police academy cadets under my command who had come from Ukraine. I must say, it was an excellent school. They were all big, bear-like, steady, good-natured fellows who observed one supreme principle: strict enforcement of the law. They had the ability to listen, to help, and to sympathize. But any deviation, any disturbance of the peace brought an instant reaction. The boys were able to show, quickly and effectively, who was boss, but if the disturbers of the peace admitted their wrong, they could count on compassionate medical assistance.

The train station in Baku was big. The busiest part of the station was "the ring."

"The ring" was a circular road where taxis and cars let passengers out. It was located below the station, which gave the hooligans an excellent opportunity to maneuver. It was the station's hottest "hot spot." The Azeri porters pointedly ignored Armenian families struggling with numerous bundles and suitcases.

The next car stopped. A big, tall, young Armenian jumped out. He had an Order of the Red Star and a medal "For Bravery" on the lapels of his jacket. He helped a crippled old man, an elderly woman, and a boy out of the car. Leaving the woman and the boy with the baggage, the young man put the old man on his shoulders and carried him to the station, obviously intending come back for the baggage and his relatives.

He had taken only a few steps, when a dozen thugs came out of nowhere and knocked the young man down. A small crowd instantly formed. The woman screamed wildly and the boy gave a piercing, heart-rending shout. The Azeris in "the ring" continued as if nothing were going on. The porters were twice as stony-faced. I was with my adjutant and two soldiers. We rushed into the crowd, and with our fists and the butts of our rifles flailing, we quickly beat back the seething crowd.

The youth and the old man were not hurt badly, only rumpled. Then some more soldiers appeared, and the hooligans ran away. A police sergeant ran up and reported: "There's a crowd forming, in the square in front of the station. There are only six of us. We can't hold them back!"

After sending a soldier to get the reserve group, I went downstairs with the rest of them. The five policemen, armed only with billy clubs, had formed a chain in the middle of the stairs and were trying to calm the crowd of no fewer than two hundred men.

As soon as I arrived, the shouts began to ring out: "Colonel, why are you defending the Armenians?"

When you talk to a crowd, it is important to maintain absolute calm. In most cases, the crowd will recognize the moral superiority of such a person and quiet down. But the Transcaucasian republics have no equals when it comes to forming huge crowds united by a single idea. A few seconds before, each of them had been going about his own business, but something flared up somewhere—probably the fight in "the ring"—and the disjointed mass instantly became a crowd.

"Why are you defending the Armenians?" This *leitmotiv* was accompanied by curses and threats.

I stood next to the policemen. The ten soldiers who had come with me thickened their chain and made it more imposing: "Esteemed comrades, I beg you, calm down! We are not defending Armenians. We are defending *people*! In Armenia the 98th Airborne Division guaranteed the evacuation of the Azeri population. It doesn't matter to us who is killing whom, and for what reason. Our job is to prevent it. Calm down, I beg you, and go in peace. I and my subordinates wish you no harm."

People from the south are hot-blooded. For the most part, they are good people; they get upset quickly, but, thank God, cool down just as quickly. The crowd began to simmer down. But then, from the depths of the crowd, a hefty-looking lout elbowed his way to the front. From all indications, he was one of the regular provocateurs and not completely sober.

"Colonel, you are a. . ." and there followed a long, unprintable phrase. That's when I lost it. I have never forgiven, and will never forgive, a personal insult. Few people in my life have been foolish enough to do so, and they have all paid for it dearly.

I forgot that I was the commander of a division and responsible for thousands of people. All I could see was my insulted ego. I rushed at the man. He turned around instantly and began to disappear through the crowd. I set off after him. My faithful and reliable adjutant, Senior Warrant Officer Viktor Alekseevich Velichkin, set off after me, and after him, I later found out, came the reserve platoon. This wedge, with Velichkin and me at its point, cut into the crowd, swiftly and furiously, and caused a panic. The crowd, crushing those at the end of the narrow passage, began to run. Velichkin caught the lout with his fist, and the soldier behind him cut him down with the barrel of his automatic rifle. The men in the crowd pushed, and I had to do a good job with my fists.

The crowd, bursting out of the narrow passageway, ran away, two pistol shots rang out, and in a few seconds the square was absolutely empty. Several people, including the provocateur, lay on the ground. Velichkin sent the injured to our medics. And a big soldier standing next to me, wiping his bloody nose, muttered, in a simple, man-to-man, way: "Don't do that any more, Comrade Colonel."

In a few minutes the square bustled along once more as if nothing had happened.

At the time, scuffles like this, or, as we called them "battles of local significance," were the norm. And they continued to be the norm until 1989 dawned and the mass exodus of the Armenian population was virtually completed, leaving only the old, the powerless, the penniless, and those who tried to mask themselves as Jews, Lezgins, Ossetians, or anything but Armenians.

January and February were spent normalizing the situation. As I saw it, our job was to be as responsive to people's requests as possible, regardless of their ethnic background, and to stop anybody from taking the law into his own hands. Soldiers helped people pack and load their belongings and repair what was broken, and joint recreational evenings.

The situation improved day by day. This, in large part, was due to work of the military commandant of the special region of the city of Baku, Colonel General Tyagunov. In spite of his venerable age, he had time for everything. He rounded up all sorts of hooligans, smoothed the way for the stores to start working again, and held a variety of meetings with representatives of the intelligentsia, clergy, and students. He cajoled, reconciled, praised, cursed—in short, used every means at his disposal to try to get life back on track. And he succeeded.

Thanks to this, by the beginning of February, it became possible to leave just one regiment in the *raion*. We said our warm good-byes to the *raion* leadership. Afiyatdin Dzhalilovich gave me a collection of the verses of Nasimi, the poet for whom the *raion* had been named, and a guidebook to the historical regions of Baku, as going-away presents. I gave him a paratrooper's commando knife, but since it is against tradition for the Airborne troops to give away knives, I took a symbolic payment of three kopecks for it, and we parted.

All the Georgians that I met at the time looked upon the squabble, as they called it, between the Armenians and the Azeris with the greatest contempt.

At the time, I did not give this any special significance, but I had occasion to recall it later.

CHAPTER 9:
ELECTIONS, MADE TO ORDER

IN FEBRUARY 1989, in the dawning day of democracy, a surprise mission was dumped on me. On the eve of the elections to the USSR Supreme Soviet, someone decided that Colonel General Nikolai A. Moiseev should run as a candidate. Since I was chief of the garrison in his electoral district in Tula, I was put in charge of ensuring that the elections turned out right.

Colonel General Moiseev paid his first visit to Tula in the beginning of February. His team, which I had met beforehand, impressed me (inexperienced as I was in these matters) with their profound knowledge of local conditions, the disposition of political forces, and the weak points of many local Party and government officials. Colonel General Moiseev came with a big entourage, the Group of Soviet Armed Forces in Germany's song and dance ensemble, as far as I remember, and about forty soldiers from Tula who were home on leave. There was also vodka, vodka, and still more vodka.

At the organizational meeting, at which Colonel General Moiseev presided, we put the finishing touches on our plan of action, and the wheels began to turn. In accordance with the immortal legacy of N.V. Gogol (see Chichikov's visits in *Dead Souls*), we visited all the "strong of this world," except for the prosecutor. The visits started with introductions and effusive expressions of joy on both sides, then the conversation would turn to business. "It would be nice if..." meaning, "What can the candidate do for me?" Potentially, Colonel General Moiseev was not stingy about making promises. And some of them were kept immediately. The meeting would usually conclude with a series of toasts.

When the visits to the Tula *beau monde* were completed, I found a good "excuse"—that I had a division to command—to skip the trips to the rural districts. I just couldn't stand it any more. And I did the right thing, because after every visit to a rural district Moiseev and his team would come back falling-down drunk and unable to speak coherently. It was at this point that I said to myself: "God forbid, Aleksander Ivanovich, that you ever run for people's deputy! You can't drink that much!"

And then it was time for the pre-election meeting in Tula. By lot, Colonel General Moiseev was the first of the three candidates to speak. I attended that meeting as an invited guest and had a chance to appreciate his mastery of the art of oratory. He praised everyone, picked on no one, emphasized his platform's strong points, and smoothly summed up the work he had already done, making it look relevant. He answered questions no less artfully: happily, naturally, going into detail on the topics he knew well and brushing off the hard questions with jokes and humorous sayings. He received a long round of applause from the audience.

The second candidate to speak was a worker. He was clearly a good and honest person, and I felt sorry for him. He took every question and answered it clumsily, sometimes confusingly, repeatedly referring to his ardent heart and his clean hands. A political figure has no right to pity, and he was a poor excuse for a candidate.

The third person to speak was an engineer. He made a brilliant speech. Afterwards, I found out that he had been trained by a psychologist. But at the end, he shot himself in the foot. Before an audience, half of which was made up of servicemen, the "demo-pacifistic" engineer blurted out that the army was nothing but a bunch of good-for-nothing moochers. The enchantment vanished, and the hall filled with indignant screams, whistling, and commotion. The engineer started getting questions as sharp as a sword's thrusts. He should have taken it back, but it seemed that his democratic "superstructure" rested firmly on a Marxist base. Like a stubborn jackass, he persisted in his errors.

Colonel General Moiseev easily and comfortably passed the 50 percent threshold required for admission to the general election, and thereby became the unopposed candidate.

The public in the auditorium exploded: "How can this be? Only one candidate, again, nominated by acclamation, just as in the old days!" A fiery verbal squabble broke out with hysterical screams and insults. Finally, it was decided to hold a runoff between the engineer and the worker, to nominate one of them, and thus create an alternative to Moiseev.

Passions died down. The commission started to get ready for the new vote. A long break was announced and the local politicos went off to have some coffee, calculating on the way that, since the military's candidate had won, they could now back one of the remaining candidates.

But soldiers need orders. Thus during the break, a command rustled across the lobby: "Abstain during the vote!" As a result, in the runoff the engineer received about 25 percent of the vote and the worker less then 10 percent, so both of them lost. There was noise, commotion, whistling, and laughter. The campaign train departed, sarcastically winking its taillights at those left behind.

"It's a done deal—the rest is just a matter of technique," said the general's campaign manager. He was the campaigns ideological inspiration. A colonel from the Caucasus who served in the political department of the Armed Forces Group—a smart, profound, and ironic person—I wish I could remember his name. He clearly had a masterful knowledge of human nature. He manipulated emotions as a pharmacist mixes medical powders: he could make medicine or poison.

From that time on, everything went as if it had been scripted. March 26 was voting day. Yes, I mean "voting day." "Election" comes from the word "elect," or "choose," and a choice was just what the people didn't have. Either it was the immortal principle ascribed to Stalin: "It doesn't matter how they vote; it's how the vote is *counted* that matters," or the long-time habit of the Soviet people to come out to vote in hope that they can pick up some rare delicacy on their way to the ballot box. But no matter how it happened, Colonel General Moiseev was unanimously elected and became a deputy of the Supreme Soviet of the USSR.

So, are we really just a country of fools? Have the lies that they've systematically fed us stuck to our ears, so that we can't shake them off anymore? It's hard to say, and perhaps it isn't even all that important anymore. You can say it's history. You can spit on it or venerate it, but you can't remake it.

After he became a deputy, Nikolai Andreevich Moiseev automatically, as someone who had received a popular mandate, became the chief of the Political Department of the Ground Forces. I was serving in the Airborne troops at the time, so I don't know how he did, in the ground forces. As a deputy, his face flickered a few times on the TV screen, and then dissolved into political oblivion. Opportunism is always opportunism.

CHAPTER 10:
THE HEARTLESS ADVENTURES
OF GENERAL SERDECHNY[1]

LIFE AND THE SERVICE WENT ON. On March 25 I flew with a group of officers to Kostroma for a week-long business trip. That was when my relations with Major General F.I. Serdechny, who had become the military commissar of the Tula oblast, worsened to the utmost. As I have already said, he was an extremely harsh and cruel man, but that harshness had only rarely spilled onto me. In many ways, he had helped me learn how to become a real commander. In short, I had every reason to feel the deepest respect for him.

After he became the oblast military commissar, General Serdechny, out of habit, visited the divisional headquarters from time to time and shared his happiness with his new job. I remember he said delightedly: "I've got ten telephones on my desk, but not a goddam one of them rings all day!" Up to that time, his career had been a hard one, nothing but front-line commanding positions, so when he got a job where he could relax a bit, you could only be happy for him.

In late March he came to me, disheveled and in an aggressive mood. After mumbling a greeting he said: "Do you know that all my vehicles are registered at your maintenance shop?"

---

[1] "Serdechny" means "heartfelt" or "warm hearted" in Russian.

"Yes, I do."

"So how do you handle the spare parts supply for them?"

"The way I am supposed to. Your vehicles form a 17 percent share of my entire fleet, so you get 17 percent of all spare parts."

"Who told you that?"

"What do you mean 'told me'? Here is a calculation signed by the division deputy commander in charge of equipment, Lieutenant Colonel Davydko."

"Davydko doesn't know crap! What 17 percent? I can tell you right off the top of my head that it's 30 or even 35 percent! And again, that's just a yearly estimate; the division has been owing it to the oblast military commissariat for the past five years!"

I refrained from adopting his offensive tone and just burst out laughing:

"Fyodor Ivanovich, let me remind you that for four out of those past five years you were in command of this division! Nothing could have stopped you from settling this matter accurately with your predecessor, General Dobrovolsky. So, let's just stick to the year that I have commanded this division."

"Well, that's bull! Dobrovolsky was a wimp, and he did not demand it from me."

Here I grinned, trying to imagine the tactful General Dobrovolsky demanding something from the explosive General Serdechny.

"But I will demand it from you and you will repay me in full—for all five years! I'll turn the whole military district on its ear if I have to, but you'll pay me back!" General Serdechny choked on his own saliva.

"Fyodor Ivanovich, I'll check it all over again tomorrow. But I'll tell you right now that you won't get anything for the previous four years, and for the current year, you'll get everything that's coming to you, strictly in accordance with the calculation, and not a bolt more."

"I don't care about any calculations of yours and of that idiot Davydko. I said, 30 percent for five years!"

"In that case, you won't get anything at all. I don't have anything at the warehouse!"

"You snotty little—" General Serdechny choked again. Then for about a minute, the conversation took an extremely ugly turn, which cannot be rendered in polite language. After that, General Serdechny stormed out of my office. We parted like arch-enemies, which—I am not going to hide it, since it is all in the past—upset me greatly. Not because of the threats—I never cared much about them, they usually had the same effect on me as a red cape on a bull—but because he had been one of my teachers.

I left for a trip. When I returned on Saturday, April 1, the division's chief of staff, N.N. Nisiforov, met me at the airfield. He reported that everything was all right in the division. Around 1900 I got a call. It was the prosecutor of the Tula garrison.

"Comrade Colonel, General Serdechny and your adjutant started a gunfight. Another person was wounded and a car was shot at."

"Well, Comrade Prosecutor, you are quite an actor! All right, enough—I believe you. Happy April Fool's Day!"

"What April Fool's? I have Serdechny's pistol in front of me and the victim's pants all covered with blood."

"Arkady! Enough of these bloodcurdling details! I told you, I believe you. April Fool's!"

The prosecutor persisted, adding more and more details. I got mad, "Okay, I'll be right there. But if you're lying, Comrade Prosecutor, and this is nothing but an April Fools' joke, then watch out!"

I called a car and went to the prosecutor's office. The prosecutor, who was usually jovial, looked depressed. A "PM" pistol lay on the desk in front of him, the clip next to it, and the bloody pants on a stool. At first glance, I realized that the prosecutor was not joking. I spent the whole evening sorting things out, and the following picture emerged. I had inherited my adjutant from Serdechny—Chief Warrant Officer Viktor Alekseevich Velichkin. He was a decent and honest person, who was deeply convinced that the general stood close to God. I rarely took him on my frequent trips—there were never enough seats in the car or the helicopter. And Serdechny, who knew when I would be away, was accustomed to use his former adjutant for his own purposes.

And that's exactly what happened in October 1988. I was away on business, and Serdechny invited Velichkin over and asked him gently: "Vitya, I would like to buy a Lada for my daughter. You know that I already have one, and if I get two, people wouldn't understand. So let's just register that car in your name."

Whatever the general said was holy writ for Velichkin. The car was purchased and registered. The true owner, Serdechny, put the car and garage keys in his pocket, and the official owner, Velichkin, went about his business with the sense of having done his duty.

This time Serdechny had told the adjutant: "You know, Viktor, I am short of cash for a new dacha, so I've got to sell the car. You own it on paper, so do me a favor." No sooner said than done. In the early morning on April 1, Serdechny and Velichkin traveled to Moscow and found an auto market.

Serdechny negotiated with a couple of drifters from Kharkov and arranged to meet them in Tula at 1600 hours in front of the "Strela" grocery store. A party meeting had been scheduled for 1500 hours, at which Serdechny was supposed to speak. The political officer of the commissariat came to remind him about the meeting and brought his prepared speech. Serdechny told the political officer to take care of the meeting as he, Serdechny, needed to practice target shooting.

Serdechny summoned his deputy and ordered him to check out and bring him a handgun. He stuck it in a pocket of his leather jacket and took off, leaving the political officer bewildered.

Soon Serdechny was in the car negotiating with the buyers. There was a heated argument over the price, but they finally agreed on 5,000 rubles. One of the buyers took out an amazingly thick wad of 50 ruble notes and counted out 5,000. His stack of rubles was still enormous, and Serdechny jumped to the conclusion that he had sold out too cheaply. He demanded at least 50 percent more, arguing that "you've got a lot more where that came from." The owner refused, and another argument erupted. Serdechny took out his gun and told them not to push him into using it. The owner of the wad of bills was stubborn. Serdechny and one of the buyers got out of the car, the other stayed behind the wheel. The heated argument drove Serdechny over the edge. He shot at the windshield. By sheer luck, the bullet missed the windshield and lodged in the frame of the car. If the bullet had gone one or two centimeters to the right, the man behind the wheel could have been killed. The buyer got scared, rammed the pedal down, and disappeared from the scene. Serdechny sent another three shots after him, one of which, as we found out later, pierced the rear tire. The enraged General Serdechny turned to the second buyer who stood, dumbfounded: "Well, you'll have to answer for this!" Two more shots rang out, hitting the ground. The third shot passed through the man's thigh. He screamed and fell, but the bullet had missed the bone. Serdechny came to his senses, stuck his gun in his pocket, and signaled for his driver. A black Volga sedan pulled over, and Fyodor Ivanovich departed from the scene, leaving Velichkin, shocked to the depths of his soul, in a crowd of onlookers.

Serdechny had been dressed in civilian clothes, but his driver had been in uniform and the Volga had military license plates. The search started, and the prosecutor followed the tracks. But there was not much to the search—there were only four black Volgas with military license plates in the entire Tula garrison. For some reason, the prosecutor started with me, but he was told that I had been away for a week on business and that my Volga hadn't budged from its place. By the time the prosecutor got to Serdechny, the latter had downed at least two glasses of something to warm himself after a hard day's work. With the consequent philosophic outlook on life, he gave the prosecutor his gun, but refused to provide any explanations, due to stress and his inebriated state.

Attempts to get depositions from the witnesses turned out to be futile. Everyone agreed they had seen something, but nothing fully incriminating. "Yes, I heard the shots! But who was shooting and at whom, God knows!"

The prosecutor told me this story and then posed the eternal Russian question, "What Is to Be Done?"[2] The second eternal Russian question—"Who Is to Blame?"[3]—did not need to be posed. And again we had to deal with the concept of equality of all Soviet citizens before the law. If a soldier or a warrant officer, or even an officer, had done something like that, the prosecutor's hand would not shake signing the arrest warrant and he would be doing the right thing. But in this case, the circumstances, were, well, extraordinary! We were talking about an oblast military commissar and major general, a deputy of the Oblast Soviet, and a member of the Oblast Executive Committee. To imagine such a figure sitting in solitary confinement in a guardhouse was beyond the wildest imagination. I reminded the prosecutor that deputies had immunity from criminal prosecution, and recommended that he file a criminal case and report it along the chain of command above him. The prosecutor accepted my suggestion with relief. He started up his legal bureaucratic machine, and I left for headquarters.

Velichkin, devastated, crushed, was waiting for me there. He looked so lost my harsh words stuck in my throat. He kept repeating incoherently: "How can it be? He just said to me, 'Vitya, why does the division commander have to know?' He said he didn't do anything illegal! That's what he said! He's a general, how could it be?" Viktor Alekseevich looked at me with the eyes of a sick puppy.

"Go home, Viktor Alekseevich. Drink your hundred grams, and go to bed. Nothing will happen," I said.

"Yeah, right, nothing will happen! He is a general, and I am a warrant officer and the owner of the car. They'll pin it all on me."

"I said, go home! On the double! Nothing will happen! He played you for a fool, that's clear, but you're not guilty of anything!"

---

[2] Which was the title of a famous novel by Chernyshevsky and one of Lenin's first tracts.

[3] Title of a novel by Alexander Herzen.

It was clear from Velichkin's eyes that he didn't believe a word I'd said. "Yes, sir!" He shuffled out awkwardly, as if made of wood. In exactly fifteen minutes I found out that Vitya knew his former boss much better than I did. The telephone rang.

"Colonel Lebed speaking."

At the other end of the line, instead of a greeting, I heard sniffling and a drunken voice threatening: "The warrant officer must take the blame for everything!"

I was somewhat startled by such arrogance.

"What do you mean *everything?*"

"Everything, including the shooting."

"The warrant officer will be severely reprimanded for the kind of riffraff he deals with in his free time. But I will defend him in everything else before the commander, the minister, or God Himself!"

> **"The general had insulted my wife. I called the District commander: 'Teach the military commissar some manners, or I will be forced to shoot him.'"**

"You. . . ." The receiver sputtered with foul-mouthed hatred. I pressed the disconnect button.

On Monday, after I reported the case to Lieutenant General Achalov, the commander of the Airborne troops, he said that the oblast military commissars were under the jurisdiction of the Military District commander. This commander, who, as I understood, already knew what happened, growled: "We'll get to the bottom of it!" But nothing happened, and the paperwork rose as high as the defense minister, Marshal of the Soviet Union Dmitry Timofeevich Yazov. I must give Dmitry Timofeevich credit for not simply putting his signature on an order to arrest Velichkin. Instead, he called me and asked what had really happened. I told him. Velichkin's name was removed from the order.

Then a likable, well-built major arrived—the investigator from the Main Military Prosecutor's Office. He introduced himself. He had the Order of the Red Star and the medal "For Bravery" pinned to his tunic.

"Are you an Afghan war veteran?" I asked him.

"Yes, I am."

"Tell me honestly, officer to officer, what have they sent you out here to do? To get to the bottom of this, or just to hush it up?"

He lowered his eyes, hesitated for five seconds, looked up and met my stare.

"I was ordered to hush it up. It makes me sick, but I have my orders!"

The drifters from Kharkov, the "witnesses," figured out that being in the spotlight would not do them any good. They negotiated with Serdechny and changed their testimony. The doctored picture began to look almost tame. It went something like this: good old friends had boozed it up a bit too much and had gotten a little hot under the collar, but had cooled down, and were ready to forgive and forget absolutely everything, including the shot in the leg. Keep in mind this was the period when the mud-slinging campaign against the army was in full swing, so the Military District commander had no desire to give the "free democratic press" such a trump card. Serdechny perked up. A new rumor was born, and the story spread that the courageous General Serdechny had repelled an attack from racketeers. In fact, he had been the buyer of the car, not the seller at all. In short, the entire military bureaucratic machine was geared up to soften, blur, and hush up the damage.

It might have worked if it had happened ten years before, but times were already changing, in some regards drastically and irreversibly. In the first place, the officers of the military commissariat, who knew their leader well and were aware of the true facts, were outraged. In the second place, the press finally managed to do its job. I do not remember the name of the paper, but I believe it was *Izvestia* that published a mocking article entitled "A General Posing As an

Adjutant." In the third place, Serdechny became so cheerful that he was careless enough to call my wife and tell her what he thought of me, using inappropriate language.

Shocked, she listened to part of the tirade before hanging up. My wife could not bring herself to render it word for word, but I got the point. I went looking for Serdechny. The general was wise enough to vanish. I am not the most hot-tempered person, but this time I was boiling. I picked up a secure phone and requested to be put through to the commander of the Military District.

Restraining myself, I told him what had happened, and concluded with a request: "Comrade Commander, I am asking you to teach the oblast military commissar some manners, or I will be forced to shoot him. I mean it!"

The phone was quiet. I was sure that I had been disconnected, but finally I heard him say, "All right, we'll take care of it, just cool down."

Eventually, the criminal case against General Serdechny was closed, on what grounds, and how, I don't know; they simply took the case file away from the garrison prosecutor, and he never saw it again. But General Serdechny was dishonorably discharged from the armed forces for discrediting himself. After August 1991 he tried to get reinstated in the military, presenting himself as a victim of political repression and of *perestroika*, but it didn't work.

All these events left me with a feeling of extreme disgust, and it's still there. It's a complex feeling—a combination of contempt and squeamishness and loathing. But there is also disappointment over what a general who had made it through a tough career could turn into, when all the higher values which had been instilled in him over the years got squeezed out and replaced by a single, all-consuming passion—the craving for easy money—under the influence of changing circumstances and the moral climate of the society. What is a military commissariat, when there is no control, when the spirit of corruption and stories of lawlessness and high-handedness are in the air? A bonanza. You can list a sick person as a healthy one and a muscled stallion as an emaciated invalid. You can conscript someone today, a year from now, or never. Who is going to count each and every Ivan? All you have to do is hustle. And once someone gets drawn in, he no longer cares about his honor and his conscience, but with remarkable ease, exploits his position for personal gain. He can become a blackmailer and an extortionist on the government payroll and will divide all people into two categories: those who can and those who cannot, allies and victims.

These animals standing at the entrance of the Temple of the Army with their greedy hands and roving eyes cause great, and often irreparable, moral damage to the military. There are not many of them, but they are energetic, aggressive, and resourceful. Because of them, the public gets a distorted picture of the entire officer corps, most of whom are smart, courageous people who love and know their profession, and are selflessly devoted to their Fatherland and ready to die for it.

CHAPTER 11:
TROUBLE IN TBILISI

ON APRIL 5, 1989, the situation in Tbilisi, Georgia, suddenly became extremely tense. At the request of the first secretary of the Georgian Communist Party, the top brass decided to send troops to Tbilisi to stabilize the situation—the Airborne troops, of course.

The first unit to get the call was the former detached "Bagram-Afghan" 345th Airborne Regiment, which, at that time, was part of the 104th Airborne Division, permanently deployed at Gyandja (formerly, Kirovabad).

The 345th survived when the 105th Airborne Division was disbanded in 1979. It was one of the first units to enter Afghanistan, and fought there from June 1979 all the way through February 1989. Not even the smallest operation was undertaken without its help. In the Bagram valley and the area around it, it was in the thick of battle. On February 15, 1989, the regiment was the last to leave Afghanistan, and was sent to Gyandja, in the Azerbaijan SSR, to Karabakh, Baku, Sumgait. The regiment, that is, had simply exchanged one "hot spot" for another. And now, the regiment was deployed in Gudauta (Abkhazia). All this was based on the principle: if you succeed once, you're the one who will be sent next time.

And it was this regiment which, on April 6, 1989, got a new mission: to make a 320 kilometer march from Gyandja to Tbilisi, and prop up the tottering regime. The regiment made the march in twenty-four hours, and entered the capital of Soviet Georgia, concentrating on the approaches to Government House. Quite understandably the mood of the officers and soldiers was ominous.

The regiment blocked the approaches to Government House and the square in front of it, where a heated, typically "southern" meeting was raging for the second day in a row. The approaches to the square were barricaded by large trucks, which were filled with fist-sized paving stones. These improvised barricades were guarded by a motley group of fighters, armed with whatever they could get their hands on, and in an aggressive mood.

> **"F**reedom, independence, and sovereignty turned into cold, hunger, poverty, and the destruction of a once-prosperous Georgia.**"**

The regiment, which had fought for almost ten years nonstop, knew what life was worth, what blood was worth, and armed with this valuable knowledge, was in no hurry. In battle, the regiment was professionally cruel and merciless. But that was in *battle*! The regiment saw no enemy here. And here, too, the habits it had learned in battle didn't seem to count for much.

Even the mission was formulated in the manner typical of the Gorbachev era: march from here to here at such-and-such a time, concentrate here. All this was concrete and intelligible. But after that came a blue fog: "Act according to the dictates of the situation. Help and assist party and law-enforcement organs in restoring order." The regiment was waiting! And while it waited, it was feverishly trying to figure out: "What do they want from us? What do they expect us to do?"

Passions at the meeting continued to flare. People of both sexes and all ages took part. Hunger strikers, protesters, and people who were simply dead tired, the weakest people at the meeting, stretched out on the lawn in front of Government House. The soldiers waited.... "Freedom!" "Independence!" "Sovereignty!" "You bastards!" "You mongrels!" Still, the soldiers waited. They gritted their teeth, but they waited.

Paving stones and steel rods with sharpened tips began to fly at the patient, steadfast, courageous Russian soldiers. The regiment repelled the hailstorm, and carried off its wounded. The stream of invective and stones got worse.

The regiment seized the barricaded trucks to escape the surging mob. This action caused a panic in the square. The stampeding protesters crushed and crippled the weakest among them. As a result, eighteen people died, sixteen of them women.

The meeting dispersed. But the conflict in Georgia was only the beginning, a war of all against all, with tens of thousands of victims. Freedom, independence, and sovereignty turned into cold, hunger, poverty, and the total destruction of a once-prosperous country. When the war ended, Shevardnadze, "The Great Helmsman," was left with nothing but a half-destroyed Tbilisi, where gas, water, and electricity were nothing but a pleasant dream. But all this was to come.

On that April 8 my division was put on alert. We marched to the airport, and an armada of airplanes took off, landing three regiments in sunny Tbilisi.

The division moved out to its designated zones of responsibility. Late on the night of April 9-10, I led the column through the city and was struck by its dead appearance. There were no lights in any of the windows. Even the street lights were out; there were no pedestrians, no policemen, no dogs. Nothing but silence, and in that silence, only one sound could be heard—the screeching of our treads.

Perhaps that feeling only came later, perhaps I had it at the time— it's hard to tell—but I felt as if this city and the people in it had crossed that invisible line of what was permissible and now, without thinking, without looking back, were ready to cast themselves into the abyss of bloody passions, irrespective of anyone's personal will.

I will touch on only two typical moments and a kaleidoscope of impressions.

The third day we were there, I went to the Kostroma regiment's zone of responsibility to hear the regimental commander's report. One of the installations the regiment had to guard was Shevardnadze's personal residence, for which a company and no fewer than five military vehicles were set aside.

I arrived at the residence just in time. The residence was a five-story mansion, with a shaded horseshoe-shaped garden in front of it. A road ran around the outside of the garden, and another road cut the garden in half and led directly to the mansion. The five military vehicles and about forty servicemen were concentrated in front of the mansion.

The company commander, Captain Levinson, deployed his men and machines as well as space would permit. But now three colonels (of unknown origin) were demanding in two languages—Russian and profane Russian—that Levinson dig trenches in the garden for the vehicles.

Levinson, for his part, argued that digging in would lead to two things: losing whatever maneuverability they had to begin with, and spoiling a nice little garden. Besides, no tank attack was expected.

But it was hard for a lone captain to hold out against three colonels. I didn't try to find out for certain, but I was pretty sure the colonels were from the military district's political department. After realizing who I was, they angrily turned on me and insisted that I personally bore the responsibility for E.A. Shevardnadze's precious life. I listened to them attentively, advised them not to stick their nose into other people's business, and gave them fifteen seconds to get out of the territory we were guarding.

The colonels beat the deadline. Levinson reported that for three days straight, he had borne the onslaught of all sorts of military and civilian officials, who in various ways tried to harass him into changing his scheme of defense of the residence.

I explained to him that since we lived in the land of Soviets, advice was cheap[1]. I ordered him to check with his battalion commander how the vehicles and posts were to be set up. They were to say, "Yes, sir!" to everyone who came with advice and recommendations, but they were to stick to the approved scheme.

The company commander also expressed bewilderment that Shevardnadze had not deigned to greet, nod, or even to look at any of the soldiers or officers guarding him.

"For him, we're even lower than cattle," he said. "We're nothing but tree stumps!"

I advised him to tell all his men to turn their faces into sphinx-like masks. They liked that idea and elaborated on it. When Eduard Amvrosievich walked to his car with a glum face, he would see faces as glum as his all around. No "Good morning!" and no "Good evening!" They would guard him like a crowd of tree stumps.

In the course of controlling our zone of responsibility, we talked to the people. All southern cities have the same characteristic: if you stop for a few seconds and talk with someone or answer a question, a big crowd will instantly form around you—noise, uproar, heated shouting.

"Well, citizens," I said, are we going to shout or talk? If you're going to shout, then I'm leaving. But if you want to talk, let's talk!"

"All right, let's talk. In the newspaper *Zarya Vostoka* (the Tbilisi city newspaper) it says that an airborne soldier chased a seventy-one-year-old woman three kilometers and knocked her down with a shovel!"

"So? The paper says! Do you have any questions?"

"What questions can there be! He knocked her down!"

The crowd got excited again, cursing and making threats.

"Quiet, citizens! Hear me out. Here's my first question: what kind of old woman could stay ahead of a soldier for three kilometers? And

---

[1] This is a pun in Russian. The word *sovety* means both "Soviets" and "advice."

my second question: what kind of soldier would take three kilometers to catch up to an old woman? And my third question—the most interesting—where were they running? A stadium? How come she couldn't find a single Georgian man in three kilometers to cut that scoundrel off?"

That hit them in the solar plexus, so to speak. They didn't have a leg to stand on. If you looked at it emotionally, sure, it made you mad, but if you took the time to analyze the report, it was a lot of nonsense!

But every time, someone in the crowd would try to divert the conversation to another subject. As, for example, now.

It was never a question but a statement of "fact" which did not tolerate any objection:

"You used poison gas on us in the square."

"Does poison gas work on communists and fascists alike?"

There was a pause. They had to think about this one. They soon came to the conclusion that anatomy had nothing to do with ideology.

"Yes. It works the same."

"So that means if I, let's say, wanted to poison you, then I'd have to put on some means of protection, or we'd both die together, right?"

"Right!" they unwillingly agreed.

"Have you seen even one soldier in a gas mask or protective clothing? Do you think the several thousand soldiers here are all kamikazes?"

The crowd rumbled and buzzed, discussing what they had just heard. People cursed Gorbachev and the first secretary of the Georgian Communist Party. Their black, southern eyes were filled with hatred, now clouded by doubt.

"Think about it," I said as I left. "I wish you all the best. Good-bye!"

I remember elderly Georgian workers with tired, knotted hands: "Don't leave!" they begged. "We have to slave away for the Mafia now, for kopecks! If you leave, then we're done for! There will be war! Many people will die! Don't leave."

Those wise old workers had already seen further than the politicians. Even then, they had a clearer and more subtle grasp of the situation.

In another incident I remember a shower of bricks as I led a column of vehicles on the street leading to the train station.

The remains of the bricks lay on the pavement, and an orange dust covered the vehicles. But people walked on the sidewalks to the right and to the left, without paying any attention to us. There was a nine-story apartment building on the left, and another one on the right. It was as if an angry housewife had decided to shake her potato peelings from her apron. Unpleasant, to be sure, but not fatal.

Officers at headquarters had rocks thrown at them, and ink jars and paint cans were rained on the enormous statue of Ordzhonikidze. They tried to wash it off, and when that didn't work, they took it away at night to some unknown location.

Command posts, patrols, trailers, additional rations, unsatisfactory sanitary conditions, squabbling, misunderstandings, meetings with people, taking care of military training—all these things, as always, converged in a mass of problems, some of which were hard to solve, and some of which could not be solved at all.

CHAPTER 12:
BLACK JANUARY IN BAKU

THERE'S AN ANCIENT JOKE that goes something like this: The commander of a regiment is arguing with his chief of staff. They bring in the political officer to act as a referee. He listens to the commander and sums up, "Commander, you're right." Then he listens to the chief of staff and says, "You're right!" The party committee secretary butts in: "How can this be? The commander's right, and the chief of staff is *also* right? It can't be!" The political officer says, "You're right, too!"

This joke is the best way to summarize the position taken by Mikhail Gorbachev to continuing troubles in Azerbaijan. Armenia was right. Azerbaijan was right. Turkey, Iran, the Armenian diaspora abroad, and in general, anyone who wished to intervene in the conflict in Azerbaijan was also right.

The inter-ethnic conflict increasingly acquired the appearance of a war. After weeks of doing nothing to stop the bloody civil strife, Gorbachev recalled his formula: Airborne troops plus military transport aviation equals Soviet Power in the Transcaucasus. On January 18, 1990, the division was put on alert.

By that time, all of the officers had acquired experience in these matters, and their opinion was unanimous. It boiled down to this: "The hell with all the Party and government leaders." Instead of nipping the conflict in the bud, they let it catch fire, persuaded that nothing would happen, and then, when it turned out that it did, they reached for their magic stick, the Airborne troops, to come to their rescue.

Believing that things would get very bad, I took two artillery batteries and a ZU-23-2 anti-aircraft battery with me. The *"zeushka"* wasn't much of an anti-aircraft weapon; the whole battery had only a 12 percent chance of knocking down a plane. In other words, if all six guns were booming, the battery could shoot down 12 percent of an aircraft. The anti-aircraft gunners liked to joke: "We can't knock 'em down, but we can scare them to death." But the *"zeushka"* was wonderful at land targets, and even against tanks. It couldn't penetrate armor, of course, but its little shells could knock everything off of a tank's body: periscopic sights, headlights, searchlights, antennas. A blinded and deafened tank can only roar in anger—its fighting capabilities gone.

Our work began the usual way: strictly at the appointed time, regimental columns marched to the airports and loaded their vehicles. The 137th Ryazan Airborne Guards Regiment was the first to leave for Baku. I took off in the Tula regiment's first plane.

It was January, wintertime. The sun rose late, and dark came early. The plane in which I flew landed in twilight at the Kala airport, about thirty kilometers from Baku. There was sporadic shooting, and the fuselage of one of our planes was grazed by gunfire. I was met by the division's chief of staff, Colonel N.N. Nisiforov, and the commander of the Ryazan regiment, Colonel Yu. A. Naumov.

Then the chief of staff reported: "The Ryazan and Kostroma boys have unloaded and are forming up in columns. They've sent scouts and are posting guards. We're ready to go except that the airport exits are blocked by barricades with KamAZ and KRAZ trucks loaded with concrete blocks and gravel. The men at the barricades have small arms. There are also groups driving around the airport perimeter, shooting at the planes. Units have been dispatched to deal with them. The regimental commander," the chief of staff said, with a hint of surprise in his voice, "will report to you what our mission is. He got it from the minister of defense personally."

The commander of the regiment, Colonel Yuri Alekseevich Naumov, was an officer of exceptional qualities: wise, thorough, able to command his regiment successfully in peacetime and wartime alike; and he had no fear of the authorities. But here, something was clearly holding him back.

"So report, Yuri Alekseevich. What's going on?" I said.

"If you permit, Comrade Colonel, I will tell you exactly what he said."

"Well, tell me!"

"The minister of defense waved his fist under my nose and said: 'Don't you dare not take it, you mother ****. Tell that to Lebed!'"

"That's all?"

"That's all!"

"Take what?"

"Baku. There's nothing else to take here."

I gave preliminary orders and went to the checkpoint to sort things out. It was thirty kilometers to Baku, and to complete the mission successfully, we first had to get out of the airport.

The checkpoint's windows were prudently reinforced with sandbags. It was guarded by tense soldiers from the airport technical company with automatic rifles. Through the gates, you could see the outlines of big trucks in the darkness. Between them, silhouettes of people flickered by, some of them also holding automatic rifles. Screams and curses rang out. I tried to enter into negotiations with them:

"I have to get out of here, and I will. The army is not a cat that you can hold by the tail. Peace be on your homes. Let us through, and I guarantee you that not a hair on your heads will be harmed."

The response was hysterical: "We won't let you through. Even if we have to die here, we won't let you through."

While we were having this delightful conversation, the airport, under cover of darkness, was bustling with activity. For three hundred meters to the right and the left of the checkpoint, the sappers had cut a hole in the airport fence, preparing the way for our vehicles. Columns of two companies, with lights out, moved up into starting position. Another company sat on top of each company's armor. "Ural"

> **"O**ur regiments were harassed nonstop. Not a single day went by without several soldiers being injured by bricks or pieces of pipe.**"**

trucks loaded to full capacity were prepared to work as pushers or pullers. On the bumper of each "Ural" were fixed two or three large logs, and on them, two or three tires. A metal screen that covered the windshield wouldn't work against bullets, but would be quite effective against stones or grenades. The drivers and the crew leaders were wearing helmets and bulletproof vests. The windows were open, and the crew leaders had their automatic rifles at the ready. The drivers had theirs on their knees.

An officer came up and whispered that everything was ready. I concluded my fruitless conversation. "Well, the hell with you! I warned you!"

In response—catcalls, whistling, malicious laughter.

"Let's go!" I ordered.

The companies broke out onto the highway through the openings made for them. In a matter of seconds, the pincers closed. The attack came from two directions, with shouts of "Hurrah!" The soldiers shot into the air to create a panic.

The blockaders, screaming, ran off to the vineyards on the other side of the road. But not all of them—ninety-two people were caught, huddled in a bunch. Not a trace was left of their former cockiness. There were no dead or wounded. Weapons were left on the ground. Their owners, naturally, were nowhere to be found—cats are gray in the dark. The "Urals" pushed and pulled the KRAZes and the KamAZes out of the way. The road was open.

The Ryazan regiment, and after it, the Kostroma regiment, moved toward Baku. I kept the Tula regiment in reserve, for unforeseen circumstances. I set up the command post at the airport in two rooms of the officers' dormitory.

It was hard going for the Ryazan boys. They had to move, scatter, or overcome thirteen barricades of various sizes. Thirty kilometers and thirteen barricades. Twice, our adversaries poured gasoline from fifteen-ton tanker trucks and set the road aflame, confronting the column with a sea of fire. At night, this was especially impressive. The column would divert into fields and vineyards, where it was subjected to pot shots.

You have to understand the soldier's psychology here. No one has ever told this nineteen- to twenty-year-old, at any stage of his education—either in regular school, or in agricultural school, or in technical school, or in college—no one has ever told him to kill anyone. No one has taught him to do that. Or to be more precise, he *has* been taught, but only in the abstract. A target is only a target; it is faceless. It has never been given the characteristic outlines of a soldier from some country or other. The kind of training intended to put meaning into this one word, "Kill!" he does not have, even with respect to the armies of potential adversaries. And here, he is not faced with "potential adversaries." This is Azerbaijan, and the soldiers have learned, at least to some degree, that this is one of our union republics, *our* land, *our* people. And with them, in the same unit, are Azeri soldiers, many of them from Baku.

A soldier is "government property." He has orders to stop the bloodshed, which must, as he sees it, be the result of a massive misunderstanding. There is no aggressiveness or spite in him. But there is grief and bewilderment. Why? Why do the Airborne troops have to do it? What are we, anyway—policemen?

Most of them go into battle in a benevolent mood, confident that if they had the chance to talk to people and explain things to them, they would understand and stop killing each other. But the benevolence is soon knocked out of them by a stream of screaming invective and bursts from automatic rifles, fired at them in the darkness. And they, youngsters, seeing that they are being killed for no reason at all, get mad and the instinct for self-preservation and the thirst for revenge take over.

The "Airborne chauvinism" that is cultivated in them also plays a role (there are no impossible missions; no one but us). Their aggressiveness awakens, and there is no trace of the sweetly smiling youths. What is left is a fierce, well-trained wolf, whose comrade has just been struck down, whose soul is full of one black passion—to get even with the sniping cowards who did it.

Those thirty kilometers cost the Ryazan boys seven soldiers wounded by bullets, and about thirty hit by bricks, sheet metal, pipes, or stakes. By 0500 the regiments had taken control of the regions assigned to them. From the east, from the direction of the Nasosnaya airport, the Pskov Airborne division entered the city. In addition there came a mass of motorized infantry, whose units were staffed with hastily called-up "partisans" from Rostov oblast, and Krasnodar and Stavropol *krais*. The same city, the same people. But in November 1988 it had been a living, cheerful, temperamental southern city, blooming with smiles and flowers. Now it was gloomy, depressed, strewn with the traces of military action and hated by everyone.

The work began—to organize a commandant's office and to rebuild and restore the city's infrastructure, work that had become familiar, but which was still difficult. Our regiments were harassed nonstop. Not a single day went by without several soldiers being injured by bricks or pieces of pipe.

I was ordered to take the Baku city port terminal, where about 150 Popular Front activists had coordinated their resistance efforts against our troops. Division headquarters planned the operation. I gave the commander of the Kostroma regiment, Colonel E. Yu. Savilov, the mission of taking the terminal.

In accordance with the plan, at 0430 on January 24, the regiment was to move toward the starting point in converging directions and take the terminal (bloodlessly, if possible) by 0530. They were to open fire only if fired upon, but if it came to that, they were to return fire so hard that the activists would never again have the urge to shoot. Everything was ready.

The first units began to move, but then Colonel General Achalov, the newly appointed commander of the Airborne troops who was in Baku, intervened. What had happened to him, I don't know to this day, but in a frantic voice he roared into the receiver: "Stop immediately!" So we stopped immediately. Troops, thank God, respond to orders. At 0600, we got a new order, from the very same Achalov, accompanied by the remark: "What, you've stopped your regiment? Devil take you! Move out, I say!"

If he wanted us to move out, then we'd move out—especially if he was going to bring the Devil into it. By 0700 the regiment had taken the terminal without any losses on either side. They captured the first-class steamship *Sabit Orudzhev*, which had been built in Finland, where the Popular Front activists' headquarters had been. The mission had been accomplished, but, as always happens in these situations, a number of circumstances influenced the course of events.

At 0705, a ship from the *Neftegazflot* (oil and gas fleet) came in, turned about 250 meters from the shore, and about fifteen or so people opened fire on the regiment with automatic rifles. In the first few seconds a sergeant and a private were seriously wounded. A bullet hit the sergeant in the small of the back and went into his abdominal cavity. In the hospital, they took out a large chunk of his intestines, but he lived. The private got a "blind" head wound through his helmet. A "blind" wound is when there is an entrance wound, but no exit. It was probably "blinded" because he had been wearing his helmet. In a month, the soldier died without regaining consciousness. The company, standing on the pier, returned fire. The regimental commander made an instant decision: four BMD-1s crawled onto the mooring, and each vehicle shot two cumulative grenades at the ship. The ship caught fire. The surviving gunmen jumped into a motorboat which was tied to the side of the ship. They got away.

Later, when everything had died down, people joked that we could even fight with the navy, since we could take care of the main problem—enticing the enemy to within range of our guns.

Among other facilities at the terminal, a restaurant had been captured, and in the restaurant, breakfast for two hundred people. And not just a normal breakfast, but *shashlik*, salmon, and red and black caviar for soldiers who had been living on dry rations for a week.

Due to the inexplicable delay, instead of capturing the 150-200 people that we planned on, we nabbed only a little over twenty. Most of the Popular Front activists had run away between 0500 and 0600. Somebody had "given away" the operation. I don't think the commander had anything to do with it. Most likely, he had been a pawn in someone else's game.

The regiment, in my view, had accomplished its main mission: The command post, the "brains" of the resistance, had ceased to exist. Tension in the city decreased rapidly, and life began to return to normal.

The Kostroma regiment remained in the city, and I concentrated the other two regiments at the Kala airport.

We barely had time to clean our feathers when I received word that a large—thirty-nine people in all—joint commission from the USSR Prosecutor General's Office and the Main Military Prosecutor's Office would be arriving to investigate the incident, and one of its main jobs was my division. They passed on an invitation from the senior member of the group to meet and organize our "fruitful work" together.

I went. The group was located in a hotel near the Salyansky barracks buildings. And herein an interesting story. The barracks got their name from a Frenchman named Salian who served during the reign of Czar Nikolai I. Where and how the Frenchman disgraced himself, history doesn't tell us. But he was sent to serve in Baku, which at the time was a wild, remote place. The Frenchman was well educated, had a lot of organizational talent, and, wanting to redeem himself, threw himself into bustling activity.

In a short period of time, three to four years, under his personal leadership, a fortress-city was built. It was beautiful and durable, taking the peculiarities of local architecture into account.

After completing construction, Salian, hoping for mercy, sent Nikolai I a triumphant letter, the point of which could be reduced to a single phrase: "Your Majesty, I am reporting that I have built Heaven on Earth in this wild place!" The emperor's response was curt: "So you've built Heaven on Earth—well good for you! You can live there!"

I couldn't find the senior member of the group of investigators, a major general (I don't remember his last name). Some of the group's investigators were people that I had met before. Others, I didn't know, but they were friendly.

There was a simple explanation for this. As Mowgli said, we were of one blood: I and people like me put out conflicts, and they and people like them took care of the consequences and tried to make at least some superficial legal order out of the boundless chaos.

I quickly briefed the investigators. One of them pushed a stack of more than 150 papers toward me. I skimmed through them. They all had the same heading: "List of Crimes Committed by the Airborne Troops in Baku on January 19-20." The texts differed, but only slightly: they said that hundreds of people had been killed and thousands wounded. An absolutely unbelievable number of cars, refrigerators, rugs, money, and valuables had been stolen. And the conclusions were always the same: we demand an immediate investigation and severe punishment.

The third from the top was the statement of Galina Nikolaevna Mamedova, the accountant of the port terminal's restaurant. From the statement, I was amazed to find that she had kept twelve thousand rubles in unpaid advances in the top drawer of her desk, and that in the middle drawer, a diamond ring and stunning gold earrings. In the lower drawer, she had kept several little boxes of French perfumes and toilet water. According to Galina Nikolaevna, the contents of her three drawers added up to about fifty thousand or sixty thousand rubles. This was 1990 and sixty thousand rubles was the equivalent of a small herd of Zhiguli cars.

Then I found a letter from the deputy director of the port terminal. From this letter, pages long, it seemed that the port terminal had been looted completely. The list, which ran to more than two hundred items, included televisions, rugs, china, and video cameras. I read this with growing amazement until I got to a the following point: "Six couches were stolen from the waiting room." The couches in the port terminal's waiting room were welded, were about sixteen feet long, and designed to seat six people.

I burst out laughing. I recommended that all this "evidence" be consigned to the nearest wastebasket. Our political officers had already asked the terminal administrators if they had claims to press against us; and instead the administrators had been effusively grateful that their buildings and equipment had not suffered any damage and that nobody had shot at the windows or chandeliers. The restaurant's accountant had been the most effusive of all. The investigators said that they believed me, but that their job demanded that they prove the obvious.

By lunchtime, the major general—the senior member of the group of investigators—called me at my command post:

"Are you division commander Colonel Lebed?"

"Yes, I am."

"According to the information at my disposal, two regiments have been taken out of the city and are concentrated at the airport. Is that true?"

"Yes!"

"I want to talk with the officers and the warrant officers of these regiments. When can you get them together?"

"Whenever you want to see them, I'll get them together for you. Is 1600 or 1700 all right?"

"Yes. Let's say, at 1700."

By 1700 the officers and warrant officers of the two regiments, and the division command and the special units, sat in the pilots' club.

He greeted me, dry and unsmiling, and went straight-away to the improvised rostrum. Several hundred pairs of eyes looked at the general with wary interest.

This wasn't a very good beginning, but I sat down behind a table and waited to hear the prosecutor's speech.

The general looked the auditorium over sternly, extinguishing any smiles, and began: "You are harboring criminals in your ranks. Either you will hand them over voluntarily, or we will have to take them by force!"

We had no idea what "criminals" he had in mind. As it turned out, they were two warrant officers, the commanders of supply platoons, who had temporarily seized two cases of Czech beer and a case of instant coffee during our raid. Deathly quiet hung over the club for several seconds, and then everyone unexpectedly burst out in mocking, disapproving laughter. The laughter was a challenge. On the benches sat officers and warrant officers of the Airborne troops, well honed, elite warriors, ready to fight anyone, anywhere. Where did this insolent fellow come from, and why the insulting tone? *Take away!*—Ha-ha-ha! From *us!*—Ha-ha-ha! *By force!*—Ha-ha-ha!

The prosecutor-general turned pale, then blushed, and the auditorium went crazy, bursting out in more and more spasms of uncontrollable laughter. It wasn't funny to me. A wave of cold fury passed over me. I picked up the phone and called the commander of the only regiment left in the city:

"Savilov, how many of your troops are guarding the group of investigators?"

"A platoon, seventeen men and three BMDs."

"Take them off that post immediately, and report when you've done it!"

It didn't take much time; in seven minutes, the regimental commander reported:

"The platoon has been taken off that post, and has returned to the company, sir!"

I turned to the prosecutor, who had been standing at the rostrum the whole time and said: "Comrade General, this conversation hasn't turned out too well, and now it won't turn out at all. I have the honor to say good-bye. Comrade officers!"

Several hundred men obeyed the command in a single instant. Up! Not a sound. Only eyes. And in this deathly silence, the prosecutor, accompanied by me, made his way to the exit.

But it did not stop there. The four hundred soldiers and sergeants remained—silent and hostile.

As we stepped outside, soldiers formed a semicircle around us. They bombarded the prosecutor with mocking questions. The prosecutor tried to field the questions, but soon waved his hand and gave up.

Realizing how dangerous the situation was, I announced loudly: "In view of the severe magnetic storms and the incessant outbursts of solar flares, question time has been postponed. Additional time will be given at a later date. Clear the way!" While the men were pondering what connection there could be between magnetic storms, solar flares, and answering questions, and in general, what their division commander was up to, they cleared the way.

We walked to his car, the general said good-bye with a nod, without giving me his hand, and left. Laughter rang out from the club. Obviously, they had been thinking about the solar flares.

In an hour, the calls started coming:

"Comrade Colonel, Aleksandr Ivanovich, bring the guard back. They'll cut us up. The chief is usually a pretty good guy. He just got a little carried away there."

"I will give you twenty-four hours to call with an apology," I said. "If it goes one minute beyond that, the question of the guard will be resolved only by the personal appearance of your boss."

In four hours, the general called. The investigators had obviously been at him, and his tone reflected this; it was completely different.

"Aleksandr Ivanovich, you know, I still don't understand what happened there. Devil take me if I do! Perhaps there was a dose of truth in what you said about magnetic storms. I apologize to your officers. Hear me out. I guarantee you that we will investigate everything quietly, impartially, and... I beg you, please send the guard back, we need to get to work!"

In about twenty minutes, the platoon returned to its interrupted duties. And they really did investigate the matter quietly. The beer and coffee lovers (they actually *had* taken something, even though it had been instantly returned) were given a dishonorable discharge.

The end of January 1990 saw a transfer of tension from the center of the country to the provinces. Information poured in, and most of it was not comforting. There was unrest in Neftechal and in Jalilabad. Something had been captured, something destroyed, the police had been disbanded, the city executive committee building had been burned down....

If my memory doesn't betray me, on January 25, I got a call from the commander of the Airborne troops, Colonel General V.A. Achalov.

"Soviet Power has been overthrown in Jalilabad. You have a helicopter regiment deployed at the Kala airport. Think about what to do about Jalilabad. Report your decision!"

What was there to think about? I called in the commander of the helicopter regiment, who turned out to be pleasant in every respect. He had been in Afghanistan twice. He had the Order of the Military Red Banner, two Red Stars on his breast, and a scar on his cheek. In short, he was just what I needed. We planned the operation quickly, I reported my decision, and it was approved.

At dawn, on January 26, five Mi-8 helicopters took off from the Kala airport and set off for Jalilabad. There were fifteen men on board each helicopter with helmets, bulletproof vests, three company machine guns, three AGS-17 grenade launchers, and automatic rifles with self-propelled grenades mounted on them. The equipment of each helicopter instilled deep respect.

Each group's mission was to take one of the roads leading to the city. They were to let anyone in, but no one out. Fifteen minutes later, another sixteen helicopters of various modifications set off from the airport. A reinforced Airborne battalion, led by the commander of the Tula Regiment, Colonel V.I. Orlov, who had seen his share of extraordinary events, set off for Jalilabad.

It all went smoothly, like a knife through butter. At the appointed time, all the roads were cut off, the landing took place without losses, and all the city's vital installations were put under guard.

Orlov reported the following interesting situation. Taking advantage of the uncertainty and terror that was hanging in the air, about a dozen enterprising men with criminal pasts (with the silent nonresistance of the rest of the people in the town) destroyed the city executive committee building, burned down the city Party committee building, and dispersed the police academy—150 valiant guardians of public order armed with automatic rifles did not offer the slightest resistance. They ran from the city in a panic, throwing down their weapons along the way.

The criminals announced publicly that Soviet rule had been overthrown, that the Popular Front had come to power, and they forced businessmen and private persons to cough up more than 350,000 rubles "for the needs of the Popular Front." But being on the lookout when the first helicopters appeared, they succeeded in getting out of town.

Orlov reported that the city residents who had gathered in the main square had greeted the battalion warmly, and had immediately elected him, Colonel Orlov, the chairman of the city's Executive Committee. After thinking it over a little, everyone, Party members and non-Party members alike, elected him chairman of the city Party Committee and, after a little reflection, also appointed him the city chief of police. Nobody had freed Vadim Ivanovich from his duties as regimental commander; he had come there to fight, and here he was met with respect, joy, and high trust. Vadim Ivanovich, despite his powerful and stern character, was a little taken aback. His report ended with a simple human question: "What should I do?"

It was a simple matter: when I was listening to his report on the radio, I split my sides laughing, although I knew that it wasn't funny to

Orlov. To his classic question, "What should I do?" I gave an almost classic answer, "Prove that you deserve their trust!"

"How? If I'm the city Party Committee, the city Executive Committee, and the police, all rolled into one. . . ."

"Very simple. Make sure that the schools, the hospitals, and the bakeries are all working. Restore and repair everything that has been destroyed, looted, and burned. Clean up the city. Then we'll find out

> **"I** *found it strange to read "Charge!" in the military regulations. In real battle, people are commanded chiefly through profanity.***"**

what sort of a city Party Committee and police you are. For me, you're a regimental commander first."

Vadim Ivanovich cheered up. By that evening, I received a report from him that everything was working again, and that they were busy cleaning, sweeping, and restoring things to their former state. The people eagerly set to work, and the directors of the local enterprises offered him every assistance. A curfew was established. They decided on what needed to be guarded and organized patrols.

The next morning, he reported that nothing had happened during the night, that the cleaning and restoring was proceeding apace, but that someone had come from Baku, introducing himself as the first secretary of the city's Party Committee.

"Now Vadim Ivanovich, don't frown. You can give up one of your jobs," I said. "In a few days, the chairman of the executive committee and the chief of police will show up, too. Then you'll be just a simple regimental commander again."

By evening, Vadim Ivanovich had reported that everything was normal, but that the secretary of the city Party Committee hadn't shown his face to anyone.

"Find out what's going on with him, Vadim Ivanovich—why the hell do we need that kind of Party secretary!"

In an hour, he reported back:

"I talked to him. He paid 50,000 rubles for his job, and he came back because he wanted his money's worth. But he had been in this city once before on some other job, and knew that if he showed up as the secretary of the city Party Committee, and people saw him, they'd kill him."

"So kick him out!"

"How?"

"In a civilized way! Drive him three kilometers out of town in the direction of Baku, let him out, and explain to him that if he walks along that road, he will sooner or later get to where he came from. And don't forget to give him a bag lunch for the road!"

"Yes, sir!"

While Orlov was reestablishing Soviet Power in Jalilabad, the other units in my division were not exactly standing still. A reconnaissance group from Ryazan, lying on the bottom of the bed of a GAZ-66, arrived at the Popular Front headquarters in Neftechal. When they were about 100 meters away, they came under machine gun fire from a nearby apartment building. The machine gunner was quickly silenced.

In the storming of the building itself, the platoon commander, Lieutenant Aleksandr Aksenov, caught two bullets in the stomach and died a day later. He was a healthy fellow with the heart of a lion, full of the joy of life, born to be a victor, who had the absolutely unfounded belief, as do all lieutenants, that Death could take anyone, but not him. "Yes, people get wounded and even killed, but only other people. Not me. I'm young, strong, powerful, and well-trained. You've got to be joking!"

This psychology is typical of youth; practically all soldiers and young officers are infected with it. Frequently, heroism is accompanied by stupidity, although it is sad to have to say so. Where there is common sense, elementary tactics come to the fore: you run in short bursts, or crawl. But a soldier or officer penetrated with the psychology of impregnability just rolls up his sleeves, sticks a cigarette to his

lower lip, carries his gun atilt, and walks forward in no hurry showing in a dignified way his eloquent contempt for everything and
everyone—for his own life and for the enemy.

On the one hand, you have to fight against this kind of psychology,
for if you encourage it, it will lead to unjustified human losses, but on
the other hand, you can't fight against it too hard, because if a man
knows for sure he will be killed in an attack, he won't attack!

I found it strange for me to read the command, "Charge!" in the
military regulations. And I have never heard it used in my whole life.
I once asked some veterans about it, and they confirmed that you could
never get people to go into a real attack with such a dry command. In
real battle, people are commanded chiefly through profanity.

I met the helicopter that evacuated the lieutenant. He looked as
though he had aged thirty years. He was conscious, and even tried to
say something with his parched lips, but I couldn't hear it over the
noise of the engines. Something in his eyes, however, told me: "This
guy's a goner." I don't know how, or what you call it, but as I mentioned earlier, I can pick out people who are not going to survive.
And not just wounded people, but even people who are completely
healthy. I learned that in Afghanistan. It's something in their eyes. At
first, I didn't believe it. But to my deep regret, I turned out to be right.

A day later, another officer died—Senior Lieutenant Aleksandr
Konoplev. He died because he knew what honor and nobility
were. This is how it happened. Our intelligence was plentiful but
frequently contradictory. One fact was confirmed by three sources:
We knew of a village where there was reportedly a group of bandits.
The task of neutralizing this group was given to the Tula regiment's
reconnaissance company, which was led by Senior Lieutenant
Konoplev.

The operation itself was led by the division's chief intelligence
officer, Lieutenant Colonel O.P. Truskovsky. The reconnaissance company was put on three helicopters, which flew to the appointed place,
about ten kilometers from the gorge in which the village was situ-
ated. That night, it made a complicated march through the mountains,

and by morning it had set up an ambush along a path that led up through the canyon.

As happens extremely rarely, almost exactly at the appointed time, the target—a well-armed group of about fifty-one people—appeared in the ambush zone. The bandits had two machine guns, two sawed-off hunting rifles, a dozen SKS carbines, and automatic rifles of various modifications, along with pistols and grenades. It was early in the morning. They seemed confident that they were safe.

When the bandit column was about twenty meters away, Senior Lieutenant Konoplev stood up from behind a rock and said: "Bandits, you're surrounded. If you don't want any bloodshed, put down your weapons and give up!" He could have shouted that from behind his rock. But he stood up to demonstrate his peaceful intentions. He stood up because he didn't want to kill anybody. He stood up because he didn't believe that anyone wanted to kill him. Nobody knows what else Senior Lieutenant Konoplev wanted to say, because it was all over in fifteen seconds.

One of the bandits standing on the path fired a long burst from the hip. One of the bullets hit Konoplev in the forehead. He died instantly. The forty-eight recon soldiers swept everyone on the path with fire from their automatic rifles. None of the corpses had any documents. Our soldiers collected their weapons.

No one wanted to hear a report on the operation. The commander didn't want to listen to it. The clerks were told to report the operation as a seizure of a warehouse full of weapons. How convenient—if you stick your head in the sand, you can't see anybody.

On February 17, 1990, I was awarded the rank of major general. A completely new dimension opened up, and the clock started ticking all over again.

CHAPTER 13:
BACK TO THE BALLOT BOX

SOON, THE SITUATION got normal enough that we could start relocating back home. The regiments returned, and again, we put the training process, equipment maintenance, and other duties back on track. In short, business as usual.

But not for long. The elections to the RSFSR Supreme Soviet were slated for March 4, 1990. Even before the events in Baku, I received a call from Colonel General Achalov, the commander of the Airborne troops, who gave me a new mission:

"You're good at elections, and if you can get the chief of the Political Department of the Ground Forces elected a deputy of the USSR, you simply have to elect the commander of the Airborne troops a deputy of the RSFSR!"

"But Moiseev was running in Tula and the neighboring areas. If you run here too, people will laugh at us," I said.

"No, I'm going to run in remote areas of the Tula Oblast. You have an artillery regiment stationed in the town of Yefremov. That will be our home base."

My memories of the last elections were still fresh. The last thing I wanted was to step on the election rake twice, but. . . .

I said, "Yes, sir!" and, cursing under my breath, set about my duties as campaign manager. Colonel General Achalov went to Yefremov, and his meetings with the local leadership were catered lavishly. He knew how to talk to people about important things in life. He discussed the latest political news, and at the same time casually promised to build bridges, renovate schools, lay water and gas pipelines, and provide machinery.

An elite group consisting of about thirty was selected for a more detailed discussion of campaign issues. It was made up of the secretaries of the regional Party committees, the chairmen of the executive committees of the regional Soviets, the most prominent industrial directors, and collective farm chairmen. Tearing themselves away from the determined crowd of *perestroika*-minded petitioners, the elite secluded themselves in a suburban auditorium where, at a well-furnished table, they continued to make the situation more concrete. They went through more than two cases of vodka. The conversation flowed, and the secretaries, directors, and chairmen took turns expressing their priority concerns, all spotted with humorous comments.

Alchalov gave his verdict: the bridge they wanted would be built by March 1. The hell with wintertime—March 1, it would be. Twenty GAZ-66 trucks were to be set aside, the required diesel fuel was to be transferred at cost, and their desired school renovation would start the very next day.

Knowing from experience that running an election campaign demanded that one be in good physical condition, I faked my drinking and tried to keep my candidate on course. But the night wore on, and soon it became clear that more detailed discussions were needed.

I glanced at my watch—it was 0300. Using my authority as master of ceremonies, I dared to interject:

"Enough drinking! You have to meet with the voters at 0800 hours."

"Nonsense!" The commander turned back to his guests: "I went to France recently and brought back a sobering-up remedy that will amaze you. I'll show you. Oleg!"

His assistant took something from his pocket that looked like a matchbox, with a curved shape. He opened it and passed it around. Everyone fished something out of it and put it in his mouth. It didn't have any smell or taste. I tried to chew on it and it gave a bit, but it had no significant effect. Politely, I turned away and took it out of my mouth. The sobering-up remedy was, in essence, a small cylinder made of yellow foam, an inch or so in diameter. The guests became preoccupied with chewing the remedy and were visibly sobering up. What will they think of next! Damned capitalists! There's no taste and no smell, but look how well it works! This isn't just some home-grown Russian remedy, like pickling brine!

Intrigued by the effect and out of pure curiosity, I asked how this sobering-up remedy worked.

The commander cocked his eye at the cylinder in my hand, took a similar cylinder from behind his cheek, and howled at his assistant: "Idiot! What did I ask you to bring? The sobering-up remedy! And what did you bring? Earplugs!"

The guests and I burst out laughing. And once the humor in the situation dawned on him, so did the commander. While they were laughing, the mirage disappeared. By the time the laughing stopped, they were falling-down drunk again. Self-suggestion is a powerful thing.

But there was still a meeting with voters at 0800. The advance promises had been given, and I started to carry out Colonel General Achalov's campaign promises. We did it honestly and with good intentions. I won't bring up how much it cost, but just mention the school, which was supposedly in need of "a little renovation." The commander of the engineering battalion, sent out to estimate how much repair had to be done, came back with his eyes popping: "What the hell do you mean 'renovation'?" The school was a wreck and couldn't be salvaged. It would be easier to build a new one. Which, in essence, is what we did, but after the elections—constructing a building like that in the winter would have been impossible. In short, the campaign machine was picking up momentum, with characteristic army flair.

But then we had an unplanned interruption—the events in Baku. Both Achalov and I were distracted. His opponents took heart. They started to spread rumors such as: "What are you thinking of doing, folks? You are voting for butchers!"

We got back a little over two weeks before the elections. The pace of the campaign race intensified. In those last two weeks, people from my division gave about 150 concerts and shows in towns and villages all across three rural regions. In record time, diesel fuel, gasoline, all sorts of spare parts, construction materials, and machinery swept into the test area like a tidal wave and reduced the other candidates' chances virtually to nil. People saw the most important thing—little talk and lots of action.

The whole election procedure at all levels in our country was defective at that time. The view toward each candidate was unambiguously consumer-oriented. The person's wit, intelligence, or knowledge didn't matter at all, only whether he could deliver the goods. That was why everybody was annoyed by the political ballyhoo that was mixed with tempting promises. There was only one question on the agenda: "Can he do it, or not?" There hadn't been a bridge here for a hundred years, and this guy said, "I can do it," and the very next day the pontoons were brought in. Wow! Vote for him, boys, he's our kind of guy!"

But nothing is *all* bad. In spite of the system's deficiencies, we managed to do many small, and some not so small, things for the good of the people and to make some progress on things that had been stagnating for decades.

But nothing is all good, either. Who paid for that stream of gratitude in the hearts of potential voters? The government—in essence, the budget. And in particular, and more concretely—my division. That meant that the division had to make cutbacks, and reconsider its priorities.

And what was the driving force behind this mechanism? It was the boss's will, which can work wonders. Masses of people from lieutenants to generals hustled to make the answer fit the problem. How? Well, for example, in order to please the voters, you had to give them equipment which was in good condition. But you can't just write off an automobile with only a few thousand kilometers on it. So, with the help of a few simple manipulations on documents, a practically new low mileage car can be transformed into a scrap heap, and in that "paper" form, can be turned over to the voters.

In essence, the commander was exploiting his official position on a massive scale for personal gain. If he were elected, he would become a deputy of the Supreme Soviet, with all of the honors, benefits, and privileges which come with it. The rest of us would scratch our heads trying to fill the holes that the campaign spending had created. If he didn't get elected, we'd still be scratching our heads, but this time for our stupidity: people would say, "These scoundrels couldn't even manage such a simple thing as an election to the Supreme Soviet!" But there is nothing you can do about it. It's a vicious circle.

Anyway, he won the election—Vladislav Alekseevich got 63 percent of the votes, and the other five candidates shared the remaining 37 percent.

One amusing episode: after the elections, the commander called me and said in a warm voice, "Aleksandr Ivanovich, you know, I'm a country boy. All these vodkas and cognacs are purified and refined, but I prefer simple moonshine, the way they make it in the heartland, the kind that leaves a stain around the edge of my glass. I like it in a large, square three-liter bottle. I call it 'Chateau des Three Beets cognac.' Go get me some."

Another tough one! In order to prevent rumors, or getting ribbed about why a division commander would need a three-liter bottle of moonshine, I turned this delicate mission over to the chief of the political department. I had no idea where he went to get it, but he came back and reported: "I have it! It's exactly what he wants—it's 70 percent alcohol, and the smell can kill flies at a distance."

It was our lunch break. We came out of the headquarters and the chief of the political department, wishing to demonstrate the latest achievements in the field of moonshine-making, carelessly opened the tail gate of his UAZik. The three-liter jar rolled out slowly and smashed against the asphalt, generously splattering nature's gift on the political officer, and partially on me. The lip-smacking smell, which hasn't completely disappeared to this day, wafted thickly across the headquarters courtyard. That's what comes from trying to hide the obvious.

CHAPTER 14:
SURPRISES BEFORE THE
FINAL CURTAIN

I NEVER CONSIDERED MYSELF a dyed-in-the-wool Party activist and never tried to reach the top in the Party hierarchy. Though I was elected secretary of grassroots Party organizations on several occasions, I never used this for my personal benefit, and the idea that you could suck something out of it never crossed my mind. Thus, I never imagined myself a delegate to a Party congress, because that was not an area where I could apply my talents. But while man proposes, God disposes. Matters beyond my control proved me wrong once again.

The 28th Congress of the Communist Party of the Soviet Union (June 1990) was justifiably considered a turning point in the life and operation of the Communist Party. The preparation for it and selection of documents and delegates began long before the congress and were conducted with scrupulous attention.

I had never wanted to become a delegate to this or any other Party congress, but my wishes notwithstanding, the very first delegate-selecting caucus put me in the middle of many interesting experiences. It all began when the 51st Tula Airborne Regiment nominated me as their candidate for a delegate's seat. The caucus was attended by Lieutenant General V.K. Polevik. He told me some believed the commander of the Airborne troops, V.A. Achalov, and the member of the

Military Council—General Polevik himself—should be the delegates to the 28th Congress.

Knowing the mood of the division and the officers, I told him that the issue could probably be resolved, but that at this stage, he would lose a vote to me. I suggested that he look for other ways to resolve the problem. General Polevik's reaction was: "We'll see about that!"

> **"At my first Party caucus, what was being said was pure garbage. I took the floor for eight minutes and was unanimously elected a Party delegate."**

At that time there were 123 Party members in the regiment. The caucus took place in the regimental club. General Polevik's clerks took the presiding reins in their hands. Everything went quite smoothly until Lieutenant General Polevik's name was put up for nomination. Only nine of the 123 voted for him. Five of them were regimental executive officers—people who had tasted the fruits of opportunism. They were sitting in the front row. It would have been awkward for them to look back to see how the rest of the audience was voting. The other four were old warrant officers who had been trained by Beria. They had no doubts: they were ordered to elect the member of the Military Council, so "Yes, sir!" could be the only possible answer. There was no counting No and Abstained votes—it would have been tactless. Even the clerks understood that. When my name was put in nomination, more than one hundred arms shot up at once. Counting them would have been pointless. The official transcript read: 123 – 9 = 114. In the club's lobby, General Polevik gave a nervous laugh and without so much as a ceremonial good-bye, got in his car and left.

I made it through the second round of the election process in an even easier and more ridiculous way. I was peacefully dosing in my fifth-row seat through the first hour of the Airborne Caucus, which was held at the Airborne Corps club. I was listening with half an ear to what was being said up at the podium. After some time, I was convinced that what was being said was pure garbage. The speeches were long and boring. People were getting off track, and their minds were wandering. I felt like putting everything back in its place, at least as I saw it. I took the floor and spoke for eight minutes. It ended with the people unanimously electing Vladislav Alekseevich Achalov and me as delegates to the congress.

And then came the first working day of the congress. It did not begin as the 28th Congress of the Communist Party of the Soviet Union. It turned out to be the founding congress of the Communist Party of *Russia*. Great Mother Russia found out that she did not have a Communist Party of her own, was very disappointed, and decided to fill the gap.

Never before in my forty years had I found myself in the middle of an assembly of this kind, and naturally I didn't know how to behave. I didn't even think of wielding any influence over the outcome. I was just happy to listen and observe.

There, for the first time, I discovered the unity of the Communist Party was imaginary. The Party's representatives had absolutely irreconcilable positions.

The founding congress of the Russian Communist Party raged for three days before the 28th Congress of the CPSU began. The external indication of this was that the number of delegates in the hall rose from two thousand to five thousand, and Mikhail Gorbachev took the top place on the Presidium.

The congress adopted a resolution to hear out each member of the Central Committee of the CPSU. The following scheme was worked out: a twenty-minute report, followed by oral questions from each of twelve microphones, followed by written questions. The overall question-and-answer session could not exceed forty minutes. In the evening of the fourth day, Aleksandr Nikolaevich Yakovlev held a small, behind-the-scenes conference with the proponents of the democratic platform in the CPSU. Some Lithuanians sneaked in a tape-recorder. On the next morning, they gave the transcripts of the meeting to the delegates, revealing that what Aleksandr Nikolaevich told a narrow circle of insiders was significantly different from what he told the delegates as a whole. Later on, I got used to politicians' two-facedness, but, back then, it was a real blow.

The rules of the microphone game were simple: the strongest one there gets the microphone. I was the strongest on the balcony at microphone number eight, so I got it. After Yakovlev's report, Gorbachev began calling people at the microphones in turn—the first, then the second.…

Finally, he reached me: "Comrade General, microphone number eight, please!" Basing my questions on the Lithuanian transcript, I said: "Aleksandr Nikolaevich, you are the author of an unpublished book entitled *My Vision of Marxism*. Why do you say you would be hanged if you published it? Who would these hangmen be? My second question: You've referred to unfortunate victims of the system. How would you look at the prospect of placing Leonid Ilyich Brezhnev in the same category? And how many faces do you have, Aleksandr Nikolaevich?"

As I was speaking, the audience grew quiet. I asked my second and third questions in dead silence. Trying to buy time, Gorbachev and Yakolev simultaneously broke out: "What? What did you just say? Repeat it, please!" As I repeated my questions, I had to raise my voice over the noise from the crowd. The uproar was so great that it took more than five minutes to restore order. That was enough time for Aleksandr Nikolaevich, experienced demagogue that he was, to recover. When the silence had been relatively restored, he said approximately the following: "The issues which the Comrade General touched on, for me, are rather like the situation concerning the Kremlin wall." He elaborated: "Does it really make sense to have a cemetary at the nation's most important venue? Are all these dear departed really so dear to us, and is it right for them to be there?" Accompanied by the tumult issuing from an audience which was perplexed by his rain of non sequiturs, he excused himself, complaining of a severe headache, and left.

It was a wonderful trick, and I suppose I should be grateful to Aleksandr Nikolaevich for teaching it to me. The rest of the congress followed an uninspiring course. Take the report of Central Committee secretary and Politburo member Zaikov, for example. Zaikov's twenty-minute speech had obviously been prepared by his assistant and he had not even read it. When he stood at the podium in front of five thousand people, he was tied in a death grip to the typewritten pages. He didn't dare lift his eyes.

But despite his care, he blundered. He came across the word "anachronism," which had been divided at the end of the line. While he was searching for the ending of the hyphenated word, he started mumbling in the extra-sensitive microphones of the Palace of Congresses: "Ana-ana. . . onanism!" The entire audience rolled with laughter. While everybody was laughing, Comrade Zaikov caught up with the ending of the word and continued to read as if nothing had happened.

In the end, Comrade Zaikov decided to say a few words from the bottom of his heart. He tore himself away from the boring text, took off his glasses, looked up at the audience with shining eyes, and said, with feeling: "Comrades, I relieve myself from responsibility for the current situation in the Party." The audience became numb. If a secretary of the Central Committee can relieve himself of responsibility, then who has to answer for anything? Comrade Zaikov realized he had misspoken, put his glasses back on, and turned back to the text: "Excuse me, comrades, I mean to say—I do *not* relieve myself from responsibility for the current situation in the Party."

It would have been better if he had just left it as it was. It would have given the delegates something to talk about in the corridors. Now it only raised suspicions about Zaikov's senility.

I thought that the second character from that pack, Comrade Medvedev, the Party's chief ideologist, would have been at least an above-average public speaker, but he wasn't. And he was tense when he had to answer questions from the microphones. Some malicious fellow had submitted a written question: "Comrade Medvedev, what is the difference between ideology and sex?"

Medvedev could have skimmed the note and put it aside, saying, "This one is just inappropriate, it's a joke." But Comrade Medvedev read it aloud, smiled in confusion, and said in a dejected voice: "Comrades, if I can still talk to you about the first, I am no longer capable of the second!"

I was used to seeing the pictures of our leaders on posters in Lenin conference rooms with the caption, "The Politburo of the Central Committee of the CPSU," where rejuvenated and retouched by an artful hand, they looked into the future, knowingly and purposefully. When I compared their pitiful, mumbling answers to the simplest questions with these pictures, the thought involuntarily came to mind: "Who are these people who are ruling us?" My God! Why does our country, which has been famous for its brilliant minds, have to be ruled by senile old men who have lost all touch with reality? Where are they leading us, and why are we following them? What is a country worth if it is "led" by pale feebleness and organizational impotence? How can people, who lack the most elementary clarity of thought, govern the country? How did we come to this, how did it become possible?

> **"W***hy is it, despite our colossal wealth, we live in poverty and misery? Why are we not masters of our own land?***"**

I remember Shevardnadze's passionate speech, delivered in his thick Georgian accent, in which he publicly confessed the only sin that had been burdening his conscience—when he was seven years old, he had written a poem dedicated to Stalin. He was ashamed of it.

Then one delegate rose and quoted excerpts from the transcript of the 25th Congress of the CPSU, in which Shevardnadze, in the best traditions of Georgian toast-mastership, had delivered an ode to Leonid Ilyich Brezhnev. And then he asked: "Doesn't that ode burden Eduard Amvrosievich's conscience?" The answer was: "No. That was the way you had to do it back then."

I remember how I.K. Polozkov was elected first secretary of the Communist Party of Russia by tricking M.S. Gorbachev in an ingeniously simple way. The day before the vote, Polozkov came up to the podium and humbly announced to the audience that he was an old "partocrat" and that the mere mention of his name would discredit the idea of renewal in the Party. So he was withdrawing his candidacy. Gorbachev believed him. He called off his pen-pushers, who were ready to fill the media with exposés. What point was there in kicking a man who was already down?

But the next morning, Polozkov again approached the podium and announced that after conferring throughout the night with various comrades, he realized he had been wrong. He was going to reinstate his humble candidacy for the post of first secretary. Mikhail Gorbachev looked as if he were going to have a stroke. Polozkov was elected first secretary.

I also remember when the delegation of the Communist Party of Russia invited Gorbachev to a question-and-answer session. Mikhail Gorbachev showed his shining face to the audience of two thousand people and declared: "We have nothing to talk about. We stand on different ideological positions." Then he just turned around and left two thousand delegates of the Communist Party of Russia, stunned. That was the end of relations between the Russian Communist Party and the CPSU.

Because I had kicked Yakovlev's butt with my questions (at least 80 percent of the delegates hated him), a lieutenant colonel proposed electing me a member of the Central Committee of the Communist Party of Russia. I was elected, as I remember, by more than 90 percent of the vote.

I went to two plenary meetings. I listened to the screaming and the useless fights. I observed the open, no-holds-barred struggle of various factions to get their people in the Party hierarchy. I saw the Party's refusal to acknowledge the changes that were happening all around them. And I was an eyewitness to the double, or even triple, standards of morality that were endemic in the Party. In its upper echelons, it had become the norm to say one thing, to do another, and to think something else. I realized that this organization and I had nothing in common. And it was at the second plenary meeting that I first had the idea, and then the firm conviction, that I would never go back there.

My faith in authority came tumbling down. I became convinced that all men are opportunists and fallible. I ought to subject everything I did to extreme scrutiny.

How did our leaders descend to such degradation, and after them the entire people? How did double standards become the rule of life? How could people who were given the greatest authority lie so shamelessly? How could we, the Russian people, who had overcome the enemy in the greatest of wars find ourselves so weak?

Why is it that in spite of our colossal wealth (not a single country in the world can compare with ours!), we live in poverty and misery? Why are we not masters of our own land? Why do we spit on the environment that will be our children's and grandchildren's after us? The dozens, the hundreds of bitter and unanswerable "hows" and "whys" spill out from our poor suffering land.

CHAPTER 15:
AUGUST 1990:
THE SIXTIETH ANNIVERSARY OF
THE AIRBORNE TROOPS

THE RUSSIAN ACRONYM FOR the Airborne troops—VDV—can be interpreted in various ways within the military, depending on the circumstances. For example, it can stand for *Vryad li Domoi Verneshsya* (Unlikely to Return Home) or *Voiska Dyadi Vasi* (Uncle Vasya's Troops), in honor of the legendary commander of the Airborne troops, V.F. Margelov. It can be spelled out in a number of near-literary and some far-from-literary ways.

But that's not the point. The Airborne troops are combat troops, always in deployment. Life is always in full swing, oversaturated with parachute jumps, air drops of combat machinery, shooting practice, and hand-to-hand combat. In short, things are never boring, and if you plan to celebrate their sixtieth anniversary, you have to recall their history and demonstrate the accomplishments of modern parachute technology and aviation. And God forbid that you mess up. If you do, your name will be blacklisted in the Airborne troops forever, and you will be treated like a leper for the rest of your life.

August 2, 1990, was the sixtieth anniversary of the Airborne troops. To celebrate the occasion, they decided to organize a big air-show on the Tushino airfield in Moscow. The job of organizing and running the event was given to the "court favorites," the Tula division—that is, to me, and to the Ryazan Airborne School. The over-all oversight was conducted by the first deputy commander of the Airborne troops, Lieutenant General Osvald Mikolovich Pikauskas.

We developed an extensive and diverse program. It included everything from an Airborne operation featuring twelve people in uniforms and parachutes dating back to August 2, 1930, when the Airborne troops made their debut at maneuvers in the Kiev Military District; to massive airdrops of modern commandos; to sport parachute jumps featuring breathtaking stunts; to an airborne insertion with a simulated battle to follow; to hand-to-hand fighting and a martial arts demonstrations; and much more. In short, the show was planned to be a stunning spectacle. But to carry it off we had to practice, practice, practice.

> **"T**he Airborne troops are combat troops, always in deployment, always in full swing—jumping, shooting, and fighting hand-to-hand.**"**

I will touch only on a few points in the mass of details. The first and the main point is that, due to the extremely bad weather conditions, both dress rehearsals had to be canceled, which made the situation extremely tense. The lead-colored clouds at low altitude did not allow us to rehearse the spectacle completely. Jumping ahead, I wish to say that the division's executive officer, Vladimir Ivanovich Krotik, did a brilliant job of putting everything together.

One disaster was a practice demonstration of the capabilities of Military Transport Aviation in fire-fighting. The Ilyushin-76 airplane with forty tons of water on board accidentally dumped its forty tons over the Moscow ring road!

According to witnesses, the scene was quite remarkable. The grass was green and the sun was shining. No sign of rain. A transport jet flew over at a low altitude and the highway was sprayed with water. Thank God, there were no casualties.

Another story: A reconnaissance company that was to demonstrate an Airborne assault and a spectacular simulated fight, decided that they needed to spice up their demonstration. During one practice when the helicopters approached the landing site, hovered about twenty-five to thirty meters over it, and dropped the special ropes for the men to disembark, the men sent a stuffed dummy dressed in military overalls falling out of the helicopter. His fall was accompanied by a heart-rending scream from one of the crew on board. It made quite an impression, so I approved the change.

August 2 finally came. From early morning, crowds of people filled the observation decks of the Tushino airfield. The weather was wonderful. The sky was pastel blue and deep, with a few feather-light clouds hanging coquettishly. There was sun and music and a sea of smiling faces; in a word, it was a holiday. On such a day, you can only win.

The many honorary guests were sitting on the VIP bleachers, and among them was the most honored guest—the former commander of the Airborne troops, General D. S. Sukhorukov.

The festivities began. Such celebrations do not happen often, and it is hard to describe them—you just have to be there.

Everything went swimmingly. But a misunderstanding arose when two helicopters came hovering at about 150 meters over the target and "Ivan Ivanych"—the stuffed dummy—fell out and hit the ground, accompanied by a blood-curdling scream. The crowd gasped. A sigh of pain turned into murmuring. Someone grabbed me by the arm from behind. I looked back and saw General Sukhorukov standing in his dress uniform. There was pain and anger in his eyes.

"Where is the ambulance? Send the ambulance to the field!"

"Comrade Commander, that was 'Ivan Ivanych.'"

"I don't care if it was Pyotr Petrovich, send the ambulance to the field!"

"It was a *dummy*, Comrade Commander."

Dmitri Semenovich was a deputy defense minister at that time, but on that day, for all the Airborne troops, he was the commander.

After the commander realized what was going on, he cleared his throat reproachfully, looked at me—his anger was gone and I could see little devils flickering in his eyes—and quietly stepped away. Using the megaphone I explained quickly to the crowd what had happened. Smiles broke out on their faces.

I had served for more than twenty years, but I had never seen a celebration like this. I remember the enthusiasm of officers, soldiers, and cadets and how easily they performed the most complex elements of their program. It was like soaring in the air or hearing a marvelous song. The mock battle was going on in full force. Parachutists rained down from the sky; helicopters were landing, hovering, and taking off. A number of hand-to-hand fighting techniques was displayed, and the units demonstrated their fighting skills with their weapons. Everything was done in a joyful and relaxed manner. It was a beautiful and unforgettable spectacle. It will remain in people's memories for a long time.

And then the show and the holiday were over, and the prose of life began again. And the first part of the prose was that the current commander of the Airborne troops, Colonel General Achalov, and I, as the owner of an especially equipped tent, had to entertain some VIP guests. So we did. A group of cosmonauts came, led by Lieutenant General Aleksei Leonov. The cosmonauts—great men, by the way—said many nice things, and congratulated us. After the cosmonauts, they said, we, the Airborne troops, were the best things on this earth.

After our guests departed, I held a reception for my own deputies, the chiefs of the arms and services, and the unit commanders.

It was a good occasion with wonderful people for a wonderful cause, but why did we have to spoil such a beautiful holiday by abusing alcohol? The ancient chronicler once said, "The Russian way of having fun is drinking." But isn't it time to break from the age-old tradition that the bigger the occasion, the more bombed you get?

CHAPTER 16:
AUTO RALLY:
MOSCOW–GOZHE-PORECHYE

IN THE VERY BEGINNING of September 1990, the 76th Airborne Division conducted its planned divisional tactical exercise, featuring an Airborne landing of the division headquarters, one Airborne regiment, part of an artillery regiment, an anti-aircraft battery, and a number of special units, at the Gozhe-Porechye training grounds in Belorussia (present-day Belarus). The exercise was to include field firing for the regiment and its affiliated units and sub-units.

The commander of the Airborne troops decided to gather the division, brigade, and regimental commanders at the training grounds to show them how such an exercise was supposed to be done. But as the old song goes, "Vast is our native land!" The commanders of some remote units (like the Ussuri brigade) were ordered to get there on their own. But all the father-commanders from the European part of the country and Central Asia were brought to the headquarters of the Airborne troops for some sort of improvised military council. At the end of the council, the chief of staff of the Airborne troops, Lieutenant General Podkolzin, told us when and where we were to board the buses for departure.

I decided to get to the Chkalovsk airfield in my official car and then send it back to the base. I estimated that my Volga would get me to the airfield ahead of the buses, so I stayed a little longer at the headquarters to tie up the loose ends. Then, after picking up two regiment commanders, Yu. A. Naumov and A.N. Soluyanov, I hit the road.

Hero of the Soviet Union Lieutenant Colonel Alexander Soluyanov, my old friend and classmate and a fellow Afghan veteran, was the commander of the Fergana training regiment at the time, so we had a lot of reminiscing and talking to catch up on.

We had left the ring road well behind when the car started "sneezing." Tolya, our experienced driver, assured us that he would take care of the problem in three minutes. Three, five, ten minutes passed. Twenty minutes passed, and Tolya was still fiercely but silently fiddling with the engine. On the twenty-third minute, the engine started up at last and we took off. Tolya, usually calm and rational, showed us his wild side—the Volga flew along the narrow highway, weaving through traffic. As we sped toward the airfield, we saw our airplane standing at the runway furiously blinking its signal lights. It was about three hundred meters away.

"Come on," I urged, "just one more push."

It turned out to be a thrust to nowhere. The plane picked up speed and took off into the blue sky.

We drove to the communications brigade, where we were told that all flights to cities near our final destination had already left or were scheduled for the next day.

I called my old friend, Colonel N.S. Yurasov at Vitebsk, the headquarters of the 103rd Airborne Division, which wasn't inordinately far away.

"Hello, Kolya! I have a problem—we missed our plane. I'm getting a ride to your place. Have the chopper ready, will you?"

"No problem! We'll be waiting for you!"

At 2100 hours we arrived at the headquarters of the 103rd Airborne Division.

The 103rd Division was one of the most distinguished in the Airborne troops. Its glorious history dates back to World War II, and it has steadfastly maintained its proud traditions. Perhaps that was why the division was one of the first to enter Afghanistan in December 1979 and among the last to leave it in February 1989. Throughout those nine years, the division was in the thick of the fighting, virtually without a break. Thousands of servicemen were decorated, and more than ten were awarded the title "Hero of the Soviet Union," including Generals A.E. Sliusar and P.S. Grachev, and Lieutenant Colonel A.N. Soluyanov.

After Afghanistan, the division came back to its home base in Vitebsk and found that everything had broken down. Some of the barracks had been reassigned to other military units, and the training grounds had been badly looted or neglected. The division, which had just come back from active combat, was faced with a solid wall of social problems. Some bureaucrats, exploiting the growing tensions in society, proposed a novel move: to make the division part of the KGB. No division—no more problems. The division was no longer "Airborne" but not yet "KGB."

Combat officers had been turned into clowns. They wore the green hats and shoulderboards of the Border Guards, blue striped undershirts, and the Airborne insignia on their hats, shoulderboards, and breasts. People aptly called this motley uniform "a conductor's suit." The officers and soldiers became the butt of jokes from the local population.

Later, after August 1991, the division was returned to the Airborne troops. And a little later, the Soviet Union fell apart and the "parade of sovereignties" began. Now, it's no longer a division, but the Airborne Brigade of the Armed Forces of Belarus. A unit with a glorious combat tradition became the victim of political opportunism. One of the great sculptors was once asked: "How do you create your remarkable works of art?" The sculptor answered: "It's all very simple, really. I take a piece of granite and cut away everything superfluous." In our case they chopped off everything that was necessary. They made a molehill out of a mountain.

But in September 1990 it was still an Airborne division and it was still a part of the VDV.

Nikolai Semenovich Yurasov was waiting for us in his office. Somehow, he did not look too confident.

"Hello, Kolya, long time no see!" I said. "What's going on? The chopper is ready, I hope."

"The chopper is ready, all right! And the pilots are the cream of the crop. All of them have Afghan experience, but...."

"There can't be any 'buts.' Thanks!"

"Wait, wait, let me finish. The chief of staff, General Podkolzin, called and relayed to me an order from the commander himself: 'If General Lebed comes to you, don't give him a helicopter.' So what kind of number did you pull to deserve such preferential treatment?"

"Nothing! Did he say anything about giving me a UAZik?"

"A UAZik? No."

"Well, then get a UAZik ready and give me two drivers, so that they can work in shifts. Preferably, Belorussians, who know the roads. Tolya is overworked."

> **"Y**ou could hear the roar of engines, the clanking of treads and bursts from assault rifles, but what was actually going on? Only God knew....**"**

While they were getting the UAZik ready, old friends and fellow Afghan veterans got together, reminisced, and talked. At 2330 hours they wished us a safe trip. There was a thick fog, and it was getting thicker. After an hour or so, the driver said, "So, where are you going?"

"What do you mean, 'where'? Gozhe-Porechye."

"And where's that?"

"What do you mean 'where'? Pull over!"

It turned out our two youthful drivers had arrived in Belorussia only two months before and had no knowledge of Belorussian geography whatsoever. With their youthful enthusiasm, they were ready to drive to Alaska—and hadn't thought of asking direction until now. Since we had expected experienced drivers, we had not brought a map. We were thirty kilometers away from Vitebsk and surrounded by milky-white clouds of fog.

"Go west!" I ordered.

We followed the signs. The fog became even thicker and our speed, consequently, dropped, but by 0800, we arrived in Grodno, only thirty-five kilometers from Gozhe-Porechye. At 0920 we were on the observation deck. We were greeted cheerfully and told that the night before, the commander had threatened that there would be hell to pay if Lebed and his adventurers did not arrive by the start of the exercises at 1000 hours.

We got a shave and a bite to eat. I placed the two regiment commanders in front of the formation, and as soon as the commander got out of his car, reported: "Comrade Commander! A group of three people has completed a maneuver along the following route: Moscow to Vitebsk to Minsk to Grodno to Gozhe-Porechye. The maneuver went off without a hitch. We are ready for the exercises. Group Leader, Major General Lebed, reporting! Requesting permission to return to formation, Sir!"

The commander grunted. There were ten minutes left before the exercises were to start officially.

"Permission granted!" he muttered.

"Yes, sir!"

People were jammed on the observation deck. We had an extraordinary experience ahead of us. Only rarely do you have such an armada parachuting at the same time. The commander invited some of the elite to observe the exercise. I had no idea who they were, but I remember that one of them was the chief military prosecutor. Everything and everyone was ready, but the Belorussian fog covered the Gozhe-Porechye training grounds like a thick blanket. One hour passed. . . . The fog still hovered. The guests started to get restless. They began to push the commander a little. Someone reported that the fog would lift in an hour. The commander perked up; by the time the troops formed up and the planes took off and were hovering over the drop zone, the fog would lift. So the order followed: "Go ahead!"

Another hour and a half went by. The fog got considerably thinner, and visibility increased... but not enough! Still, the armada was on the way. The clock was ticking. A decision had to be made... and it was.

The armada rumbled in the fog above our heads. I could imagine small figures separating from huge transport planes and falling into the haze. Then, after whistling through the air on their pilot chutes, their canopies would open in a flash. I could imagine that, but it would have been impossible to *see* it. And *seeing* it was the reason the VIPs had come all the way to Belorussia. And of course the mock battle in the landing zone was conducted in the fog as well. You could hear the roar of the engines and clanking of the treads and short and long firing bursts from assault rifles, but what was actually going on? God only knows whether things were going well or not. The fog hid the successes and the shortcomings with equal effectiveness.

All sorts of reports came in. One person reported that the nearest mission was accomplished and the unit was on the designated range. Another worried that he was missing about ten people. Some regimental commander was demanding, loudly and without bothering to watch his language, that this farce be stopped, and that we make a "tactical pause" and wait until the fog lifted.

They stopped. They began to gather and count personnel. The fog, as if it were mocking them, quickly cleared. It turned out that due to the fog, two or three vehicles had landed in the woods.

There was a rescue team on the lakes, but they too were blinded by the fog. They managed to save one person. He was lucky. He landed in the water ten meters away from the rescue boat. But the other three, wearing all their gear, sank to the bottom like stones. When they were reached, it was too late. The reports started to come in, and a deathly silence settled on the observation deck. When they heard about the casualties, the prosecutor was the first to leave. The rest of the guests melted away. The commander was left alone to face the consequences of his decision.

Finally, the commander, saying he needed to inspect the scene of the accident and report to the minister, recommended that we learn from what we had just seen, and left. But was there anything to see and anything to learn? Any fool can leave corpses behind.

The exercise continued sluggishly, lacking the tiniest spark, as if in slow motion. I would not even call it a parody of an exercise. We were all left with a heavy burden on our hearts.

CHAPTER 17:
POTATO PICKERS IN UNIFORM

ON THE EVENING OF September 8, 1990, I received yet another vague order over the telephone from Colonel General Achalov: "Put the division on alert!"

Some officers got caught up in guessing games, but couldn't figure out where we could possibly be going. Some exclaimed, half mockingly, half seriously: "My God! What progress we've made! All this time, we've had to clean up other people's messes; maybe this time we'll be able to prevent something before it starts!"

Not knowing is always worse than sure trouble, because it generates anxiety and lack of confidence. For example, we had adopted the practice that if, say, we were going to Azerbaijan, we'd leave the Azeri guys behind in the barracks; if it was Armenia, it would be the Armenians; and if it was Georgia, the Georgians. Not because we didn't trust them, but because after it was all over, they'd have to live there! There's no need to turn a twenty-year-old into a human time bomb that could blow up at any time.

This time, the soldiers were laughing and making bets among themselves on who would be staying "home": the Armenians? the Azeris? the Lithuanians, maybe? As a sidelight, I should mention that for some reason I have had many ethnic Lithuanians as my subordinates. Physically strong, well disciplined, and cool under pressure, they made excellent soldiers and absolutely marvelous sergeants. I am grateful to all of them, and it was a pleasure to serve with them.

Late in the evening of September 9, we got a directive: The Kostroma and Ryazan regiments were to be formed up at 0600 on September 10 on the parade ground of the Frunze airfield. Destination: Moscow. When I relayed this order to my subordinates, someone said: "So there it is! What are we going to do now, leave all the Russians behind?" Seventy percent of the officers and soldiers were ethnic Russians. I responded: "I'm not sending out our fellow Armenians and Azeris alone to invade Moscow. Everybody is going!"

The division was well trained, so the march went off without a hitch. The regiments were on the airfield by 0530.

Other regiments were on the march, too, and it is easy to imagine that Moscow was receiving ominous messages from various regions that added up to just one thing: "All the Airborne forces are on the move and headed your way." It made no sense at all, and that made it all the more terrifying. The panic rolled on like a snowball.

> **"You can find nasty people anywhere. But there is a higher concentration of them in legislative bodies."**

At the checkpoint of the parade ground, a company of soldiers held back a crowd of hysterical journalists fighting to sink their claws into me. But what could I tell them?

I was summoned to the headquarters of the Airborne troops to see the commander. The commander was keyed up:

"All right, here's the thing! You came here to prepare for a parade. Understood?"

"Understood!"

I left and went to the Operations Department to find out what was going on.

A regimental commander can place a battalion on alert for training. A division commander can put a regiment on alert. The commander of the Airborne troops can put one division on alert. In this case, two divisions had been put on alert, and another three were ready to go on alert. Obviously, the commander couldn't have done this on his own. Formally, only the minister could give the commander such an order. But this was unlikely because the minister, Marshal of the Soviet Union Dmitri Timofeevich Yazov, had more than forty years of service behind him, and was a disciplined and cautious person. That meant that it had to have come from even higher up. One could only speculate as to who this might have been.

But the minister and everyone above him could not be implicated in the scandal of putting us all on a false alert. So the commander was given the assignment of giving a credible explanation of what we were doing.

In short, when the defense minister climbed onto the podium of the Supreme Soviet of the USSR to explain the confusion, everything was just fine! He reported, calmly and convincingly, that the Airborne troops were conducting large-scale maneuvers. He slapped his palm on an explanatory map prepared by our operations people.

The plan of the maneuvers, the minister said, had been developed by the staff of the Airborne troops. The map was signed by the commander, and he, the minister, had approved it. Now the plan was to get the soldiers involved in harvesting potatoes in the fields near Moscow. So, distinguished comrade deputies, there was no reason to worry, none whatsoever!

You can find nasty people anywhere. But there is a higher concentration of them in legislative bodies. The rest of the hearings were like a fencing bout. Thrust, parry; feint, parry.

"What about helmets?"

"There is a shortage of harvesting buckets for potatoes."

"And bullet-proof vests?"

"People get cold."

"And the armored vehicles?"

"A parade is to follow, and they are all included in the parade line-up."

"And what about the ammo?"

The minister threw his hands in the air:

"Well, you know how these Airborne guys are trained.... No matter what you tell them, they always drag their ammo around with them."

Some people in the audience were growling, others laughing, but the minister was stony-faced. Maneuvers-potatoes-parade; potatoes-parade-maneuvers.

A little later, some journalists tried to have some fun with the idea of "potato pickers in uniform," but it was too late. Disciplined Airborne troops had been holding maneuvers.

"Get ready for the parade!"

"Yes, sir!"

"March to harvest potatoes!"

And we found enough buckets so as not to embarrass anyone with our helmets. The people were happy. And we combined our potato harvesting with preparations for the parade.

CHAPTER 18:
THE LAST PARADE

THIS WAS MY FIFTH PARADE. The preparation for it started with the potato ordeal and continued in the same vein. The men on the parade ground were experienced, but the soldiers weren't performing well. The daily evaluations were more like chewing-out sessions, and with every chewing-out, performance decreased.

I probably contributed to the tension, although unwittingly. As I found out later General K.A. Kochetov, who was in charge of the parade, wanted to put camouflage paint on the parade vehicles. Realizing how much this luxury would cost, the commander of the Moscow Military District, Colonel General N.V. Kalinin, told the unit commanders not to mention camouflage in Kochetov's presence, and if the issue arose, they were to report that the parade colors of green with white trimming were an unbreakable tradition.

I did not attend the orientation, and so missed these instructions. At the next rehearsal, General Kochetov raised the issue of camouflage.

"What do you think about it, Comrade Generals and Officers?" he asked.

The well-coached commanders caused a commotion, the basic meaning of which was, no way!

"Comrade Officers!"

The formation snapped back to attention.

"What is this? A marketplace? We don't answer all at once here. Each person will express his individual opinion."

He walked along the line. The commander of a motorized rifle brigade reported that the parade colors were beautiful and that he was all for them. The commander of the Taman division said that they were what he was used to, so he was all for them, too. The commander of the Kantemirov division said that they were a tradition, and he was also all for them.

And then it was my turn.

"So what does our paratrooper have to say about it?"

"Comrade General, I think we need to camouflage the machinery. Combat machines should look predatory."

Kochetov went no further.

"The paratrooper is right; you are conservatives! Nikolai Vasilievich, repaint the machinery by the next training session."

The line let out a collective groan.

I won't reproduce what the district commander and his officers told me. Sputtering with rage, the army machinery was set in motion, and in three days, the vehicles were all repainted in exemplary fashion—and the results unexpectedly, unwillingly, impressed everyone.

"Parade colors" make vehicles look peaceful and theatrical. Repainted in a camouflage pattern, they appear an avalanche of predatory armor. One result was that the troops instinctively and suddenly smartened up their parade ground performance. The same superiors who just a few days ago had been threatening to blacklist the Tula Division as long as I was commanding it, said, in a conciliatory tone, that although I was, of course, a big jerk for making them go through three days of sweat and toil, it turned out all right after all.

But no sooner had I survived the "camouflage scandal" than the division was struck with a new misfortune. The commander of the Airborne troops called me in and informed me that U.S. Defense

Secretary Richard Cheney would be visiting the Soviet Union from October 10-15. My division would be one of the stops on his itinerary. And we had to demonstrate to the capitalist world's top military man the power, might, and valor of the Soviet Airborne troops. I was to report my plan in three days.

I was on my own, and it was daunting. For two days, I examined every foot of the exercise ground and the landing site of the Tesnitsk training center. But soon I was pressed for time.

My days became hectic. The commander of the Military District, who was responsible for the preparation for the parade, demanded my constant presence on the parade ground. The commander of the Airborne troops was no less insistent that I be present at division headquarters. I was between a rock and a hard place. I quickly got sick of this, and I raised the issue of working out a schedule not too easy on me but at least physically possible. The commanders thought about it and reached a compromise.

When the commander of the Airborne troops reviewed our dress rehearsal, he was satisfied; but there was one final hitch.

"For the first time in history, your division will be visited by an American defense secretary. What kind of commemorative gift are you going to present to him?"

"A fountain pen and a pennant!" I blurted.

"A fountain pen? Forget it! He's got plenty of his own. A pennant isn't enough. Tula is a city of master craftsmen. You need to get something authentic. Don't you think it's strange that I have to teach you? You've been commanding the division for three years."

Yes, Tula has been a city of master craftsmen since the time of Peter the Great. I had always been struck by the remarkable beauty and perfection of their work, and also by their poverty. At this time people were just starting to realize that their unique works of art were being sold for one-thousandth, or even less, of their true value.

I visited the masters and explained my situation to them. They opened their storage bins, and I saw marvelously hand-crafted rifle butts and stocks and outstandingly beautiful walnut cases for hunting rifles. There were exquisitely crafted knives of all kinds and sizes, and sheaths for them; lacquered boxes and holding cases, big and small. The masters had rediscovered the secret formula for Damascus steel. One could shave with a knife made by them, then skin a moose, and shave again—the blades were self-sharpening. I chose two Damascus steel knives in a walnut case for the American and a finely hand-crafted dagger for our own minister.

> **"W**ith the American delegation, we drank often, but the shot-glasses were microscopic. Secretary Cheney told various funny stories, and Marshal Yazov read poetry.**"**

The artisans had a little conference and announced their price—3,500 rubles for everything. I explained to them that even though I was a division commander and a general, my salary was only 612 rubles a month, excluding Party dues.

We were all embarrassed and became silent. My conscience would not allow me to take this precious work for nothing, and they could not afford to give away their labor and creative inspiration.

But they respected me and sincerely wanted to help. Besides, they had the healthy self-esteem of the Russian master craftsman, whose work, bearing his family name, could cross the ocean and demonstrate to the Americans that the craftsmen in Russia were still going strong.

Of course, this was a situation which could only be resolved with the help of a half-liter bottle. And that's what we did. The youngest of them brought out a bottle of vodka, we all agreed that we had to think further on what to do, and... clicked glasses on it. The decision turned out to be the right one. There was a stack of colorful booklets on the edge of the table. These artfully arranged and beautifully published booklets depicted samples of sport and hunting rifles, manufactured in Tula, decorated with exquisite carvings and marvelous inlay work.

"Is it your work?" I asked.

"Yes, it's ours."

"What's the most expensive thing in the world?"

"Who the hell knows?"

"Advertising. So let me be the one to advertise you. You give me the knives and a stack of your booklets for all of my guests. I'll promise to give one of these to each of the Americans, and recommend—insistently—that they waste no time, and purchase one of your remarkable rifles."

"Hey, the general's talking business—let's do it. Let's make ourselves known."

We shook hands on it.

The day finally came when the helicopters carrying the Americans were to land in Tesnitsky. Everything was ready, and morale was extraordinarily high. My only concern was the October weather. But even the weather did not let me down. It was dry and cool; the skies were high and virtually cloudless.

The guests landed. We introduced ourselves, and the show began.

On that day everything worked out perfectly. My deputy division commander in charge of Airborne equipment, Colonel Petr. Semenovich Nezhivoi, an expert with outstanding experience, made his calculations precisely. The planes flew over the landing site and left behind chains of paratroopers. All the targets were blown to smithereens, and the recon men did miracles on the obstacle course. The commander was on cloud nine. So was I. And I could tell from looking at the American that he was impressed.

The demonstration ended with the traditional banquet. Before the banquet, I received a "behind the scenes" report that everybody was alive, and there were only two minor injuries. The weapons were unloaded, and the ammo was taken away. I insist that this kind of report is the most important part of any exercise or demonstration.

At the banquet, I handed each member of the American delegation a set of booklets. Everyone was interested, including Marshal Yazov. Then, I realized that I had slipped up in not asking how much these rifles cost. And everyone was asking. I had no idea because I am not a hunter and I have never held a hunting rifle in my hands in my entire life, but hoping for the best, I gave them a broad ballpark figure: "From $15,000 to $100,000 depending on...." To tell the truth, I had no idea what it might depend on. I'd have come up with something if I'd had to, but, luckily they didn't let me finish. The Americans were all but smacking their lips in admiration of the contents of the booklets.

> **"D**id I have any sense that this was my last parade? Perhaps not, but I sensed the government was breaking down... drifting."

We drank to the Soviet Airborne troops, to the Tula craftsmen, and to the friendship of the Soviet and American peoples.

We drank often, but in small quantities. The shot-glasses were microscopic. A friendly, casual atmosphere reigned in the tent. Cheney told various funny stories, and Marshal Yazov read poetry, both his own and that of others. I was amazed by the marshal's literary erudition. The commander shot me a meaningful glance: "The banquet will end soon!"

I took out the holding case, which was finely carved and decorated like an Easter egg. I opened it, took out the knives, and briefly told the story of how the method of making Damascus steel had been rediscovered, and mentioned the names of the master craftsmen. I ended by announcing that since it was against Airborne custom to give knives as gifts, I could only sell that remarkable set to the American defense secretary.

I paused, waiting for the interpreter to finish his translation. The Americans, and Yazov along with them, made long faces. The minister's eyes said something like: "Just you wait, you businessman from hell!" There was an awkward delay of about a second. Then I said, "So, I'm asking five cents! It's a bit expensive, of course, but the secretary is welcome to bargain with me!" Everybody burst out laughing. But I had unwittingly created yet another awkward situation. I categorically refused to take any banknotes of any denomination, and the secretary and his entourage had no change. Fortunately, one of the secretary's assistants ran outside and found a dime. The purchase took place. Cheney and I shook hands on it. Marshal Yazov had his five kopecks ready, so I had no problem there. I have kept these two coins as a memento. A memento not so much of the two ministers, who have since left their posts, but of the Airborne troops.

We parted warmly. One load off my back. Now I could concentrate on getting ready for the parade. If the situation on the parade ground itself was going smoothly, the situation outside it was heating up. Soldiers and officers were frequently being insulted by the townspeople. There was loud mockery and profanity. They would even throw some nasty stuff at us. It was despicable and petty beyond all measure.

A soldier is "government property." Today, a young man may be studying, working, or standing in a park playing the guitar, but he could get called up tomorrow and be put in formation. When the time comes, he will be discharged and go back to studying or working again. So, why do they have to take it out on the soldier, who is an integral part of what we call "the people"? It's not just his military honor that is being insulted; it's his dignity as a man!

Because of incidents of this kind, we had to restrict allowing soldiers to go to the theater or to concerts as incentives for good performance.

We had to go to our night rehearsals along a corridor of soldiers holding back an abusive public.

After the first nighttime rehearsal I became seriously concerned. The route of my armored columns to Red Square went along Petrovka Street, and Petrovka Street is long and narrow. The old mansions facing it were undergoing extensive renovation and remodeling and were fenced off, which made the narrow street even narrower. Piles of construction debris were around the fence. I was thinking: if some militant democrats from the ranks of the "new Russians" used the cranes at the building sites and dropped ten or fifteen concrete slabs to block the street, I'd be trapped. The narrow alleys on the left and right were not suitable for maneuvering a big group of armored machinery.

I reported my doubts to the commander of the Airborne troops.

"Forget it! The division has been using this route for decades. We'll just set up the cordons and nothing will happen."

But my doubts were not relieved. I decided to stage a small preemptive scene, to avoid a bigger one at the parade. At the next meeting of the command staff, after Colonel General N.V. Kalinin finished giving his instructions, I asked an innocent question: "Comrade Commander, what gear should we use to roll over the citizens of the heroic city of Moscow in case they feel like lying down under the caterpillar treads?"

The commander blew a gasket:

"You are a general, Aleksandr Ivanovich! I've known you for a long time, and I thought much better of you. What kind of nonsense is this? To ask such idiotic questions at a working meeting! Sit down!"

I sat down. But an hour after the end of the meeting, officers from the commandant's office rushed over to me and notified me that my route had been changed. Now I would be speeding along with the main flow along Tverskaya-Yamskaya Street and no longer have to worry about getting caught in a "stone trap."

All was going well, until at the final nighttime rehearsal a drunken schizophrenic, waving the ID of a member of the RSFSR Supreme Soviet, tried to stop the column and give a sermon. The police officers did the humane thing—they made him hug a lamp post, and then they handcuffed him. After the column passed, they let him go.

The parade went smoothly, but it left a heaviness in my heart. The festive mood that I was used to was gone. Despite all the measures we took, I hardly saw any smiles. When the parade was over, I felt no exhilaration, only that I had just finished a thankless and humiliating job.

I organized the railway boarding of the Ryazan regiment's armor, and then I went back home to Tula.

Did I have any sense that this would be my last parade? Perhaps not, but I sensed that the government was breaking down, and that the country was drifting under my feet. Something big, dependable, and fundamental, the basis of my life and my military service, was crumbling away.

CHAPTER 19:
THE CALM BEFORE THE STORM

THE DISTRESSING FEELING that something had broken did not go away, even when I returned home. On the contrary, it got worse. People who had eagerly accepted *perestroika* had become morally weary after five years of fruitless attempts at restructuring, and were deeply disappointed, both in the idea itself, and in those who carried it out. Everyone was sick of the *nomenklatura's* stupidity and the Party's arrogance, laced with impotence and organizational weakness. Everyone knew that nothing would come of this monster called *perestroika*, but no one had any idea what to do next.

This lack of clarity, of definition, this hopelessness and melancholy made people mean, and as a consequence, there was a wave of crimes and suicides. On a larger scale, this led to inter-ethnic conflicts. The price of human life dropped precipitously, until it came to rest at the level of a mongrel dog. If you killed one of them—oh well, sorry and all that—you grieve for a few minutes and then get on with your life.

Life, if you could call it that, went on. Children got used to stepping through corpses on their way to school. And this will come back to bite us. We were the ones who put these "delayed-action mines" in our children's souls, and they will go off, again and again, for a long time to come.

Society rapidly split into three main groups. The smart, clever, and enterprising people went into the cooperative movement[1]. Those who were stupid, but big and strong, went to guard them or became racketeers. And the workers were left behind.

As always in times of trouble[2], all kinds of kooks came out of the woodwork; clairvoyants, hypnotists, magicians, wizards, faith healers, and astrologers. They healed by words, by touch, and by water which they had blessed. They healed in person and from the television screen. They made astrological predictions for the near and distant future. They warned of floods and earthquakes, landslides, fires, and other sorts of Divine punishments.

> **"A**fter perestroika, *a wave of filthy rubbish rolled across the country like a tsunami. And all this time, the Party idols went on dividing up power among themselves."*

All this was made possible by the growing uncertainty, grief, and anger in society. Something had to be healed. People needed to find some solace somewhere. And suddenly, it turned out that almost everyone had become believers, half-believers, or quarter-believers. Even people whose jobs prevented them from believing—party officials of all ranks—believed. Along with the traditional faiths—in Christ, Mohammed, Buddha, and Jehovah—a variety of other, smaller, sectarian faiths sprang up and flourished. Hare Krishnas, outlandish in appearance, began appearing in the streets, and other "brotherhoods" began to be fruitful and mul-

[1]One of the reforms of *perestroika* was to allow people to hire others to work in small businesses, as long as there was no "exploitation of man by man." These small businesses were called "cooperatives."

[2] The author uses the words *smutnie vremena*, which has echoes of the "Time of Troubles" in Russian history between the death of Ivan the Terrible and the accession of Mikhail Romanov. See note to the afterword on this subject.

tiply. Naturally, as always in such cases, each new convert became "more Catholic than the Pope himself."

Among the more enlightened, political parties, foundations, and social organizations began to multiply along with the religious sects.

These parties could have as few members as ten. The foundations were usually made up of their founders and honorary chairmen alone, but all of them had imposing sounding names, with the obligatory word "democracy." "Communists for Democracy," "Democrats for Democracy," "Ochlocrats [supporters of mob rule] for Democracy."

The parties, sects, and astrological computations and calculations grew and multiplied, but nothing changed for the better. This led to a new wave of disappointment, to a discrediting of authorities, to faith in a miracle, a "hero." And again, the old, latent thought began to stir: The Czar. The czar is a deity, an object of admiration. Everything good on this earth comes from him. If we could just elect or appoint a good czar—everything would be better. Not completely all right, because under a czar, there were always boyars (noblemen) who strove to move the deity away from the people. But that was inevitable.

There were endless painful and fruitless attempts to get out of this dead end. Society's foundations were being shaken. Movie and television screens were filled with "consumer goods" of three sorts: sex, violence, and soap opera serials. The numerous vending stands and market stalls were packed with the same poisonous slop: medals, tunics, and uniforms with ribbons and decorations (before which the only proper response was to doff your hat) were suddenly up for sale; and there were *matryoshka* dolls of Gorbachev and Yeltsin. While the ruble was still worth something, they did business in rubles; later, they moved to dollars.

With the influx of inferior literature, not just the ideologized Soviet classics, but even the innocent Russian writers and poets started disappearing from the shelves. And not just classical music, but even the best sort of popular music vanished. The pounding rhythms of the "rock" pseudo-musicians, with wild, frequently profane lyrics, filled the stage. Anyone who tried to resist this, anyone in whom there was a spark of spirituality, who couldn't accept this sticky filth, was simply destroyed, like the poet, composer, and singer Igor Talkov, a Russian to the marrow of his bones.

A wave of rubbish rolled across the country with the speed of a tsunami. And all this time, the Party idols, who had no idea what was going on, were voluptuously dividing up power among themselves. Gorbachev, our Helmsman and Architect, progressively became the "best German," the "best Jew," the "best American." He was the best everywhere except his own country. In his own country, by that time, he had become simply "Mishka the Marked Man."[3]

There is nothing new under the sun. Twenty-four hundred years ago, Plato wrote a treatise on the state. Plato was a far-sighted man: "Let us examine, dear friend, how tyranny comes into being.... When a democratic regime, athirst for liberty, gets bad cupbearers as its leaders, and gets intoxicated by drinking too deep of the unmixed wine of liberty, and punishes its leaders, if they are insufficiently mild and do not dispense liberty unstintingly.... In such an order of things, a teacher is afraid of his students, and fawns upon them.... Horses and asses walk proudly, with complete freedom, bumping into passers-by if they don't give up the right of way... citizens become sensitive... anything compulsory upsets them." And they end by paying no heed even to the laws, "so that no one or nothing can have power over them."[4]

And the army? This instrument of the state, this instrument of the "continuation of politics by other, violent, means"? In such a situation, only a lazy man will refrain from kicking the army. In such times "army" and "prison" become synonyms. In record-short times, through the efforts of the mass media (Korotich's *Ogonek* was espe-

---

[3] A reference to the birthmark on his head.

[4] Plato, *Republic*, Book VIII, 562a-563d.

cially vehement in this respect) all thinkable and unthinkable evils were concentrated in the army.

The point of departure was when the army was forced into functions which were not properly its own in the Transcaucasus and Central Asia. Was this a new phenomenon? In his book, *The Path of a Russian Officer*, General A.I. Denikin[5] says in a passage pertaining to the beginning of our century: "Putting the army to work suppressing disorders is a crime. The army has a specific mission—to fight with external enemies—and it has the weapons and technology, the psychology, and the specific mentality which correspond to that mission. In short, the army is part of the people. Giving the army police functions, restricting the army by strict rules of engagement, when officers and soldiers are not prepared for that sort of activity, can only lead to one thing: to bitterness, and to the army being unjustly insulted by the crowd."

The army was separating people who wanted to cut each other's throats. These screaming fools, in turn, were dragging away the army's property, weapons, and vehicles, so that they could kill hundreds at a time. When the army tried to resist, a chorus of "democratically inclined" journalists poured buckets of offal on them. They called them "murderers," "gendarmes," "mongrels," "bastards," and worse.

Dogmatism ran rampant. Slogans included words like "destroy," "annihilate," "smear," "wipe out." The atmosphere was full of hatred and spite, which led to the most shameless lying, demagoguery, populism, and pandering. No longer did anyone even bother to appeal to the national interest. The national interest had become unfashionable.

Everything concerning the army became fertile ground for the most monstrous myth. Anything negative, criminal, and perverse that did take place in the army was multiplied a hundredfold.

---

[5] General Anton Ivanovich Denikin was one of the leaders of the White Army during the Russian Civil War. The following notes refer to the period immediately following the 1905 revolution.

Society was running somewhere, at a faster and faster pace. It was rushing headlong, not too careful about which road it took: nobody wanted to stop, rest, and think: Where are we running? Why are we running?

The rejection of a peaceful, natural, evolutionary path of renewal for the country, the total and *fatal* unwillingness to think, and the desire to profit from the political mudslinging led to a dead end at the very outset, and, in the end, to the collapse of the state.

The best and most loyal Soviet people were indifferent to the army. Most citizens called soldiers "martinets" and "militarists" to cover up their fears. Society was permeated with the ideas of pacifism, and forgot the well-known truth that a country that does not feed its army will end up feeding the enemy's army.

And there is another well-known truth: every Russian knows all about three things—agriculture, soccer, and military construction. And the more remote a man is from agriculture or military construction, the more confident he is that he can "take care" of the problem. Progress, culture, and the humanities have ostensibly made war impossible, and since this was "true," everyone began to talk in chorus of a small, economical, professional army. But in a country like Russia, the army simply cannot be small. And a professional army cannot be economical. Suffice it to say that there are only two purely professional all-volunteer armies in the entire world: in America, and in Great Britain. Even such highly developed countries as France and Germany have a mixture of draftees and volunteers. But all that didn't matter, those were insignificant details, problems that the military had to deal with.

The people's deputies, pandering to populist sentiments, triumphantly announced their achievements in exempting more and more categories of citizens from military service. And in the army, harassed and under fire, the number of soldiers was sharply cut, and the intellectual level of those who remained dropped off noticeably.

According to legislation, young people with one or two criminal convictions (for hooliganism, for example) were called up to the military construction units, which guaranteed that these units would be completely uncontrollable. They became "construction *gangs*." The army became a "workers' and peasants' army"[6] before our eyes. And insofar as that was true, it gave the people all the more reason to pick on us.

At the end of January 1991, the commander of the Airborne troops, Colonel General V.A. Achalov, gathered the division and brigade commanders for an operations meeting. But the meeting was the last thing on his mind; his main purpose was to announce some serious personnel reshuffling in the Ministry of Defense and the Airborne troops. Achalov told us that he had been appointed deputy minister of defense of the USSR, and that Major General P.S. Grachev had been appointed commander of the Airborne troops. Then he unexpectedly asked me and my good friend, Major General V.A. Sorokin, the commander of the 104th Airborne Division, to stand up, and announced that from now on, I would be the deputy commander of the Airborne troops for combat training and military schools, and Sorokin would be deputy commander for Airborne training. Both of us had intended to go to the General Staff Academy. Nobody had talked to us; nobody had informed us of the impending decision. So both of us exclaimed, with one voice, "But what about the academy?"

Achalov pretended to be upset: "Just look at them! The deputy minister of defense appoints two major generals to positions normally filled by lieutenant generals, appoints them deputy commanders of the Airborne troops, and all they can do is mumble something about going to the academy! What's left to teach you—you're scholars enough already! Stop all this back talk! Go and get ready to turn over your divisions. The order will come in a few days. And if you really

---

[6] The old name of the Soviet army was the "Workers' and Peasants' Red Army" or RKKA. In this case, however, the author is calling attention to the fact that the quality of recruits was declining fast. Earlier, in Chapter 4, he used the expression in a more positive light, as a way of saying that the "fortunate sons" did not have to go to Afghanistan, and it was the common people who fought there.

want to study, serve for a few years, and then apply again when your age permits. That's all! This decision is not subject to discussion."

From my very first days in the new job, I had to deal with a number of difficulties not covered in the regulations or in any orders. Units of the Airborne troops were deployed on the territory of nine union republics. And in these republics, centrifugal tendencies were growing. I had training grounds, tank parks, and firing ranges in these republics. Local authorities examined every activity on these training grounds for signs of imperial ambitions and demonstrations of force. It became virtually impossible to come to any agreement with them.

> **"O**ur French guests knew a stunning number of songs. An army whose officers know that many patriotic songs is the strong army of a country with deep self-respect.**"**

Then an unimaginable number of environmentalists appeared, whose bustling activity reached the heights of the absurd. Suddenly, they started "discovering" all sorts of dumps and buried trash heaps. Demands piled up to remove it, immediately, or be fined. We were also fined if we disturbed beavers or rabbits. Local authorities came out with a mass of decisions to create national parks, to give citizens their own garden plots, and to create buffer zones around reservoirs or rivers to prevent water contamination. The land for all of them came from my training grounds.

As I lost land, so, too, did I lose men and money. The normally sluggish process of desertion became a hemorrhage after January 1991. A mass exodus of Lithuanians, Latvians, Armenians, Azeris, and Chechens began. Soon Ukrainians followed. And the financing of the armed forces in general, and of combat training in particular, fell catastrophically.

The presidential campaign then under way in the country inspired no optimism. The gang of competitors for the post of "First President of Free Russia" broke into ritual incantations, gave assurances, and made promises from our television screens. If you listened, each of them promised Russia the road straight to Heaven. Their speeches had everything: "let the sun shine on Russia," "God is with us," "forward... to a bright past," "believe me, people."

The leading economic minds were pulling out their wigs, organizing heated theoretical races to see "who could make Russia the Third Rome[7] in the fewest days." The bright face of revolution peered out from the pages of their programs. They had all forgotten, first of all, that revolution is always bad and always fraught with negative consequences; and second, that they had earned their wigs and academic robes, their professorships and doctoral degrees by running the horse of the socialist political economy into the ground. Three days, five days, one hundred days.... Aleksandr Isaevich Solzhenitsyn said at that time that even in five hundred days[8] it was only possible to ruin Russia.

And by the way, everyone, including all the presidential candidates, had nothing but contempt for Solzheritsyn's article "How Russia Should Be Rebuilt." They said that "The Hermit of Vermont is an eccentric! He's got all these hair-brained schemes! What can we say—he's a Nobel laureate."

Three events from this period have etched themselves into my memory: the visit of a French military delegation, led by General de Courege, the commander of the French 81st Airborne Division; the visit of Russian presidential candidate Boris Yeltsin to the Tula Airborne Division's training ground; and the visit of the chairman of the U.S. Joint Chiefs of Staff, General Colin Powell, to the same place.

[7] In Russian tradition, the First Rome was Rome itself, Constantinople was the Second Rome, and Moscow would be the Third Rome.

[8] At that time, an economic program known as the "500 Day Program" was being pushed by Russian reformers. Gorbachev never adopted it.

I remember all these visits because I was the one who had to organize and run them.

The French arrived at the end of April. In preparing for the visit, I carefully studied biographical information on each of the generals and officers in the delegation. This information did not come from spies; it was normal army information and had been sent by the French themselves. From this information, I learned that the division commander was fifty-eight years old. The director of the academy, next in rank to him, was fifty-four. I had a misconception of what our guests from the banks of the Seine would be like. I imagined that the generals would be overweight, bald, elderly, and looking the worse for wear. But I was pleasantly surprised when I met them at the airport in Domodedovo. Two generals easily and informally walked down the airplane's gangway. Both of them were well built and in wonderful physical condition.

The program was planned for five days. The simplicity, the grace, the informality, and the unpretentiousness of the Frenchmen impressed me.

"So, would you like to jump with us?"

"No problem!"

"But I'm warning you, it's dirty out there on the drop zone!"

"What are you taking about? We're soldiers!"

They took out their camouflage field uniforms, and right there, they changed into them. We showed them the parachutes. They were surprised: "These are strange parachutes."

"Why are they strange?"

Their parachutes, as it turned out, had the main chute opening behind, and the reserve chute in front. Ours were the other way around.

"Well, it doesn't matter," they said. "Let's jump in these strange parachutes!"

Every one of them jumped. Even their military attaché, who had arrived just half an hour before the jump. And they wallowed in the mud like pigs, it didn't matter.

"Would you like to shoot with us?"

"No problem."

They had never seen grenade launchers like ours before, but it didn't matter.

"We'll figure them out. We're professionals."

They figured them out. Every one of them shot, and they were good shots, too.

And they sang wherever they could. The division commander led the singing. They sang songs about knightly heroes of the Middle Ages; they sang songs from the colonial wars, lauding the courage of the French soldier; they sang songs of the French Resistance. I especially remember a song about a soldier who was dying for France in the Algerian desert. In his delirium just before his death, his mother appeared to him and gave him her blessing. The song's main theme was: France and Mother, Mother and France, Mother-France.

They knew an absolutely stunning number of songs. All their songs were patriotic, and they sang them well. It could not have been improvised; to sing like that, you have to sing constantly. An army whose officers know that many patriotic songs is the strong army of a country with a deep sense of self-respect.

I asked them as much as I could: about their service, about their daily life, about relations between the army and the local government, and learned a great deal.

Why, for example, did the attaché, who had just gotten out of the car in his dress uniform, jump with us into the mud only half an hour later? It turned out that if you wanted to become a French officer, along with the other tests, you had to make three parachute jumps, in order to demonstrate that you had the will, the courage, and the ability to keep cool in extreme situations. Afterwards, if you didn't want to jump, it was your business. So all the officers in the French armed forces, regardless of their military specialty, were paratroopers.

All positions in the French army are held for a certain time period, and no longer. In tough jobs like company commander or regimental commander, you serve for two years. If you become a regimental commander on January 1, 1990, then you can be sure that on January 1, 1992, you will no longer be in command of that regiment. Where you go after that—up, down, or sideways—will depend on you.

A general in France serves until he is sixty years old. He goes into retirement on his sixtieth birthday. If you're not simply a general, but a general and a scholar, you'll keep your salary, take off your uniform, put on a business suit, and go off to do the same work.

The president personally presents each regimental commander with the documents that give him the right to command a regiment, and by tradition, all of the officers and generals who have ever commanded that regiment, no matter how high they are now, get together for the ceremony of one commander turning the regiment over to his successor. Failure to show up at such an event would be very bad form. The ceremony lasts about three hours. It is long, complicated, and beautiful. It concludes with a banquet.

I asked: "How many people attend? Fifty to seventy?"

"No. Six to eight hundred, and sometimes more than a thousand."

"But who pays for all this?"

"The municipality."

"What does the municipality have to do with it?"

"Good question! First of all, people have a deep respect for the army, and are proud of the unit based on their territory. Second, if the mayor and some other high functionary in the municipality break this centuries-old tradition, they are dead men as far as their political future is concerned because it would appear that they are not patriots; they do not love France, because they do not love her army. Such people cannot stand at the helm of any government. And if you get your documents from the president himself, and honored generals make heartfelt speeches at your ceremony, if hundreds of people raise their glasses to your health and success, and if the mayor and other public officials express their hopes that you will make the regiment even better—just try to do a bad job commanding that regiment!"

The base pay for a serviceman is calculated on the basis of the average *reasonable* subsistence wage, and not on a bare subsistence wage, as it is here, and I'm talking about the average *in France*. A number of coefficients are applied, depending on one's position and rank, and another 80 percent can be added on top of that for incentives. Again, unlike us. The counting does not go "from the bottom up" (if you behave, we'll give you a bonus at the end of the year), but "from the top down," i.e., if you do everything right, you'll get 185 percent of your base pay.

"And do you have 'relations not covered by regulations' in France?" I asked.

"What are 'relations not covered by regulations'?"

I explained that it was a Soviet euphemism for hazing and abuse—usually by senior enlisted men—of new recruits.

"Oh, no!" came the answer. "One regiment is staffed completely with volunteers. The other, with draftees, who serve for one year. If a career soldier strikes, insults, or in any way offends a draftee, he becomes something of a leper. And he is severely punished, from a financial standpoint."

"And what about religion?"

"What about religion? You can believe in whatever you wish, as long as you keep it to yourself. For five days a week, you're in the service, you're a soldier. On Saturday or Sunday, you can pray, cross yourself, bang your head against the floor if you like."

I had a good impression of these Frenchmen: they were free, highly professional, deeply patriotic officers, who served out of conscience, with a firm grounding in common sense.

The assignment to receive Russian presidential candidate Boris Yeltsin in Tula came just a few days before his May 31 arrival. It came from the commander of the Airborne troops, General Grachev. Yeltsin was not going to visit the division, but a visit to the training ground was on his Tula itinerary.

I coordinated plans with the oblast Party committee secretary and the chairman of the executive committee of the city soviet. Because the runway at the Tula airport was deficient in some respect, the Tu-154 landed in Kaluga instead, almost one hundred kilometers away, but General Grachev brought the future president to the training ground right on time.

The division put on a masterly demonstration. At one point a military vehicle with paratroopers inside was dropped from a plane and landed about eight hundred feet in front of the observation deck. A lieutenant and a sergeant untied the vehicle from its chute, started the engine, and drove up to the reviewing stand to make their report.

> **"T**he result of our demonstration for General Colin Powell was one fractured skull (he died), eight broken legs, three broken arms, and one broken collarbone.**"**

Yeltsin beckoned to the Chief Bearer of the Briefcase. The bearer opened up the briefcase and gave him two watches. Boris Nikolaevich thought for a bit, took off his own watch, and put it in his jacket pocket. He put one of the new watches on his wrist and the other in his pants pocket. The lieutenant appeared. "Comrade. . . ." the lieutenant stumbled, "Comrade Presidential Candidate. . . the team. . . ." Yeltsin took off his watch and gave it to the lieutenant: "Thank you, son, from the bottom of my heart." He took the second watch out of his pants pocket and handed it to the sergeant with equal gratitude. The lieutenant and the sergeant left, assuming that presidential candidates carry a minimum of two watches—one to wear, and another to keep in their pockets, just in case. Yeltsin then took his own watch out of his jacket pocket and put it back on. We went to the next observation point. The end of the demonstrations was followed by a twenty-minute meeting with the paratroopers. Soldiers and junior officers stared, goggle-eyed; it wasn't every day they could see a presidential candidate.

Boris Nikolaevich said something about reviving Russia, and about how Russia should have a Russian army, with Russian soldiers and officers serving in it. He should have used the word *Rossiiskii*, which referred to the Russian state, but instead he said *Russkii*, which means "ethnic Russian." A major, the political officer of a battalion, ran up to ask what to do if the battalion commander was a Ukrainian, the executive officer was a Belorussian, he, the political officer, was a Russian, and the ordnance officer was an ethnic German. Yeltsin, annoyed at the interruption, waved him off. "We'll sort things out!" he said, and went on to announce that he intended to give the glorious Tula Division five hundred apartments. The crowd reacted with rather faint applause. Boris Nikolaevich had expected a more enthusiastic response. He frowned, involuntarily. The commander hurried to close the meeting, and the whole cavalcade set off for the banquet table.

When he got to the hunting lodge where the banquet was to be held, Yeltsin said that he liked to swim in cold water whenever he had the chance. He quickly stripped down to his birthday suit and crawled into the pond next to the hunting lodge. His chief bodyguard, A.V. Korzhakov, went in after him, wearing the same thing. The waitresses and cooks, who had had their noses pressed to the windows facing the pond, scurried off inside the building. Boris Nikolaevich Yeltsin and Aleksandr Vasilievich Korzhakov, now refreshed and wrapped up in sheets, went into the banquet hall. Yeltsin was accompanied by the commander of the Airborne troops, the division commander, and other officials. I stayed outside to make sure everything went all right.

A patrol (a lieutenant and two soldiers, armed with automatic rifles) was walking around the outside of the parking lot. Another patrol was walking around the pond. Seven of Yeltsin's bodyguards came up to me:

"Who are they?"

"Patrols!"

"Do they have ammunition?"

"Of course!"

"Would they shoot at us?"

"You're our guests!"

"Oh.... All right!"

The bodyguards dove into the cellar and, in half an hour, according to the division supply officer's report, "talked him out of" seven bottles of vodka, one for each of them.

We've got to protect His Majesty
From people he doesn't wish to see.
Oh, a bodyguard gets up early in the morning....

Forty minutes later, the banquet was over. Everything that was poured out was finished off. They all walked out into the fresh air feeling as if they loved and respected the whole world and were loved and respected in return. The motorcade stopped three times in the first seven hundred meters for repeated good-byes.

Later came the elections; Boris Nikolaevich Yeltsin became Russia's first president and Lieutenant General P.S. Grachev, the commander of the Airborne troops—one of the president's dearest friends and most loyal comrades—became Russia's minister of defense.

There's one other visit I have to mention. It was in July. The chairman of the U.S. Joint Chiefs of Staff, Colin Powell, arrived in the USSR. A visit to the Tula Airborne Division was on his itinerary. As we awaited Powell's arrival, the wind was blowing at twenty to twenty-six miles per hour, and gusting up to forty-two miles per hour. I reported to General Grachev that we couldn't jump in that wind. He thought we could. I insisted we couldn't, saying that Americans were Americans, but we Russians would be the ones breaking our legs. Hospitality was a good thing but not when carried to that extreme. The commander seemed to agree. I asked permission to give the appropriate orders.

The commander asked: "Are the planes in the air?"

"Yes, the planes are in the air, but we can turn them around again, no problem."

The commander suddenly, sharply changed his mind: "Go ahead with the jump! Stop your whining! Let them see what Soviet paratroopers can do! See to it!"

Colin Powell and his entourage of high brass were on the observation deck. The buzzing of the airplanes could be heard somewhere on the other side of the forest, but the planes couldn't be seen. In order to land in the drop zone with the wind blowing like this, they'd have to jump from far off.

Let's go! Waves of "kamikazes" floated out onto the drop zone, and hit the ground with terrifying speed, rolling head over heels, putting out each other's parachutes, getting out of their harnesses, and attacking. They attacked fiercely and indomitably. And that was understandable. If someone knocks you to the ground like that, you'd get up fighting mad too. I know from my own experience.

The four-star American general was rushing about the observation deck, asking over and over: "What are you doing?" And that, for some reason, was the most painful of all. That damned American was a guest; he should have sat there quietly, coolly, and watched as the Russian gladiators broke their legs. Then your hatred of imperialism could grow and grow. But he was a human being, and a general; he knew the price of blood and life; he had a conscience, and that's why he rushed around the platform, asking: "What are you doing?"

And that made it not just painful, but also unbearably shameful. The result of this demonstration of our capabilities was one fractured skull (he died), eight broken legs, three broken arms, and one broken collarbone.

Colin Powell's question still rings in my ears: "What are you doing?"

CHAPTER 20:
A SPECTACLE CALLED A "PUTSCH"

IN 1991, for the first time in many years, I managed to take a leave in August. I had big plans. I had just gotten hold of a plot of land, and I wanted to plant something, watch it grow, and make some improvements on it. So I decided to visit my mother for a week or so, and then concentrate on working on my land. The sun, the fresh air, the water, the physical work—in short, the whole program.

On August 15 I arrived in Tula, where I had an apartment. I spent all of the next day planning the work I would do. I had wanted to start on the morning of the 17th, but like all Orthodox Christians, I put it off until Monday.

At 1600 hours on August 17, I got a phone call. It was the commander of the 106th Airborne Division, Colonel A.P. Kolmakov.

"The commander of the Airborne troops wishes to speak to you. It's urgent."

"First of all, I'm on leave, and second, where does he want to speak to me? On the telephone there, or in Moscow?"

"Here. It's urgent!"

"Well, send a car for me then."

The commander of the Airborne troops, Lieutenant General Grachev, ordered me to get the Tula division ready for action, immediately.

I tried to find out where I'd be going, but Grachev only promised: "You'll find out later."

The division commander and I gave the necessary orders. The regiments and separate units were set in motion with no real problems.

Naturally, we wondered where we would be going this time. We learned that somewhere on the border between Armenia and Azerbaijan, forty Interior Ministry troops had been taken hostage. Perhaps they would send us there to free the hostages and restore order. We decided to get a detailed description of the area, but we didn't have the right maps, and when we requested the maps from the Airborne command staff, they turned us down. Mystery hung in the air.

By midnight all the regiments were ready. I tried once again to find out what we would be doing. I was instructed not to bother the commander with dumb questions. It was good that he warned me, because the next thing he said was completely unintelligible: "You'll be going south, but through me!"

The night was spent waiting.

At 1100 hours on August 18 I got a call from the chief of staff of the Airborne troops, Lieutenant General E.N. Podkolzin. He clarified a few minor issues and in passing dropped a phrase: "Wait for an emergency message at 1800 hours." Time dragged. Finally, the clock showed 1800 hours, but there was no emergency message. Nothing had happened by 1900 hours or 2000 hours. . . . Midnight came and went, and still nothing. So I got fed up and went home after ordering the division commander to sleep by the phone.

At 0400 on August 19 the phone rang at my apartment. It was the division commander reporting: "We have orders to send the three regiments on a march in the following directions: Kostroma–Moscow; Ryazan–Moscow; Tula–Moscow, and to concentrate our forces at the Tushino airfield by 1400 hours. Further instructions will be given later on."

At 0450 the wheels and the treads were already turning and the march began. The so-called "operations group" consisted of me, myself, and I. That being so, I decided that my place was at the division's forward command post vehicle. I reported the positions of our regimental columns to the commander every hour, and every time I asked about our mission, I got the same laconic answer: "Just keep moving!"

By 10:30 the forward command post vehicle turned onto the Moscow ring road. I told the commander that I intended to go ahead to Tushino, establish a complete scheme of communication arrangements, and accommodate the regiments. Grachev approved my decision. Along the route on the ring road we encountered tanks moving in groups of two or three, sometimes even alone. The tank crew members stuck their heads out of their hatches, and they had what I can only describe as overwhelmed expressions on their faces.

I arrived in Tushino and set to work. Soon I got a call from the chief of staff of the Airborne Corps, Lieutenant General Podkolzin.

"Aleksandr Ivanovich, here is the commander's order. You, personally, are to go to the RSFSR Supreme Soviet building, establish contact with the chief of the security service there, and use the 2nd Battalion of the Ryazan regiment to maintain the security and defense of the building."

Here is the dialogue that followed:

"What means of communication can I take with me?"

"None! Take a UAZik and one officer and go there in person."

"Whom am I supposed to contact? What's the person's name?"

"They'll meet you there."

"And where's the battalion?"

"It will get over to the Supreme Soviet [building]."

I put down the phone. At approximately 1350, the division's deputy political officer, Lieutenant Colonel O.E. Bastanov, and I drove a UAZik to the RSFSR Supreme Soviet building. We pulled into the parking lot. Feverish work was going on around the building. The nature of the work was obvious—they were erecting barricades. The people looked excited, and their actions were frantic and inefficient. They used just about anything they came across: trolley-buses, passenger cars, whatever they could get their hands on.

I asked a police officer where we could find the chief of security. Only later did I realize that I should have been looking for the president's chief bodyguard, A.V. Korzhakov. The patrolman pointed around the corner, "Over there."

I was confused. Unlike the people who had been watching television, I had heard none of the proclamations made by the Government Committee on the State of Emergency (GKChP)—the faction of government that was attempting to seize power by force, kidnapping Gorbachev, and threatening to attack the Supreme Soviet. The people who were constructing the barricades looked like ordinary good-hearted folks. So, if I were to take a battalion and organize the security of the Supreme Soviet, then I would have to organize my defense with these people. But—the natural question obtruded—against whom?

My conversation with the police officer didn't take long, but a crowd had instantly formed around us. I was wearing a combat camouflage uniform, and I heard shouts:

"Major, are you really going to shoot at us?"

"Major, remember your oath!"

"Assholes!"

"Hey, he's not a major, he's a *major general*!"

The crowd went wild. I was followed by a train of about two hundred people screaming threats and obscenities. Thoroughly confused, I reached the back gate of the Supreme Soviet. I saw a police major armed with an automatic rifle and ordered him to get the chief of security. The major passed the command onto a patrolman, and the patrolman started making phone calls.

The crowd kept on roaring until I barked at them, telling them what "brave warriors" they were—two hundred of them against the two of us. Things cooled down a little, and the major came back and reported that the chief of security was ready to meet with me in the reception room of the Supreme Soviet.

There, I met a police colonel, accompanied by a lieutenant colonel. The colonel's hands were shaking. He introduced his deputy and himself. He was the chief of security, Ivan Yakovle-vich Boiko. I introduced myself: "Deputy com-mander of the Airborne troops, Major General Lebed. I have a mission to use a single Airborne battalion to organize the security and defense of the Supreme Soviet Building. I arrived here to coordinate our actions."

> **"I** *explained to the protesters the battalion had come to take over security, but that the army was a child of its country and wouldn't shoot its people.***"**

The colonel began to babble something about not knowing the sit-uation completely and not having any control over it, and that he him-self had been denied access to certain sectors. Then he frowned and said: "You and your camouflage uniform, Comrade General, you'd better leave here!" The lieutenant colonel never said a word.

I asked for a telephone. I called Grachev and reported that my conversation with the chief of security had not gone well. The com-mander blew a fuse and barked: "Tell him to go f*** himself.... Find the battalion and carry out my order."

I said good-bye, left the reception area, and under a barrage of insults cut through the crowd toward the car. By that time the situa-tion at the barricades had changed quite a bit. Cranes, concrete blocks, and steel rods had appeared, and the number of the people had increased. I got in the UAZik and tried to get out. It was not to be. All the exits were already blocked off. I finally got through across the lawn to the staircase and drove down the steps to the embankment.

"Find the battalion!" That was easy to say, but all I knew was the general direction it would be coming from. I had no communication equipment on me. After an interminable series of twists and turns around dug-up narrow side streets and road blocks made of concrete slabs, I eventually got out to the Garden Ring road near Barrikadnaya Street. All the lanes were flooded with an unending—and unmoving—sea of cars. There was no way to get through.

I left my UAZik on a side street and entered the office of some organization dealing with environmental issues. I went up to the second floor and pushed the door of the office that was closest to me. A few women were working at their desks. I greeted them and politely asked for permission to use their phone. I reported to the chief of staff of the Airborne troops and asked: "Where is the battalion?" "Call back in fifteen minutes, I'll find out right away." I told the ladies that I would have to make another call in fifteen minutes, went out to the hallway, made myself comfortable on the couch, and started reading some old newspaper.

In five minutes or so, a tall male figure dressed in a white suit emerged in front of me, and, after an elegant introduction said, "Comrade General, I was told that you ordered us to clear the premises and leave our money and documents behind. How much time do we have to get everything together?" Later I realized that one of the women working in the office must have had a wicked sense of humor, but at that moment it pushed me over the limit. I had dealt with environmentalists before, and I suppose they are good folks, but I snapped at him so badly that he instantly disappeared.

In fifteen minutes I called back and was told to come to the headquarters of the Airborne troops. There were traffic jams everywhere, and I had to take many detours. When I finally arrived, the commander did not see me, but I was told: "Since another deputy commander of the Airborne troops, Major General Chindarov, has met the battalion and led it to Kalininsky Prospekt, you will return to the RSFSR Supreme Soviet building, find the battalion, and carry out your mission to protect the building."

I went back along Kalininsky Prospekt. The battalion wasn't there. I looked for it on the nearby side streets and finally found it at a construction site about 325 meters southeast of the Supreme Soviet building. The battalion was encircled by BMDs covering different directions, the same way the Zaporozhian Cossacks protected their camps. In the center of that relatively small space were columns of men, lined up by company, with drivers at their vehicles. Around them were piles of construction debris and some giant structures shaped like an upside-down letter U. I could read bewilderment and confusion on the faces of the men, who had no idea what was going on.

The old familiar crowd was raging nearby, ridiculing the soldiers and admonishing the officers. My appearance was met with a sigh of relief: "Here's the general, he'll explain everything." But I didn't know a goddamn thing!

I had to do something, so I climbed on a concrete block. The crowd turned on me. Some of them looked wary; others, full of hate. I made a short speech. I explained to them that the battalion had come to take over the security of the RSFSR Supreme Soviet building, that the situation was unclear, but that the army was a child of its country and would not shoot at its people. I asked them to calm down and not to stir up the situation unnecessarily. I refused to take any questions—I had no answers. I still didn't know what was going on. To this day, I cannot forget such a humiliating situation.

I ordered the men to set up camp and double the guards. As the men got to work, the crowd calmed down. I turned to the crowd with a request: "If any of you has access to the Supreme Soviet building, please call for a representative of the president or anyone else who can tell me what is going on."

There was a man in the crowd who had once served in the Airborne troops. His apartment was nearby, and we went there to make some phone calls. I reported the situation to the commander.

When I got back to the battalion, I found a delegation of five people—V.M. Portnov, A.V. Korzhakov, and V.I. Rykov among them. I was told President Yeltsin was waiting. I took Lieutenant Colonel Bastanov with me.

All the approaches to the building were already blocked off. Numerous barricades bristled with steel rods, pipes, and boards. Many more people had arrived. I visually estimated that there were seventy thousand to ninety thousand people there. We were taken behind the barricades along convoluted pathways known only to our escorts, walking in single file.

We got to entrance #24 and went up to the fourth floor to the office of State Councilor Yu. V. Skokov, who greeted us. Skokov told us about the State of Emergency, that Gorbachev was either seriously ill or had been arrested, and that President Yeltsin and the Supreme Soviet of the RSFSR had decided to offer fierce resistance to this anti-constitutional coup. When I was informed of the composition of the GKChP, I was amazed. How could these people "seize power"? They were the embodiment of power: the vice-president, the prime minister, the minister of defense, the minister of the interior, and the head of the KGB! But I remained quiet.

After filling me in, Skokov offered me some hot tea, left the room for a moment, and came back to say the president was ready to see me. We were shown into the office. The president was in his shirt-sleeves, and his white "diplomatic" bulletproof vest was hanging on the back of his chair. He shook hands and offered us seats. Skokov, Portnov, and Korzhakov went with us into the office. Yeltsin started asking questions.

"What is your mission?"

"To organize the defense of the Supreme Soviet building, using the forces of a single Airborne battalion."

"On whose order?"

"On the order of the commander of the Airborne troops, Lieutenant General Grachev."

"To protect and defend it from whom?"

I answered him evasively:

"Against any person or group of people who threaten it."

The president was satisfied, and he expressed his concern for Gorbachev's fate. Then he began to ask me about the armed forces' reaction to the coup. I told him that there was no reaction, because they didn't know about it. Yeltsin said nothing, but this clearly amazed and even irritated him.

But finally he said that he believed me and saw no reason to impede the redeployment of the battalion.

I explained that there was virtually no way to bring the battalion in. I had already tried to argue with that crowd. The smallest spark could lead to a powerful explosion. A burst from an automatic rifle—from the crowd at the battalion, or from the battalion at the crowd, it wouldn't matter—would leave a pile of corpses. There would be nothing left to explain.

There was only one solution: for Yeltsin to introduce me to the leaders of the barricades and order them to help us get through the barricades and take up defensive positions.

Yeltsin agreed with my plan and ordered that the leaders of the barricades be summoned.

In about an hour, the barricade commanders—about forty men wearing headbands and armbands—were seated at a long table in a small conference room. I sat on a chair by the wall.

In a few minutes, the president walked in. He greeted everyone, thanked them for their courage, and announced that an Airborne battalion, under the command of General Lebed, had gone over to the side of the people. He introduced me, told them what they had to do, and suggested that they get started. I demanded that a couple of the more authoritative leaders explain to the crowd what was going on. Meanwhile, I would go back to the battalion and give the order to form into a column.

Yeltsin asked Korzhakov: "Why must the general walk across the square alone? See to it." Korzhakov saw to it, and I was given two bodyguards: one was Russian, the other was either Chinese or Korean.

When the people at the barricades learned that the battalion was officially on their side, there was a gush of euphoria.

The battalion and the reconnaissance company attached to it started moving. The plan was simple. Each of the four companies would cover one side of the building. We had to come up from the embankment, cross Kalininsky Prospekt to the right of the former headquarters of the Council of Mutual Economic Assistance, pass in a wide arc around the right corner of the Supreme Soviet building, climb up onto the platform, and concentrate around the building. A path was left between the barricades for us to do that.

I walked in front of the first vehicle, and the crowd roared in triumph. Their enthusiasm only made things harder. Either they all rushed at once to roll away a big pipe that was blocking the way, and crushed someone as a result, or they couldn't cope with the thirty-nine-meter bars, and in knocking one board out of the way, made all the rest of them fall down. The battalion was moved at a snail's pace.

The lead company rounded the turn and mounted the platform, proceeding along the facade on the far side of the building, moving into defensive positions.

But a serious incident took place with the second company. The one at fault was people's deputy of the RSFSR and the USSR, Colonel Tsalko. We had met each other at the 28th Congress of the CPSU. He noticed me, and rushed off to greet me. The "Chinaman," who had been trained to cut off any sharp movements, reacted instantly: he took the little Tsalko by the collar and the seat of his pants and threw him aside. Tsalko picked himself up, crawled into the crowd, and shouted "Provocation! Provocation!"

I had no idea that he was talking about me and paid little attention. But I should have! Not three minutes had passed before movement stopped completely. About two hundred people blocked each vehicle. I got up onto the front of one of the BMDs and saw the scared face of the driver.

I tried to explain to the crowd, but their reaction was strange: they frowned. If you pushed them away, they wouldn't resist, but they didn't move away either. I ran up onto the platform and looked down at the whole picture. People were blocking every single vehicle. The battalion stood, stretched all the way around the arc. Since I could do nothing there, I went into the Supreme Soviet building.

There were about ten people in Skokov's office—Korzhakov, Portnov, Rykov, Colonel General Kobets, and a few others. I asked them to look out the window and explain what was going on. They looked. From the height of the fourth floor, it was especially impressive.

That's when I remembered the episode with Tsalko and his cries of "Provocation!" Clearly that was the key to the riddle. They called for Tsalko, who confirmed what I said.

I asked Korzhakov: "Aleksandr Vasilievich, were you the one who gave me the Chinaman as a bodyguard?"

"Yes, I was."

I turned to Tsalko: "Who threw you aside?"

"The Chinaman."

I summed up: "Korzhakov's Chinaman threw aside People's Deputy Tsalko. What do I and my subordinates have to do with this?"

It was a purely rhetorical question. Everyone sat there quietly, thinking.

"We've got to get the column moving again," I suggested. "Who will come out with me onto the square and clear up this misunderstanding?"

Again they paused, deep in thought. I turned to K.I. Kobets:

"Comrade Colonel General, you're the senior officer here, make a decision!"

"Cool down! Wait a minute! Let's think about this."

After thinking a little longer, Konstantin Ivanovich suddenly said:

"Ah, we have Litvinov here. He's a people's deputy, a paratrooper, and a lieutenant colonel. Bring Litvinov in to me."

They summoned Litvinov. Kobets ordered him to go with me to clear up the misunderstanding.

I knew Litvinov well. When I was commanding the Kostroma regiment, he was one of my company commanders. I had appointed him the regiment's chief intelligence officer, and promoted him to major. Now, he was a lieutenant colonel.

I said that Litvinov alone wouldn't be enough—he wasn't well enough known as a people's deputy. Again, deep silence reigned.

"Since Tsalko was the one who caused all this mess," I proposed, "let him be the one who comes with me!"

They agreed immediately, and sent for Tsalko again. He came, but without his deputy's pin on his lapel. I said that it wouldn't have the same effect without his pin. Tsalko went back to get it, and in the meantime, Rutskoi appeared and said from the doorway that there was no reason to bring vehicles in under the walls.

"Put part of your vehicles on the embankment, and the rest—over there!" He gestured vaguely toward the window.

"Either I deploy my vehicles the way I personally agreed with the president or I will send them back where they came from," I objected.

Aleksandr Vladimirovich reminded me that he was the vice-president and I was only a deputy commander. We argued a bit. It ended with Rutskoi and Skokov going off to settle the matter with the president.

About forty minutes later, Skokov returned and announced that the president had backed the vice president's decision, and I went off with my team to move the vehicles according to the new plan.

It probably looked quite funny from the outside. Tsalko went up to the nearest vehicle, raised his deputy's pin, and shouted: "Comrades, I am People's Deputy Tsalko. There has been a misunderstanding. I ask you to let the machine pass. Let General Lebed and Colonel Litvinov deploy them, according to plan!" Tsalko was short, and his voice was weak; the crowd showed no reaction.

Finally, Litvinov and I decided to resolve the matter another way. We got up onto the front of the two nearest vehicles and told the drivers, "Start your engines! Move out, with all the people riding on you!" The vehicles, with people on top of them, began to move slowly. The BMDs inched forward, and the crowd accompanied them.

It was getting dark. Leading the first vehicle to its assigned position, I said that for at least today, it would stay put. Persuaded that we had no aggressive intentions, the people let the rest of the vehicles through, and I put all the BMDs in position and organized sentry posts.

Colonel Kolmakov, the division commander, arrived at the Supreme Soviet building and reported that one of the battalions had tried to defend the Moscow Soviet building, but due to the escalating situation, had moved off toward Dinamo Stadium. Another battalion was at the Ostankino television and radio station.

> **"I** *returned to Achlov's office. I later found out that the media had spread the rumor I had shot myself."*

I reported to the commander who said: "Make sure that the security and defense of the Supreme Soviet building has been organized properly, go to Dinamo Stadium and Ostankino and check that everything is all right. Then go to Tushino." So I did.

I was in Tushino, as ordered, when the phone rang at 0550. It was the commander. He began curtly:

"What have you done? Where did you put the battalion?"

"What do you mean where? I put it in front of the RSFSR Supreme Soviet building, on your orders."

"You misunderstood me."

I went nuts: "Comrade Commander, all my directives, instructions, and orders are written down by three operators and put in my operations log."

My experience, after numerous investigations, had taught me long before to document every order I received. The commander changed his tone a little: "Well, don't get upset! You just got a little confused, that's all! By the way, the chief's upset."

"What chief?"

"What do you mean 'what chief'! The minister, that's who! Remember, you just got a little confused. You put that battalion there; now go and get it back."

I hung up the receiver and thought about it. Like any normal person with some character and pride, I didn't like being anyone's puppet. And I had spent a whole day rushing about, cursing, squabbling, dealing with conflicts and obeying orders, whose purpose was still an enigma.

But orders are orders. At 0800 I was at the Supreme Soviet again. I walked into Skokov's office and told him that I had received an order to pull out the battalion. Yuri Vladimirovich took the news calmly, although he regretted our departure. By 1100 hours the column was moving toward Leningradsky Prospekt. People were throwing candy, cookies, and ten-ruble banknotes into the hatches of the combat vehicles.

After making sure that all the vehicles had cleared the passage in the last barricade, I discovered that my UAZik had disappeared. I took a quick walk around a couple of blocks and found it squeezed by a fire engine.

A liaison officer found me there and told me to appear by 1345 hours at the General Staff building in the office of the deputy defense minister, Colonel General Achalov.

Suddenly, I was attacked by a crowd of journalists throwing questions at me: "Where did you take the battalion, and why?" "Why are you withdrawing?" "Who are you?" and so forth. They were persistent and aggressive. The situation was grim, but I choked with laughter. Where did I take them, why was I withdrawing them—who the hell knows! But I couldn't tell them that.

I brushed away the journalists and went to the General Staff. In the fifth floor reception room of Achalov's office, I met the commander of the Airborne troops, Lieutenant General Grachev. He asked me to step into an adjacent room for a talk.

"Are you ready?" he asked.

"Yes, I'm ready."

I am always ready, but it would be nice to know what I was supposed to be ready for.

"Well, then, hang on!"

A lieutenant colonel burst into the room and announced, "The Defense Minister wants to see Major General Lebed!"

I followed him through long corridors to the minister's office. The adjutant announced me, and I presented myself. The minister stared at me for a few seconds and said, "I got a report that you shot yourself!"

"I see no reason to have done that, Comrade Minister."

The minister exploded. He gave a graphic opinion of the mental abilities of his intelligence officers and gave me permission to leave.

I returned to the reception room of Achalov's office. Grachev was not there. An adjutant passed on the instruction to wait. I later found out that the mass media had spread the rumor that I had shot myself. Jumping ahead, a new story reported on the twenty-first that I had been held hostage by the defenders of the White House (another name for the Supreme Soviet building). It didn't seem to bother anybody very much that I had committed suicide just the day before.

After fifteen minutes, I was invited in. Twenty or so people were sitting at a long table. Colonel General Vladislav Alekseevich Achalov was pacing back and forth around the room. He invited me to go to the head of the table and take his seat. The first person on my left was General Valentin Ivanovich Varennikov, on the right at the end of the table sat Grachev, looking disheveled, Colonel General B.V. Gromov, the commander of the "Alpha" group, Major General V.F. Karpukhin, and other people, some in uniform, some in civilian clothes.

I don't know what they had been talking about before, but as soon as I appeared Grachev jumped up and said, "Here's General Lebed. He spent quite some time near the walls of the Supreme Soviet building—let him brief us."

I reported that there were about one hundred thousand people at the Supreme Soviet building and that the approaches to the building were fortified by numerous barricades. There was a well-armed security guard unit inside the building. Any use of force would lead to great bloodshed. That last remark was pure intuition, since I supposed this would be the main issue.

Valentin Ivanovich interrupted me. Flashing his glasses at me contemptuously, he said, "General, you are full of pessimism and uncertainty." I had always respected Varennikov—a Hero of the Soviet Union, winner of nine combat decorations. But at that moment, the contemptuous flash of his glasses rubbed me the wrong way.

I had been taught by some pretty smart people, and they considered it an indisputable truth that you had to report the situation the way it really was, and not the way someone wanted to hear it. That was the only way that the right decision could be made.

After pacing around a little more, Achalov closed the meeting. At Achalov's order Major General Karpukhin, Lieutenant General Golovnev, and I stayed behind.

Achalov turned to the three of us and suggested that we reconnoiter the approaches to the Supreme Soviet building. It was a suggestion, not an order, which was very strange—not at all like Achalov. When Vladislav Alekseevich had been in charge of the Airborne troops, I had been the commander of his "favorite" Tula division and knew him to be cruel, overbearing, and self-confident.

We went downstairs, got in Karpukhin's car, and drove off. It was a weird reconnaissance mission. The driver was dressed in plain clothes, and I wore camouflage, as did Karpukhin, but without any shoulderboards. Golovnev had an everyday uniform on. I didn't understand who we would be fighting against or why, and that made me mad. Golovnev was quiet. Karpukhin was ranting.

We drove around the Supreme Soviet building, constantly bumping into pits, barricades, and concrete blocks. We crossed over to the other side of the Moscow river. We got out, had a smoke, and enjoyed the view of the Supreme Soviet building, bristling with logs and steel rods. Then we exchanged glances, got in the car, and went back to report.

Everything was clear and, at the same time, nothing was clear at all. From the purely military point of view, it would not be hard to seize the building, although as I pointed out previously, at the cost of much bloodshed. Later on, I had to testify at the hearings of one of the parliamentary commissions. They asked me:

"Comrade General, could you have taken the White House?"

I answered confidently, "Of course."

"How? We had defenders, we had barricades...."

"Look at the walls around here."

"Yes, they're beautiful, aren't they? What about them?"

"They're beautiful, but they're finished with wood paneling. You also have a very beautiful plastic drop ceiling. Parquet floors. Carpets. Plush furniture...."

"Get to the point!"

"That *is* the point. Say that twenty or thirty anti-tank guided missiles were fired at the building from two different directions. Once all this beauty starts to burn, or even worse, to smoke, and all the polish, varnish, paint, wool, and synthetics start melting, all I'd have to do is pull the riflemen closer and wait until the people inside started jumping out the windows. The lucky ones would be jumping from the second floor, the unlucky ones—from the fourteenth."

They thought a little bit and agreed.

So, this point was clear. But something else was unclear—why the hell did we have to do this?

We returned to the General Staff and briefed Achalov. When Karpukhin and Golovnev left, Achalov held me back.

"Could you draft a plan to blockade the Supreme Soviet building?"

I rarely get emotional, but his words made my eyes pop out.

"Well, I'll be damned! The battle has been in full swing for two days, and now they realize they need a plan? All right, let's do it by the book. What are the resources available, sir?"

Achalov was about to blast me, but realized that it would really be impossible to draft a plan without any knowledge of the available resources. He informed me that the operation would involve the Dzerzhinsky division, the Tula Airborne Division, the Teply Stan brigade, and the Alpha group. I drafted the plan in five minutes, right there, on a large-scale map with a dull pencil. I assigned the sealing off of the facade and the right side of the building to the Dzerzhinsky division, and the left and rear sides to the Tula division. I positioned Alpha behind the Dzerzhinsky division and designated the Teply Stan special forces brigade and part of the Tula division as the reserve.

Vladislav Alekseevich, that magnificent Vladislav Alekseevich, who had always demanded accuracy and neatness when working with maps, just looked absent-mindedly at the plan I had scribbled down and approved it.

"Good. I'll call Gromov right now. Go coordinate the plan with him."

While he was dialing, I folded the map and stuck it in my pocket, and a few minutes later another deputy commander, General Chindarov, and I were zooming in Achalov's car to the Interior Ministry. In the back of my mind I kept wondering—I had done a lot of planning in my life, but I had never managed to come up with such a unique plan in such a short time.

The chief of staff of the Internal troops, Lieutenant General Dubinyak, was in Gromov's office. Gromov looked at the plan for a minute or two and said it was good. I had never served with Gromov, but all the officers who knew him said that he was a competent, scrupulous, and extremely secretive person. All his operations in Afghanistan had been carefully planned by a limited number of individuals. If it were possible to announce the mission only fifteen seconds before its implementation, that's when General Gromov would announce it—not twenty, not eighteen, but precisely fifteen seconds in advance. And now this man had just approved my scribbled plan and ordered Dubinyak to coordinate his activities with us.

Dubinyak barely glanced at the map and said, "Everything is clear. We'll be there on time."

Chindarov and I simultaneously let out a trial balloon: "And what about the chart of the code names for the executive officers and the signaling system for troops control and interaction?"

Dubinyak's response was rather strange: "I don't have it with me. But it doesn't matter! You leave us your phone number, and we will call you and tell you."

After looking at each other, we decided to leave him in peace. That was *just* the sort of information we could pass on over the public phone lines in a situation like this!

We returned to the General Staff, reported on the completion of our mission, and were dismissed. From a military man's standpoint, something unimaginable and absurd was taking place.

We arrived at headquarters and reported to the commander. Chindarov was dispatched immediately for the division in Tushino. I stayed behind. I told the commander just what I thought of this madness, which I was taking part in against my will. There had to be something behind this scheme, because if we really did what I was being ordered to do, we were nothing but a bunch of idiots. I finished:

"Comrade Commander, put your cards on the table! I don't play these kinds of games! You know that I am always ready to carry out any order, but I need to understand the reason behind it. I don't make a good puppet, and I refuse to start waging a war that I can't comprehend in the middle of our nation's capital, a war which in essence would be a civil war. Any use of force on the approaches to the Supreme Soviet building would lead to mass bloodshed. And you can report that up the chain of command."

The commander beamed at me:

"I can see that I taught you well, Aleksandr Ivanovich! I have always trusted you, and it's great to see that I was not mistaken. Let's do it like this: you, personally, drive to the Supreme Soviet and find a way to let the defenders know that the siege and, possibly, the assault will start at 0300 hours. Then, go to Medvezhie Ozyora and arrange for the arrival of two regiments from the Bolgrad Division."

But that was not at all to my liking. I was in an ambiguous position. I was the author of the siege plan, which I had personally coordinated with two deputy defense ministers, even though I had felt that we were playing some idiotic game. Just like the theater of the absurd! And now I had to go and betray my own plan. What the hell!

Moreover, I didn't understand the second part of the assignment. I had to ask, "Should I go to Chkalovsk airfield and receive the regiments there?"

"No, you'll be directing the process from the office of the commander of the communications brigade."

I took the license plates off my UAZik, and my driver and I took off our striped undershirts and removed all distinguishing marks from our uniforms.

Outside the Supreme Soviet building, I fished the most trustworthy folks out of the crowd, passed the information to them, and requested that Skokov or Korzhakov be notified. I gave them not 0300 hours, but 0200 as the zero hour, the so-called "corporal's margin of error." Figuring that at least two of the three messengers would deliver the information, I left for Medvezhie Ozyora.

Total chaos was brewing there as well. The most important thing was that even from the brigade commander's office, I could see that there was a major mix-up at the Chkalovsk and Kubinka airfields. The Bolgrad division had enough experience to be able to land just about anywhere, but their airplanes were falling behind schedule, taking off in the wrong order, and landing at the wrong airfields. The units of the regiments were mixed up, and their unit coordination impaired. The division commander landed in Kubinka instead of Chkalovsk. And behind all this disorder, I could sense someone's strong organizational will.

Grachev called me a little after midnight: "Get back here, on the double!" I came back. The commander was wound up. Karpukhin called and said that Alpha would not be taking part either in the siege or in the assault. The situation with the Dzerzhinsky division was unclear; it looked as if their vehicles were coming, but it had not been confirmed. He suggested that I call to the division's checkpoint and find out what was going on. A sergeant answered in a sleepy voice: "Vehicles? What vehicles? They're all right here. Nobody's gone anywhere!"

Suddenly, it was clear. The Dzerzhinsky division hadn't moved. The Tula division hadn't budged either. And the Teply Stan Special Forces brigade had disappeared altogether. I couldn't find it through any channels of command communications.

Grachev was nervously pacing around his office and saying something, but I was too tired to hear him. I asked him for permission to leave and rest. I told him that I would be in my office. Without taking off my clothes, I lay down on the couch and fell into a deep sleep, like a bottomless pit.

I leaped up off the couch at 0600 to find that blood had after all been shed—three persons had been killed. I had not been a witness to those events, but later I had to deal with some who had, as well as some of the participants in the tragedy.

The picture was more or less as follows. On the order to patrol the streets given by the Chief of the Military District, General Kalinin, an army company was moving along the Garden Ring Road in BMPs (infantry fighting vehicles). Eighteen to twenty year olds were sitting in these vehicles, and if their generals didn't know what was going on, how could they be expected to make heads or tails of it?

The company entered the tunnel under Kalininsky Prospekt, leaving the Supreme Soviet building behind them, on the right.

There is a saying that you can get a failing grade in tactics for three things: delivering a nuclear strike on your own troops, going through a river instead of across it, and "advancing" in the opposite direction from the enemy. Considering that the company was supposed to be advancing on the Supreme Soviet, the moment it hit the tunnel it had earned a failing grade.

Any tunnel, moreover, is a trap for a military column, whether of tanks or trucks. The company commander could not help knowing that. The company entered the tunnel because it was moving on its own turf, had no intention of attacking, and the officers and soldiers were naive enough to think that there was nothing to fear.

They were wrong. The "New Russian Revolution" needed some sacrificial blood. The tunnel's exit was blocked by motor vehicles, and the column barraged by sticks and stones and Molotov cocktails coming from the side ramps. When some people tried to seize a BMP, warning machine gun shots were fired.

> **"The Soviet Union no longer exists. Those who do not regret its disintegration have no heart, and those think it can be restored have no brains."**

Those shots accidentally struck down three victims. But the troops had to act quickly. An infantry fighting vehicle was set on fire by a Molotov cocktail. A nineteen-year-old boy, a sergeant, under a hail of sticks, rocks, and insults, acted like a real man and a true commander. He led his crew out of the blazing vehicle, turned on the fire-extinguishing system, and organized an effort to quell the fire. There was a full combat kit inside the vehicle: forty rounds for the turret gun, five guided anti-tank missiles, and four thousand rounds of ammunition. If he had lost control and let the fire spread, the vehicle would most likely have blown up and caused havoc.

I have seen what happens when a vehicle blows up with a full supply of ammunition inside it. Its mutilated turret ends up lying about 160 feet away; the rest of it looks like a giant tulip opened up by an inhuman force. The crew just evaporates. You'd be lucky if you found a piece of a boot with the owner's heel still inside it. The earth would be scorched dead for a 150- to 250-foot radius, and for triple that area, tree branches and buildings would be damaged by the fragments. If this had happened here, in the center of Moscow, the windows in the entire neighborhood would have been shattered. Not 3, but 303, or maybe 1,333 people would have paid with their lives for that thought-less and unprovoked aggression. We should thank that young sergeant. We should thank God for people with common sense, for putting a stop to this high-handed behavior toward soldiers who were guilty of nothing.

And I must give credit to the courageous woman investigator who later took charge of the case. I don't know her name, but she was able to rise above the hysteria and opportunism and conduct an unbiased investigation of the accident, and exonerate the soldiers.

As a human being, I am sorry that lives were lost. May they find their way to Heaven, and may their souls rest in peace. But the fact that they became the last Heroes of the Soviet Union, the last in that country's history, being awarded the title posthumously from the hands of the people who were getting ready to liquidate the Soviet Union, sounds more and more blasphemous with each passing day and month.

The drama's finale came on August 21. The pitiful coup attempt failed miserably. In the afternoon, Russian President B.N. Yeltsin said: "I express my heartfelt appreciation to Major General Lebed, who, together with his men, prevented the putschists from seizing the polit-ical center of new Russia."

Gorbachev was discovered unharmed and now safe, and the arrest of the members of the GKChP followed. An investigation was launched immediately—even prematurely, because investigations shouldn't be conducted until passions have cooled. Emotion must not replace reason.

I testified at the hearings of three parliamentary commissions and talked to a great number of investigators. There were sensible people among them, but there were also intolerant fools who were fixated on one thing: "How could you obey criminal orders?"

I would answer: "In any army worthy of the name, orders are not questioned, but obeyed according to regulations, precisely, implicitly, and on time. On orders, I brought the division to Moscow, and on orders I withdrew it again. I didn't kill or wound anybody; I didn't insult a single Muscovite. We didn't fire a single shot, or even cause a single traffic accident. Any complaints?"

I retained the rank of major general and my position as deputy commander of the Airborne troops for combat training.

Like a log cabin eaten away by termites, the Soviet Union was eroded by the triple immorality of thinking one thing, saying another, and doing something else. And now, the Soviet Union no longer exists. Those who do not regret its disintegration have no heart, and those who think that it can be restored in its original form have no brains. But there is something to regret: there is a *big* difference between being a citizen of a Great Power, with many shortcomings, and being the citizen of an emaciated "developing" country.

But Russia is still here, and the same termites are still inside her. Our Party elite, our peerless leaders, have become stronger as the result of many years of selective breeding, and they have learned to be resilient and keep their noses to the wind. It seemed that we were all on the way to a bright future together, but as soon as the wind started blowing in a different direction, they, our leaders from the *nomenklatura*, were smart enough to lag behind a little, throw their Party cards in the trash, and hoist democratic banners. Once again, they were ahead of everyone, leading us now to a no less brighter future— this time a capitalist one.

Is there a single known case, during the August spectacle-putsch, in which the secretary of some Party committee stood, gun in hand, like Salvador Allende, to defend the government which had brought him up and nurtured him? No. Everyone retreated calmly to his previously prepared commercial and political position. And once again everyone is fat and happy.

Look around you and see who's in power. Yes, you recognize all the faces. Until recently, many of them stared down at you from posters with the caption: "The Politburo of the Central Committee of the CPSU." True, there's something in the Bible about people who "betray twice," but not everyone can understand the Bible. If they did something wrong, they will get paid for it in the next world. With hot coals.

And what happened to the repeatedly praised community of people called the "Soviet people"? Where were they looking when their beloved country was being torn apart right in front of them? I cannot answer for everyone, but it isn't hard to guess. When the tension near the walls of the White House was at its peak, there were no more than one hundred thousand people there—only 1 percent of the population of the hero city of Moscow. What were the other 99 percent doing? They were feverishly buying up macaroni and pretending that nothing was going on. Was there another crowd standing under red banners somewhere close, itching to enter the fight? By the time of the spectacle's denouement, there was nothing left but an enormous crowd, not united by any idea that rose above ethnic preoccupations with nothing in common, most of whom were thinking "how can I survive," while the rest were looking for a way to profit from the chaos.

Sometimes, when you open a nut, it's empty—or, more accurately, not exactly empty. There's a fat, insolent worm sitting inside grinning at you and asking, "Makes you mad, doesn't it?"

So are we really a nation of fools? Could it be that there are intelligent and courageous individuals among us, but that in the aggregate, we are a foolish nation? Perhaps the Russian poet Vladimir Semenovich Vysotsky was right when he wrote this ringing line: "The whole history of our country is the history of an illness." Is that a diagnosis? Or the normal condition of our heart and soul?

CHAPTER 21:
IN A TAILSPIN

The troops, who still didn't completely understand what they had taken part in, returned to their permanent bases. The soldiers and officers were given a hero's welcome. They shook their heads, trying to figure out what they had done that was so heroic, but accepted the praise and gifts. In Tula, and especially in Ryazan, there were souvenirs and flowers by the truckload. Democratic euphoria reigned in the cities.

Returning to Tula, I was immediately plunged into this ocean of joy. I was congratulated, hugged, and thanked. I was even asked to autograph the official flag of the RSFSR that was, apparently, going to be displayed in a museum and dedicated, I assume, to the Second Russian Revolution. People made joyful plans about who needed to be thrown out from where and what organizations had to be closed. The radical democratic citizens did not even rule out the possibility of arrests. Buzzing like honeybees loaded with nectar, volunteer and professional spies of all kinds were swarming in from different directions.

"So-and-so drove off in the evening with two boxes in the back of his UAZik. You've got to investigate this!"

"What's-his-name left work carrying something huge in his briefcase!"

"They've got to be hiding something in that garage!"

"I really lit into him! I told him that we've had enough of him trying to lord it over us!"

There was something dirty about it all. A mile away one could smell the stool pigeons ready to settle personal accounts. I was not happy. I refused all honors and gifts. I did not allow people to take pictures of me. I signed no autographs. I didn't care what they thought of me.

I was tormented by the sense that something big and important had just passed me by, and that I hadn't seen it, hadn't understood it, and now it was too late to figure it out. That made me envy those who did understand, and I felt terribly irritated with them, too.

On August 23, 1991, a rally was held in front of the balcony of what was now the "former" Tula Oblast Committee of the CPSU. I was invited to attend. Against all expectations there were only about three thousand people, but most of them were cheerful and excited. A priest ceremonially blessed an enormous new Russian flag. Accompanied by the new Russian anthem, it was hoisted on the staff over the Obkom building.

The speakers talked about the hateful regime that had finally fallen, they spoke of freedom and a new era, and in general they rang with the age-old Russian motif of retribution. Such jabs were greeted with exclamations of approval from the audience; some cried, others spat, and still others waved their fists, threatening God knows whom.

Then they gave me the floor. After citing Plato, who was so dear to my heart, I spoke briefly and quite harshly about how we mustn't get drunk with our new-found freedom and give way to the old Russian habit of slipping from one extreme to the other. I called on them not to tolerate the reprisals that everyone had been hinting at, and to be calm and restrained. If someone was guilty of something, that was for the courts, and not the crowd, to decide.

My speech was not well received. Tula's democrats quickly lost interest in me.

Nevertheless, from the moment of my return on August 22, reporters of all sorts harassed me. They ambushed me in front of my home, next to division headquarters, any and all places. They called me on the phone, and the more I brushed them off, the more persistent they became. At last, I blew up and announced that I would answer all their questions on August 24 at 0400 at division headquarters. About twenty-five people gathered at the designated time.

The press conference could be divided into three acts. In the first act, the reporters tried to congratulate me with questions: "Wasn't it great, General, that you defended our democracy at such a critical time?"

I got up and explained that I was not a democrat and that I couldn't care less about democracy. It was not democracy that I had been defending; it was common sense. "I am a Russian general, and there is nothing that can make me shoot at the Russian people."

Disappointed, the reporters went on to act two. Its main theme was: "Wasn't it great that that darling General Lebed switched over to the side of an even bigger darling, General Rutskoi?" Here, I tactlessly said that all Soviet generals were brought up in roughly the same way, and that Rutskoi was just as much of an army hard-ass as I was. Making "the people" stand at attention was all he knew about democracy.

The essence of act three could be formulated as: "Well, well. We thought you were different."

There was no need for an epilogue. I do not know what they had expected, but they left hurt, angry, and disappointed.

In the meantime, the number of defenders of the White House was growing at an extraordinary rate. According to my calculations, when the tension was at its peak, there could not have been more than a hundred thousand people there; now the count ran into the millions—ten thousand doctors alone! They called the defense "heroic," but it could have been heroic only if there had been an attack on the White House, and there hadn't been. People *had* been ready to defend the White House, but there was no attack.

I was invited to go on a live broadcast of "Good Evening, Moscow!" The program's host, Boris Notkin, told me what he would be asking me and suggested how my answers should go. I nodded in agreement.

When the show started, Boris spoke in an impassioned tone, getting more and more heated, "So, when I heard that General Lebed's troops crossed over to the side of the people's uprising, tears of joy came to my eyes." He finished with the question, "How does it feel to be the defender of the White House?"

I spilled out all the rancor that had accumulated inside of me: "As we now know from history, about three thousand people helped Vladimir Ilyich Lenin carry that log on that famous *subbotnik*.[1] Now there are more than three million defenders of the White House. Since I am afraid of getting lost in this vast heroic crowd, I hereby officially renounce my status as 'Defender of the White House.'" For the rest of the live broadcast, Boris tried to tone down my appalling tactlessness.

I was appointed to the Government Commission of the Reform of Political Organs (in the Armed Forces).

But by the third session I was told my further participation in the commission's work was not recommended. I didn't try to find out who was behind my removal. It just made me love democracy even more. This was a true example of democracy, army-style. They tell you to go to hell, and you go wherever you like!

Getting kicked off that learned commission didn't bother me much. I soon found other work. The former union republics declared their sovereignty, one after another. After all, Boris Nikolaevich Yeltsin had told them, "Take as much sovereignty as you wish!" And they

---

[1] A *subbotnik* is an event in which people "volunteer" their time on a Saturday for some public clean-up project. The *subbotnik* to which Lebed is referring was the first of that tradition. There is a famous picture, taken on that day, of Lenin helping someone carry a log.

weren't shy; they took it. Moreover, each union republic claimed as an essential attribute of sovereignty all Soviet army units stationed in its territory. They grabbed anything they could get their hands on whether they needed it or not; they'd sort it out later.

A group of negotiators was quickly formed, led by USSR Deputy Defense Minister Colonel General B.E. Pyankov. It was made up of representatives of all branches and services of the armed forces. I represented the Airborne troops.

In this "diplomatic" capacity, I repeatedly participated in talks in Kiev, Vilnius, Minsk, and Kishinev. The Belorussians were the most civilized. Belarus was perhaps the only republic where logical argument, common sense, and feasibility held some weight. I would give second place to the Lithuanians (close to the Belorussians, but with subtle nuances).

The Ukrainians would come in third, but they were peculiar. During the breaks, we were all friends and brothers; there were jokes, laughter, we all smoked and spat[2] together. But as soon as we sat down at the negotiating table, under the watchful eye of the "democratic political commissars," we put on our official masks and that was the end of it—we were worlds apart. At the next break, we'd have jokes and laughter again.

The most outrageous diplomat I had to deal with was the defense minister of Moldova, General Costas. You can't call it "negotiations" when seven out of every ten words a negotiator uses are obscene. There is a different word for that. We were talking about the 300th Airborne Regiment, which was deployed in Kishinev and commanded by my brother, Colonel Aleksei Ivanovich Lebed.

"I'm taking the regiment!" Costas said.

"How can you take it when 96 percent of the regiment doesn't wish to be taken?"

---

[2] Coarse, unfiltered Russian cigarettes often leave tobacco particles in the mouth, making spitting part of smoking.

"It's on our territory, and that means it's ours! We'll block off all the exits with concrete slabs."

"Even if you block it off, that won't make it yours."

"Then we'll seize it!"

"Listen! We're talking about a regiment here! A re-gi-ment. It'll be just like in the old Russian fable: 'I've caught a bear.' 'Well, bring it here.' 'He won't come!' 'Well, then come here yourself!' 'He won't let me go!'"

This was the end of the relatively printable part of the negotiations; the high-level negotiating parties moved on to a "more elegant style." In short, God had sent me a real pig to deal with, and I apologize to pigs for making this comparison. General Costas was a short, twitching, nationalistic little man. He was like a frog, trying to puff itself up to look like an ox. He tried to compensate for his lack of education and good breeding with the strength of his voice and his revolutionary fervor.

My "diplomatic activity" led to one more responsibility: to check out the proposed new bases for the Airborne units withdrawn from what were now called the countries of the "near abroad." So I took an Antonov-12 transport plane, loaded with three UAZiks, ten barrels of gas, a hundred dry rations, and thirteen or fifteen officers from the headquarters of the Airborne troops, and off we went to investigate potential new bases for four divisions and one detached regiment.

Because of my various "diplomatic" activities, the only thing that I had time to do along my direct line of responsibilities was to give a graduation exam at the Airborne troops' 242nd training center in Lithuania.

Spring 1992. Free Lithuania. There was an "occupation" training center on its free territory. The Lithuanians were setting up checkpoints on the highways, or they were accusing us of selling concrete slabs belonging to their airfield on the black market, or posting complaints about our alleged environmental violations. Whatever they did, they did in a cultured, polite, and calm manner.

Their "home guard" set up a checkpoint at the entrance to the airfield. That didn't bother us; let it stay there. But for some reason they decided to dig trenches across from our positions. They were poor excuses for trenches, but nevertheless, they were trenches.

I ordered the deputy director of the training center, Colonel Gladyshev, to set up a model entrenched position for a single squad one hundred meters from the Lithuanian positions. I told him to do it by the book, leaving enough space for a BMD in the trenches, and to have the whole thing sodded and camouflaged. We'd give our Lithuanian brothers a little lesson in army engineering.

They didn't come for the lesson, but when they passed by, they drew the appropriate conclusions and filled in their trenches. So we filled ours in as well.

On June 19, 1992, the armed conflict in Transdniester broke out with renewed force. Hundreds of people were killed, thousands wounded, and tens of thousands made refugees. On June 23 I took off for Tiraspol under the name of "Colonel Gusev" with an Airborne Special Forces battalion to make me look more authoritative.

CHAPTER 22:
WHY AM I MAD ABOUT
OUR GREAT POWER'S FATE?

TRANSDNIESTER, 1992: it has a special place in my heart—"a land which I fought for, and nursed back to health." When it comes to Transdniester, I would either have to write about it in detail or not write about it at all. At this point, my disappointment is still too great. Perhaps someday I will write about those who were courageous in battle, but helpless before insolent scoundrels at home. I could write about how good people were played off against one another for selfish political interests, and about how the human urge for freedom is being shamelessly exploited to create a little principality, where the wildest excesses reign supreme. Perhaps. But not now.

Now I want to write about what has happened to our country, and to come to some conclusions.

I was born on Russian soil, and I shall die here. As the poet Anna Akhmatova once wrote:

We are not laid in Russian soil; we become part of it,
And that is why we are so bold as to call it our own.

There is nowhere, and no reason, for me to run from this land; my children and my grandchildren will live here, and I am far from indifferent to its fate. Russia is a great nation, and we have nowhere left to retreat; where we are standing now is our own Kulikovo Field.[1]

In their gigantic labors over the past thousand years, the people who have created Russia have rested on three great foundations: the spiritual might of the Orthodox Church, the creative genius of the Russian people, and the valor of the Russian army.

> **"I** *was born on Russian soil, and I shall die here. A Russian poet once wrote: 'We are not laid in Russian soil; we become part of it.'* **"**

People who had forgotten where they came from began to shake the first of these foundations on a national level immediately after the 1917 revolution. They completed their diabolical work in the 1930s by blowing up thousands of churches, burying their Motherland's spirituality beneath their rubble, driving it underground for decades, and trying to turn it into something shameful and unworthy.

The repression of the second foundation—the people's creative genius—was completed at the end of the thirties, when everyone "able to make up his own mind" was either put up against the wall and shot or sent to frigid outlands not far from the North Pole. The rest were bent down and leveled.

They tried to destroy the third pillar of this great power—the army—and even succeeded to a certain extent, but the crime against Suvorov's descendants did not succeed. The army gritted its teeth, produced brilliant new military leaders from its ranks, and filled in the gaps created by Stalin's purge with new, reliable warriors. At first, it survived. Then it managed to win the greatest war that mankind has ever seen, writing a new and glorious page in the annals of History with its sword.

[1] Kulikovo Field is the site of the great battle in which Dmitri Donskoi finally drove the Tatars out of Russia.

The German fascists and our allies spoke about the USSR and Russia as if they were the same thing, calling all of the soldiers of the Red Army "Russians." And they were right in doing so. It was the great, multi-ethnic Russia that had fought and won this war, showing the world the greatness of the Russian spirit, confirming the glory of Russian arms, proving once again that the tradition laid down by the great Russian warriors had not decayed.

And what did the army of the Russian state stand on? What does it stand on now, and what will it stand on in the future? It stands on principles that are simple, strict, and therefore eternal. In the spiritual realm, it stands on the primacy of mind over matter. In the area of building up the armed forces, it stands on originality ("We are not like other European peoples"), and on the superiority of quality over quantity ("You can't win by numbers alone").

In the area of education and training it stands on religion and national pride ("We are Russians, and God is with us!"), on being aware of one's own mission ("Each soldier must understand his own maneuver"), on showing individual initiative, even in the lower ranks ("Someone closer to the scene can make a better decision. . . . If I say 'go right' and you ought to go left, don't listen to me"), and on encouraging those at the top to let their subordinates show this initiative ("Don't try to second-guess your subordinates when they already know the risks facing them, and don't tie their hands").

In the area of strategy: "Look at the big picture." In the area of tactics: "Judgment, Speed, Keep Up the Pressure." On carrying through what you've started: "The forest that you don't chop down grows back." And crowning it all: victory, victory "at little cost in blood."

These immortal precepts, these wise instructions, gave our forebears great results.

What is the Russian army? It is bravery, quickness on the uptake, toughness, a complete lack of pretentiousness, and discipline. That is the Russian soldier.

In addition to these qualities an officer must add public spirit (not to keep silent, for example, out of opportunistic, careerist considerations, when you see stupidity bordering on the criminal—"Honor above all else!"), and the ability to accept responsibility.

What good is all the personal bravery and tactical training in the world, if an officer is unable to say, "I made the decision" when the chips are down, and act in a situation in which he has to depend upon himself, his reason, and his strength of will. When an officer makes a decision, he should see victory in his mind's eye, and not the military prosecutor breathing down his neck. "I am personally responsible for my own decisions, and nobody else!" And then victory will come. The great Suvorov formulated this clearly and concisely: "A soldier must be brave; an officer—indomitable; a general—courageous." And as to whether there is such a thing as courage in this world—let every man decide for himself.

And there is one more factor which is especially important for the army. An officer, from the rank of platoon commander to that of battalion commander, will never say: "When I commanded the fifth company. . . ." No. He will say with pride, "When I was serving in the 331st Airborne Guards Regiment. . . ." And by doing so, not always consciously, he will be emphasizing the unique spiritual nature of the regiment. Yes, spiritual; a regiment is not only a tactical unit, it is also a spiritual phenomenon. Regiments bear the spirit of the army, and a regiment's spirit depends on its commander. Therein lies the great calling of the regimental commander.

Anyone who wishes to restore the Russian army and the Russian military art on a Russian foundation must always remember this. The brigade-corps system may be a good thing, but for the Russian army, it is just the same old "Prussian ringlets and braids"; in renouncing regiments, we are depriving the army of its spiritual foundation, we are knocking the Russian spirit out of it, and there will be no army left. Or rather, it will be only a parody of an army.

An army built on these Russian spiritual principles will be invincible. And while such an army is still alive, the nation will continue to live as a great power. But this formula can be turned on its head; to ruin a great power, one must first ruin its army.

Take a look at the last few years: first you have to drop the army into the political muck, as they did in Hungary, Czechoslovakia, and Afghanistan. Since the political goals of these operations were vague and confusing, and the military ones unattainable, force it to wash its hands in blood. When you think that this has gone on long enough, blame the army for the miscalculations, blunders, and rank stupidity of the country's political leaders. Call the army "criminal," and then undercut it by reducing the army's intellect through exempting students of all types, the sons of the elite, and so on, from the draft. Create the opinion that serving in the army is like serving a prison term, and implant this in the public mind. Place at the head of the army people who place their personal loyalty to the incumbent "czar" incomparably higher than their loyalty to the country, and thereby undercut the moral authority within the army. Drive a wedge between officers and enlisted men; sow mistrust and hostility between them. Take measures to reduce the level and scope of combat training sharply and destroy discipline. Scatter vehicles and weapons along ethnic lines, and the officer corps along political lines, and start playing them all against one another. And finally, plunge the country into bloody chaos and danger of political collapse.

If one looks closely at what is taking place, it would seem that we have been through all this before. That is to say, *we* haven't, it happened before our time, but it did happen. Take a look at the history of the Russian army, written by honest Russian officers, under the leadership of Russian Colonel Aleksandr Yevgenievich Savinkin.

"The harsh lesson of the Russo-Japanese War took a double toll on the army's heart and soul—its officer corps. Its main mass—mid-level and junior officers—quickly set about restoring Russian military might, which had been undermined, and quickly and fruitfully worked through the whole bitter experience of the lost campaign. But the army's senior officers were deeply shaken and depressed by the military catastrophe: customs which had seemed unshakable had been destroyed, and it was too late to start all over again.... So at that time, at the same time as spontaneous creative work was going on in the thick of the army—among its lower ranks—and the healthy blood of the military organism was healing its wounds remarkably quickly, at the top of the Russian armed forces, one could see that its leaders were crestfallen, downcast, vacillating, and hesitating. . . ."

Doesn't that sound like us?

And this is what Savinkin writes about relations between the army and society at the turn of the century:

"There was an extremely negative and contemptuous attitude toward the army and the officer corps in society. General Vannovsky, who had been appointed Minister of Education in his declining years, could think of nothing better than to force the most unruly students into the army. This absurd measure greatly harmed the army, turning it into something like a place of exile or a prison. It also hurt the prestige of military service in the eyes of the people by portraying one's military obligation as the equivalent of serving out a prison term. People had contempt for the uniform—Kuprin's short story 'The Duel' is a monument to the disgraceful attitude that Russian society had toward its army. Military service was considered to be an unworthy occupation: according to the ideas reigning in the intelligentsia at the time, only fops, stupid people, or failures could become officers; a cultured person could never have anything to do with the military, which he considered a holdover from more backward times. Miliutin's regulations of 1874, which exempted virtually all educated people and even half-educated people from military service, put all of the burden of military service on the illiterate. The intelligentsia, which were not subject to being called up, were completely unfamiliar with military life, and by the beginning of the twentieth century, thought that the barracks were a prison, and that military service consisted of nothing but 'running the gauntlet.' Out of more than two centuries of glorious military history, they have retained only one thing—spiked whips!!!"

A strikingly familiar picture, which has to be updated a bit—you'd have to replace "running the gauntlet" with "relations not covered by regulations." The rest is exactly the same.

But what about the military ministers? What was the situation like with them at that time? Let's look. Here's one: "A man not without ability, General Sukhomlinov was distinguished by his ambition, and at the same time, by his remarkable superficiality. He impressed the Czar, who liked him for his cheerfulness and permanent optimism."

Don't tell me there's no such thing as historical coincidence! And here's a second example: "Guchkov—with the assistance of the servile General Headquarters—conducted a real massacre of the top-ranking generals. The army, which had just survived the most dangerous hour of its existence, was decapitated. . . . Adventurers were put at the head of military districts after being hastily raised to the level of staff officers. For this scoundrel of a minister, the military hierarchy simply didn't exist."

History really does repeat itself: once as tragedy, and the second time as farce!

And there's more. This is what they say about Kuropatkin: "General Kuropatkin only had the lowest of the military virtues: personal bravery. . . . More than any other, Kuropatkin lacked 'courage' in Suvorov's sense of the word. An excellent administrator, General Kuropatkin made a poor commander, and he realized that. That's why he had no self-confidence. . . . Kuropatkin was used to doing things only after receiving permission and approval, and he never did anything without them. He had the kind of fear of his superiors wherein all his mind, education, rank, knowledge, bravery, and honesty came to nothing before his timidity before anyone above him, and his dread of taking responsibility. The Czar could not command an army which was over three thousand miles away. He gave Kuropatkin full authority. . . ."

Why did this happen? The answer is given in the book, *Lessons of the Japanese Campaign*, written by General Kuropatkin himself. "People with strong character, independent people, unfortunately, were not promoted, but persecuted; in peacetime, they seemed to their superiors to be far too restless. On the other hand, people with no character, no convictions, but were obliging, always ready to agree with their superiors' opinions, moved up the ladder."

My first conclusion: there is nothing new under the sun.

My second conclusion: if a lion stands at the head of an army of lions, victory is assured. If a lion stands at the head of an army of asses, the chances are fifty-fifty. But if an ass stands at the head of an army of lions, you can call it quits!

Officers and soldiers. Soldiers and officers. What were they like, these forebears of ours, in those years before the storm? Relations between them led first to a split in the army, and the country came crashing down.

"For the soldiers in 1914, officers were the older members of the regiment's great family, the people who had educated them. Relations between officers and soldiers in the Russian army were suffused with simplicity and affection, unlike any foreign army, or even other strata of the Russian people. The armed people of 1916, on the other hand, saw their officers only as 'gentry,' and brought to the reserve regiments' barracks, and from there, to the trenches, all of the sharpness of the social contradictions and class strife growing in the country as a whole."

Another year would pass, and they'd be tearing each other apart.

And now, a few words—Savinkin's again—about the excessive "democratization" of the army, which was carried to absurd lengths: "At the end of April, that turncoat Polivanov finished his 'Declaration of the Rights of the Soldier,' which, in General Alekseev's words, was 'the last nail in the coffin of our armed forces'. . . .

"According to this 'Declaration,' servicemen received all political rights (the right to vote), they could join any political party, they could have any political convictions ('Down with the war!' 'Down with officers!'). In military units, both in the rear and at the front, you could get any publications, without exception (including anarchist publications). The obligation to salute was abolished. And finally, all disciplinary action was abolished. The army ceased to exist as a regular armed force. . . ."

If anyone thinks that it takes much work or thinking to make any army decompose morally to the molecular level, he is deeply mistaken. You don't have to do anything, or even think. All you have to do is say: "Boys, you can go ahead and wear your stripes, and collect your pay, but please, I beg of you, don't do anything. At ease!" And that's all. You don't need to do anything more: the "boys" will start planning a process of decomposition that no General Staff could think up in its wildest dreams.

And if you combine this "doing nothing" with corresponding proportions of party rivalry and religious hatred, you will be the happy owner of an absolutely unique gang of thugs. And if you give the creation and organization of this gang of thugs a legislative underpinning, at the very highest level? And do it so that the whole country becomes one big gang of thugs? What would happen then?

You don't need to exercise your imagination. It has already happened. Let's turn back to Savinkin's history: "All of Russia was turned into an enormous insane asylum, where a handful of criminals had given the crowd of madmen incendiary shells, and the administration followed the principle of giving these madmen complete freedom in the name of the 'precepts of democracy.' The country could only be saved by dealing harshly with the traitors and reining in the enraged masses. But to do this, the whole bankrupt system of governing would have had to be changed—highfalutin' phrases would have had to be replaced with decisive measures."

That's how it happened then, the first vicious circle with far-reaching consequences.

Could the political background be different now? Unfortunately, similar causes give rise to similar effects. Let us turn the floor over to the History once again: "We won't go into all the details of our Motherland's revolutionary disgrace. The eight months from February to October 1917 were a dirty page in our thousand-year-old history. That unprecedented filth later had to be washed away in blood.... The savage experience of 'one-hundred-percent democracy' from March to November of 1917, the institution of a new and untested form of government in wartime, the complete disregard of the state in the name of bookish principles, which turned out to be good for nothing—this crazy experience went into our history under the name of the *Kerenshchina*, named after the most characteristic, and the same time most 'characterless' political figure of that time, Alexander Kerensky."

And now a little about the political scoundrels of the past. *Our* scoundrels. From *our* past. And *our* present: "People who had not, up until that time, had the slightest idea of how to run the state, took it upon themselves to run a great country. The passengers took it upon themselves to drive the locomotive, with only a textbook as their guide, and they started by destroying all the brakes.

"The instinct of how to run a state system, the concept of the national interest, all this was completely unfamiliar to liberal democratic society. It was possessed by two passions: an instinctive hatred for the 'old regime,' and a fear of looking 'reactionary' in the eyes of the Soviet of Workers' Deputies. There was no blow against their country which these people would not strike, in the name of this hatred and this fear...."

And now, let us remember the moods which prevailed in Soviet society in August-September 1991. Let us remember the euphoria. Let us remember the "Square of Free Russia":

"The outbreak of patriotism which seized Russia in July 1914, in spite of its power, did not last long. Like a heap of straw, this enthusiasm burned with a bright flame, and quickly burned out. This was the fault of the government, which was unable to turn this exclusively favorable event to its advantage, which was unable to create a 'storage battery' to use this energy which had suddenly appeared over a longer period of time, and most of it was wasted. It was also the fault of society, which proved to be unable to sustain an effort of will, and soon returned to its usual condition of sarcastic skepticism and passionate criticism, which was fruitless because it was so malicious. The inertia of three generations of useless people won out in the end...."

Perestroika, shoot-outs, name-calling... a flaming arc.

Impartial Mother History says this about the government institutions, about the great-grandmothers of the contemporary Russian

Duma, the parties and the party programs: "The National Defense Council—a many-headed anarchical organism—turned out to be absolutely unable to cope with the complex and responsible task set before it. Sessions of this motley Noah's Ark were absolutely chaotic. Stolypin referred to the Council's sessions as 'bedlam'; the Grand Duke Sergei Mikhailovich called them 'a concert of cats'; and General Palitsyn, one of that institution's founders, called it simply a 'pigsty.'

"The Duma produced many good orators, but not a single statesman. Its participation in running the state was very limited. The government continued to be staffed by representatives of the bureaucratic world, and was not responsible to the Duma....

"The party and the party program represented the holy of holies for liberal revolutionary society. The Russian *obshchestvennik*[2]—whether he was a Constitutional Democrat, a Socialist-Revolutionary, or a Bolshevik—firmly believed in the infallibility of his party's dogmas. For him, nothing existed outside the party. It wasn't the party that served the interests of the country; the country was supposed to serve the interests of the party. If a party program conflicted with common sense and the demands of life, so much the worse for common sense and the demands of life. The party program remained infallible in all its particulars.

"The doctrinaire nature of society flowed from its inexperience in running the state. It got all of its knowledge of this area from foreign parliamentary practice, naively thinking European parliamentarianism the height of perfection, and dreaming of imposing the same model on Russia. Armed by their theoretical knowledge, the advanced Russian intelligentsia burned with ambition. It longed to replace the 'obsolete Autocracy' in power so that it could apply its theories in practice. None of these arrogant doctrinaires had any doubt that it was possible, and even easy, to run an enormous country with one eye on a manual, a foreign manual, to boot."

---

[2] A representative of Russian educated society, opposed to the government.

When you read this stern, serious history, it makes you want to cry. The Russian spirit of contradiction is quite strong. People will do the dumbest things. There's even a fairy tale about it. A Russian fairy tale. A folk tale.

Once upon a time, Ivan the Czarevich woke up in the morning with something very wrong with his body: there was an enormous screw where his belly button used to be. That really sent everybody scurrying! Doctors and mechanics came from every corner of the kingdom. The things they tried to do with that screw! But nothing worked. The damned thing just sat there, and didn't budge a millimeter. They found some wise *boyars* who told him: in a far-away kingdom across the ocean, they have master craftsmen that are far better than ours—they'll take care of that screw right way. So in as much time as it takes to tell this story, or even faster, Ivan the Czarevich, by horse and by water, reached the appointed region. And the masters really were far better than ours. They started fussing around, and brought out a mechanical-medical instrument, and, with a triumphant cry, took out the screw. But when the screw fell on the floor, Ivan the Czarevich's butt fell off. The moral of the story: don't risk your butt looking across the ocean for something you don't need.

> **"B**rother Slavs (and non-Slavs), in trading totalitarianism for democracy, haven't we just traded one bad thing for another?**"**

These are "pictures at an exhibition," eighty to ninety years old, but how fresh and topical! Smart people learn from other people's mistakes. Stupid people learn from their own. Social development moves in a spiral everywhere else; does it move in a circle for us? Who are we? How many times must we tread in our own footsteps? Why must a "Time of Troubles" be a normal environment for us? Can't we ever start simply living, instead of struggling for existence?

We're all guilty, all of us, of letting the broom of our great power unravel. Seventy-three percent of the people voted for the Union—and we let it fall apart! Some of its twigs writhed in the fire of fratricidal war; others bent and broke under the pressure of economic burdens, became impoverished, and split, split, split. The Union fell apart. Now, Russia is falling apart, too. Sovereign republics, sovereign oblasts, sovereign cities. Soon, we'll get to sovereign farms, or even sovereign households. Feudal Russia! Now we've started "aping" other countries. As usual, we're following the example of our "heroes": the U.S.A., Germany, and Japan. We used to try to "catch up to them, and surpass them." Now, we just try to imitate them.

All self-respecting people and self-respecting countries have their own mind. Stupidity is not lack of thinking; it is a certain kind of thinking. Perhaps it isn't so bad to imitate other countries at first, but we have to adapt foreign experience to our own soil, taking into account our own political, economic, religious, and other conditions. Otherwise, we risk getting something we hadn't expected, as we already have.

The whole world community is striving for integration and union; we are cutting off age-old ties with a steady hand. They are opening their borders and lowering customs duties; we are erecting tough customs barriers where none existed before. In Western Europe, a single monetary unit, the ECU, is being introduced, while here, a parade of national currencies have appeared, most of which are good only for papering the bathroom wall. There, they are doing everything to make people live better, to remove a mass of artificial burdens from them; here, it's the other way around.

In all the political squabbling about reforms, democracy, and human rights, someone lost sight of the person nobody had any need for, the former Soviet citizen. Most of these people have now fallen into dire poverty, and when they look up, they see no guiding star in the dark firmament.

Man lives by hope; no matter how hard things are, hope alone will help him overcome anything. Man can live in desperate situations for a period of time, but when he thinks that the rest of his life will be lived in such conditions, he loses hope. And then corpses, wrapped in cellophane bags, will begin to fill the cemeteries.

The first victims of this "life" under extreme conditions will be the elderly—the victors in the greatest of all wars, who lost their health and strength in the attempt to "catch up to and surpass" the West, and now, in their declining years, have been robbed by the state.

And the children, most of whom are having a rough time in their families. Their fathers and mothers are overstrained by their fruitless attempts to make ends meet, and take out their bitterness on their kids. Families break up; children run away. And they end up in orphanages. Statistics show that one out of every three people who come out of orphanages becomes a vagrant, one out of every five appears in court, and one out of every ten commits suicide.

Can this be called human society? What has happened to our soul? To our brains?

The ever-growing mass of illiterate, embittered people, trusting no one, with no future, mentally unstable, will bury all the timid shoots of progress beneath them. And the law of the jungle will take over.

The elderly and the children.... The children and the elderly.... The past and the present.... The present and the past.... They are one of the main indicators of a society's moral health. We must not bury our future. We must not kill off hope, for today, the death rate already exceeds the birth rate. When there is hope, people live and bear children, and the country gets stronger.

Brother Slavs (and non-Slavs), in trading totalitarianism for democracy, haven't we just traded one bad thing for another?

Czar Alexander III once said that "Russia has no friends." Nothing has changed since then. Legions of *nouveaux riches* are crawling over our land. They promise billions, and they buy up our national wealth and our souls at warehouse prices. With the help of turncoats, they do their black deeds with one goal in mind—to make sure that Russia has no future. They work in an organized way, without sleep or rest, and in every dimension: political, economic, moral. They spend liberally, because these expenditures, compared to the money it would cost to resist a great power, are nothing!

You will never be able to make a Soldier or a Citizen out of boys who have gotten used to begging, reselling "Coca-Cola" bottles or packs of chewing gum, and watching all sorts of sexual and violent nonsense. You will never be able to make a Citizen and Mother out of girls who are surrounded by all sorts of sleazy men who promise them that they will become models and make them into common sluts.

But our people are modest and courageous. No matter how bad things get, we will be able to overcome all our economic difficulties as long as we observe two conditions: as long as we prevent our future from becoming decayed, and as long as we start being guided by our own Russian mind.

We must always remember that we are the heirs of a thousand-year-old Orthodox Russia, the House of the Romanovs, which lasted three hundred years, and Soviet power, which lasted almost seventy-five years. We have no right to renounce anything, or anyone, in our history. Without the past, there can be no future. If you shoot at the past with a pistol, the future will shoot back with a cannon.

History teaches us that we have passed through the stage of appendage princes. We've lived through the three hundred-year Mongol-Tatar yoke! But that was physical servitude; our faith was alive then, and the people had the strength and courage to produce a St. Sergius of Radonezh and a Dmitri Donskoi. And Russia revived.

In 1612, standing at the edge of a precipice, facing the threat of the collapse of the state, the Russian people advanced citizen Minin and Prince Pozharsky from their ranks. The Time of Troubles was surpassed. And Russia revived.

Peter the Great, prevailing against intrigues and stagnation, creating an army, suffering defeats and failures and forging them into victory, knocking through a window to Europe, strengthened the state with his heavy hand. And Russia revived.

In 1812 an "invincible" army, headed by the emperor of France arrived on Russian land. Napoleon's prowess was so great he captured Moscow... in flames. And then His Majesty the Russian People rose up, and the "invincible" army was no more. Leo N. Tolstoi, in his novel *War and Peace*, said quite accurately that the war was won, not by Napoleon, and not by Kutuzov, but by the Russian spirit. The Russian Cossacks drove the last nail in the coffin of the French adventure in Paris. And Russia revived.

Then came 1941. This invasion was the most serious. It was so serious that we had to remember all the history we had been forced to forget, and put the portraits of Alexander Nevsky, A.V. Suvorov, and M.I. Kutuzov back up. We held out. We went to work. We threw them out. We won the war. And Russia revived.

The new, creeping, slimy, rotting yoke advancing on our land from all sides is directed not only against our country's material shell, but against the Spirit of its People. The enemy is terrifying because it is invisible. You cannot cross swords with it. You can't kill it with a bullet. But it is there. It is shaking and destroying our fundamental moral foundations, laid down by our ancestors, and replacing them with foreign ideas. It is giving rise to all sorts of sects, parties, and murky public organizations, and is preaching Orthodoxy to Orthodox Russia in English. It is creating political and economic chaos, and setting ethnic groups off against one another.

But Slavs get ten times stronger when they are backed up against the wall; nobody understands how this can be. Russians may take a long time to get the horse harnessed, but when they get started, they ride fast. The spring of Russian patience has been stretched almost to its limit, and if it is stretched still further, it will straighten out powerfully, and with cleansing force sweep away all the scum, muck, and filth that has accumulated over the years. And Russia will revive.

Our great forebears bequeathed to us a great power. They were able to show the world their strength, power, greatness, and nobility. They paid for everything in full measure, in blood, for every clump of

Russian land, and often, more than once. They were Warriors and Creators.

Why have we squandered this great inheritance? Why have we become destroyers? Let us return to the History of the Russian Army: "One can and must speak of the plots of Russia's enemies. But it is important to remember that these plots took place on favorable soil. The intrigues may have been English, and the gold may have been German or Jewish. But the nonentities and the traitors were our own; they were Russians. Without them, Russia would have nothing to fear from all the gold in the world or any plots."

Our enemy is inside us. That is why, despite our colossal wealth of land, we lead a pitiful existence. And that is why I rage about the fate of our great power!

And meanwhile, where are we going? Let us ask Plato: "Tyranny arises, of course, not of any other regime, but out of democracy; in other words, out of extreme freedom, the greatest and harshest slavery appears. . . democracy is undermined by a disease marked by the appearance of a special sort of people, idle and profligate. . . whom we will liken to drones. . . the most poisonous of these drones make speeches, and transact business, and the rest of them sit as close as they can to the speaker's stand, buzzing, and not letting anybody contradict them. . . . In the end, when they see that the people, deceived by these slanderers, are ready to kick them out, not out of spite, but out of ignorance, they indeed become supporters of oligarchy. . . . So it is clear that when the tyrant appears, he comes out of precisely this root, that is, as the people's champion. . . . Having an extraordinarily obedient crowd in his hands, will he refrain from shedding the blood of his fellow-tribesmen? On the contrary, he will start taking them to court on false accusations and defiling himself by taking a human life. . . punishing people by banishment and threatening them with the death penalty, and at the same time hinting at the abolition of debts and the redistribution of land. . . his first task will be to get his citizens into wars, so that the people will have need of a leader. . . . And if he suspects someone of free thinking, or of rejecting his rule, he will annihilate them under the pretense that they have been traitors to the enemy... the tyrant will have to annihilate them all, until in the end, he will have no one worthy left, either friend or foe.... He is bound by the blessed need either to live with a crowd of scoundrels, who hate him, or to say good-bye to his life.... And then, the people will know, by Zeus, what a creature it gave birth to, and even raised lovingly...."[3]

Plato was a remarkably profound man. He wrote these lines 2,400 years ago, and life has confirmed his diagnosis many times over. Yes, it's less than a step from democracy to oligarchy. Yes, when you're drunk on unmixed freedom, the high is wonderful, but don't forget the next morning.

And so we've come to the age-old Russian question: "What is to be done?"

Whoever wants to lead Russia successfully must be able to give at least satisfactory answers to five questions:

1. *What should Russia's nationalities policy be?* There are 132 ethnic groups in Russia, split religiously among Orthodoxy, Roman Catholicism, Islam, Buddhism, Judaism, and a mass of sects. What can unite and bring together this enormous mass of tribes and languages? What strings must be played to touch the hearts of all these people and get them to work together and stop trying to destroy one another?

2. *What should Russia's regional policy be?* There are eighty-nine regions, or as they are customarily called, "subjects of the Federation"; seventeen of them are "non-Russian." There are republics, krais, oblasts, and mega-cities (Moscow and St. Petersburg). There are off-shore zones, free economic zones, and zones of maximum economic prosperity.

[3] Plato, *Republic*, 562b-569b.

Ethnic boundaries, as a rule, do not coincide with geographic boundaries. Everyone wants a great deal of sovereignty and all the privileges that go with it. How can we make sure that no one pulls the blanket too far over to his own side to the detriment of the national interest?

3. *What should Russia's economic policy be?* We have an overdeveloped military-industrial complex, an underdeveloped agro-industrial complex, and a fuel-extraction complex that is *losing* money. We have a mass of unprofitable enterprises, some with backward technology. We have a number of nuclear power stations and chemical enterprises just waiting for an accident to happen. The environment is a mess. Everybody wants to live like people do in the West, while working as they did under socialism. They want a three-day work week and a four-hour work day. Any rise in salaries leads to another inflationary spiral. The domestic producer is being kept down. To what extent should foreigners be involved in the economy? How can we embrace the unembraceable?

4. *What should Russia's tax policy be?* The state wants to fleece the producer of 93 of every 100 rubles he earns, and sometimes as much as 116. But if you want too much, you get too little. It is becoming unprofitable to produce, so the state is getting nothing, or more accurately, a handful of little MMMs.[4] There is such a thing as the Laffer curve: if the government raises taxes to a critical level, there are two consequences: a massive decline in production, and massive tax evasion. And the state cannot live without taxes. Another vicious circle. How can common sense be introduced into our tax policy?

5. *And finally, what type of state do we want to build in Russia?* Only a fair-to-middling chicken coop can be built

---

[4] MMM was an investment pyramid scheme, run by Sergei Mavrodi, which went bankrupt in 1995, costing many Russian investors their life savings.

without a blueprint; everything else requires some planning. And this pertains to building a state. If we know *what* we're building, then we'll come to an understanding of *how* to build it. One president of a non-Russian region when asked "What are we building?" answered, "We're building something good." Can we formulate the task more specifically?

We will begin to rebuild our Motherland when we provide a substantive answer to these questions. An answer that knows what we want and that takes into account the countless difficulties we have to overcome. There is no other way. We are Russians—we can do anything.

Am I ready to answer these questions now? Yes, I am! But that is a topic for a separate, serious discussion.

Contemporary Russia is linked not only to the former Soviet Union, but, to the thousand-year-old history of Kievan Rus', Russia under the *boyars*, czarist Russia. These still matter. We should be the heirs of czarist Russia as it was in February 1917. Then we can restore the link between our present and our past, and the historical succession of generations. We have inherited the debts, but we have also inherited the interest from the numerous investments that have been made over time, and—it is pleasant to imagine—the principal as well. We will pay our debts—all of them. But we will also restore the prestige of the Russian state and remain decent people in the historical sense, and that kind of decency is worth much.

Countrymen! Three waves of emigration have been scattered by an evil Fate all over the world. The Armenian diaspora. The Chechen diaspora. But who has taken the time to think of what it is like for the Russian diaspora in the "near-" and "far-" abroad? Are people who are now in New York or Paris no longer Russian? Have the twenty-five million people who, in the blink of an eye, against their will, wound up in a foreign country in the "near-abroad" ceased to be Russian? Doesn't their heart ache for Russia as ours does? Why have we forgotten about them?

We are all different; some see and imagine Russia's revival differently from the way we see it. And that's all right. We all come into this world different, and that's how we leave it. And in this variety, this multiplicity of views, opinions, and judgments, the truth as always is found somewhere in the middle. One proves that he is right, not with his fists, but by logic, reason, and experience. What really deserves glory is

> **"So let us remember what Russia stands on, and return to the Church, to its bosom, and create a powerful spiritual state."**

not conquering by force, but by persuasion. Today, the descendants of fervent monarchists and the descendants of no less fervent communists find themselves together in emigration. There's nothing separating them any longer. We are all children of Russia, and it is time to extend our hands to one another.

What do we take as the beginning of this new age? The autocratic government and the Bolshevik Party. Czar Nikolai II and V. I. Lenin.

These two men died a long time ago, but both remain alive in the pages of the history books. Both of them knew earthly glory, honor, and greatness.

They should be buried simultaneously. It should be a national event, accompanied by the sound of church bells all over the country. With flags at half-mast. To the sound of a thousand-piece funeral band.

This age split the once-united officer corps of the Russian army, dividing it into Whites and Reds. Russian officers—of one blood, faith, language, with the same glorious tradition—began to shoot and cut each other down. Mercilessly. Russians did not take Russians prisoner. Hate became a religion.

And after the officer corps, the whole country was divided into Red and White. The Civil War sank into the river Lethe. World War II rumbled to its conclusion. Several generations had come and gone.

Man split the atom. Fearsome diseases were being cured. We took our first steps in space. The world had changed, but one thing remained unshakable—Whites and Reds. These two colors are like the mark of Cain.

This fire can and must be put out by putting up in Moscow's Red Square a simple monument to the innocent Russian people who were killed. It would be a wondrous spiritual balm for our sick national soul, which has repented of what it has done and has asked for forgiveness. And the national revival could begin.

We have to recreate that national core: nationalism and Orthodoxy. Russian nationalism is like a bear hibernating in the winter. It's hard to wake him up and get him moving. But if he gets started, don't stand in his way! He will cause terror. He won't let others live. And soon he won't let himself live either.

But our people's thousand-year-old Orthodox faith has more than once inspired it to great feats, has more than once saved it. This faith is inextricably linked with the fatherland. But let us turn back to the history of the Russian army: "Suvorov taught us that 'We are Russians—God is with us.' They didn't understand him, and began adopting foreign 'doctrines' and 'methods' designed for the hearts of other armies. We stopped being Russians.... And God stopped being with us...."

So let us remember what Russia stands on, and return the Church, which was separated from the state, to its bosom and create a powerful spiritual state institution. And seriously, thoughtfully, as we can be when we want to be, let us reform the army and bring it back to its former might and grandeur. The Church strengthens the army; the army defends the Church. And on this restored spiritual axis— the two forces of our great power—we can begin to feel like Russians again. This spiritual might and bravery, united, will give rise to creative genius. A triangle is a tough, unshakable figure.

You have to know your Motherland; and knowing her, you love her. You have to know her great past, her geniuses and villains, her sayings and legends, the colors of her flag, the shape of her coat of arms, and the melody of her national anthem. If people automatically stand up and are silent at the sound of their national anthem, that country is healthy.

Only owners of their own land with their three birch trees and a modest little stream can really love their Motherland. They have something to defend; they have something for which they can die. This doesn't mean forty million little "property owners" with their three shares of MMM in their bottom dresser drawer, which they don't know what to do with. No, I mean people who work for themselves, their children, and their grandchildren, and for their country.

Such people don't have to be commanded; all they have to be given is one thing: a reasonable degree of freedom. When a man like this begins a new venture, he risks his own money; a bureaucrat risks the government's money. A man like this works for a positive result; a bureaucrat is indifferent to the result.

We have to stop fighting and start living. People are not trash, they are not fertilizer for the fields. Human blood is not water. It has a price.

On January 15, 1905, thirty demonstrators were killed and wounded, and that day was called "Bloody Sunday." In February and March 1917, five thousand people were torn to pieces, and they called it a "bloodless revolution." In 1989 eighteen people died during the well-known events in Tbilisi, and it caused a stir around the world. In October 1993 hundreds were killed in Moscow, and it was met with silent indifference. Today, tens of thousands of people are dying in Tajikistan and where is the indignation?

There is no conflict that people or states could not solve without bloodshed, if they showed some good will. All of the wars in the history of mankind, even those that lasted for a hundred years, ended in negotiations and peace without exception. Why don't we start at the final stage for once?

It is long since time to stop pouring ashes over our heads. No foreigner will come to pull us out of the gutter of our own making. It is the Russian scholar, the Russian businessman, the Russian merchant, worker, and soldier, who are the hope of our country. We do not need to talk—we need to work!

It will be hard going. Not everyone will make it. Some will die along the way. Some will stop. And some will get lost. But we, the Russian people, will get there.

The prevailing feeling in our society over the last decade has been envy, as in: "Ivan, have you been in prison?"

"Yes, I have."

"I have, too. But Pyotr hasn't. Should we put him in prison?"

No, dear countrymen, we won't get far with that kind of thinking. If we have to fight, we should not fight to make sure there are no more rich people; we should fight to make sure there are no more poor people.

And we must finally stop lying. What mountains of lies we have piled up! Yet we continue because the same people are still in power. There is only one truth—big, beautiful, and pure. But in practice, it turns out that there is Transdniester truth and Moldovan truth, Armenian truth and Azeri truth, Georgian truth and Abkhazian truth. Tajikistan has two truths, all to itself. And all of these little streams, which go under the name of truth flow into the swamp of lies. It's time to let the crystal-clear torrent of truth wash away all the filth and blood. We have to do it ourselves!

The History of the Russian Army says: "We should always remember that we are surrounded by enemies and people who envy us, and that we Russians have no friends. We don't need them as long as we Russians stand up for each other. We don't need allies either: even the best of them will betray us."

We must learn to look at things clearly and simply, renouncing mysticism, which clogs and darkens the national consciousness. The Russian people is far from being a "God-bearer," a people with a divine mission, as people, great in spirit but unable to think in political terms, once thought. Our people are both farmers and warriors. No other people have been able to combine the plow with the sword as we have. The Russian people have their virtues and their short-comings. We should eradicate these shortcomings as much as we can.

When these difficulties seem insurmountable, when you are just about to drop your hands and lose heart, look back and ask Peter the Great, Rumyantsev, or Suvorov for advice. And the universe will shake once again from the deeds of Russian arms.

I believe that we have greatness and glory ahead of us. For man is strong only in faith. The age of destroyers is reading its sad, inevitable conclusion; another age—the age of creators—is on the horizon. The age of creators of a great Russia.

CHAPTER 23:
RUSSIA'S STRIFE

ON JUNE 16, 1996, the "people of the Russian Federation" (what that means exactly is still not clear)[1] were faced with a choice: Yeltsin or Zyuganov. It was a choice between "bad" and "very bad."

Yeltsin had withdrawn from the actual running of the government. He had never been a democrat, and his advanced age and poor health gave no reason to hope that he would ever become one. He was capable of reigning in his own way, and of issuing decrees, most of which no one intended to carry out anyway. He had enough strength for palace intrigues, but he never condescended to grapple with the problems of the "rabble." He could not remain in people's memories as a great builder. He would go down in history as a destroyer.

Why has Yeltsin been able to stay in power? Because of the West's support? In part. Money? In part. Biased journalists and actors? That, too. But none of this would have helped if the people had not con-

---

[1] Lit. *narod rossiiskii*. In Russian, there are two words for "Russian": *russkii*, which refers to "ethnic Russian," or Russian language or culture, and *rossiiskii*, which refers to the country of Russia. The "Russian" people in this second sense, includes ethnic Russians—but not ethnic Russians living abroad—as well as Russian citizens of other ethnic backgrounds. Lebed's remark reflects the fact that the expression *rossiiskii narod* sounds very strange to Russians.

sciously voted against the communist "alternative" to prove that it would not prevail in Russia—even in its improved, more civilized version. And to be fair, if Zyuganov had come to power, our fall would have been even more headlong, and probably more bloody.

As a son of my people, I also made my choice. I became secretary of the Security Council. Did I do it because I wanted the perqs that went along with being a government bureaucrat? No. I'd never make a good bureaucrat—my backbone's not flexible enough. Did I hope that I'd be able to make a career for myself in the corridors of power? No. For the people who dominate the government today—most of whom were third-rate members of the Party *nomenklatura* during Soviet times—I was an outsider.

So why did I do it? To do the one thing that could be done quickly—end the bloody nightmare in Chechnya, which the shameless bureaucrats wouldn't even call a war.

And I achieved my goal by having the power, platform, and influence to convince even the most thick-headed and greedy people that peace was more profitable than war.

There was no way to win the war in Chechnya—and it *had* become a total war. Any talented military leader can win a battle against an enemy army. But when an entire people begins to fight, there's nothing a military leader can do. Any people—whether in Transdniester, or in Chechnya, or in Abkhazia, or in Karabakh—forced to fight a total war are invincible. Anyone on the wrong side of such a war—Napoleon and Hitler, for example—loses. The Americans had to pull out of a war like this in Vietnam, and Soviet troops had to pull out of Afghanistan. Fighting on the wrong side of such a war is like trying to knock down a wall by banging your head against it.

I made the political decision to end the war in Chechnya, and I'm proud of that. The president, as always, had nothing to do with it. When the war began, he had problems with his nasal septum. When I put an end to it, he had problems with his heart—and, I would hope, with his conscience.

The peace in Chechnya was the main result of my 133 days in government, though Yeltsin appeared to consider it my first "mistake." The second was to argue that we must keep the glorious city of Sevastopol Russian, as is our legal right.[2]

"Who owns Sevastopol and what damage, or risk, will there be if the Russian Black Sea Fleet has to find another base?" I posed these questions at the beginning of October, appealing to the sailors of the Black Sea Fleet in an open letter, and exposed myself to a firestorm of criticism. Now, the much-esteemed mayor of Moscow[3] is repeating them, veterans are publishing open letters, and television is showing the negative consequences of moving the Black Sea Fleet's base to Novorossiisk.

There can only be three kinds of relations between the peoples of Russia and Ukraine—good, very good, and wonderful. All the inconveniences (economic, military, demographic, and moral) connected with the hasty divorce ought to be resolved in a civilized way, on the basis of international practice and international law. The question of who owns Sevastopol is a question for qualified international lawyers to work out. It is not a question of war.

My third "mistake": revealing secret government files that proved that when Academician Likhachev said that Chernobyl was the beginning of the Apocalypse, he was closer to the truth than many realized. The files proved that the government doesn't have the money for any of its nuclear security programs. The nuclear reactors have not been dismantled on more than a hundred of the submarines on the list. Of Russia's twenty-nine nuclear power plants, nineteen are obsolete and will have to be shut down by 2010. Half of them are "twins" of the Chernobyl Nuclear Power Plant, with the same design, and

---

[2] Sevastopol, the home of the Black Sea Fleet, is located in the Crimea, which is now part of Ukraine, and remains an object of dispute between Russia and Ukraine.

[3] He is referring to Moscow Mayor Yuri Luzhkov, who made a controversial trip to Sevastopol and proclaimed that the city was Russian, which caused a diplomatic incident between Russia and Ukraine.

the same shortcomings. And the government hasn't the wherewithal to do anything about it. Three of the navy's four nuclear waste storage facilities are full. There's no hope of building another one. Today, we can't find the dozens of billions of rubles to solve these problems; tomorrow, we'll be forced to find hundreds of trillions.

> **"C**apitalism, as it is being practiced by the present Russian bosses, is missing its most attractive side—free competition.**"**

My fourth "mistake" was to force the government to deliver much-needed food and energy to the far north. Over the past two years, a third of a million people have been forced to leave the far north. Hundreds of thousands have again been faced with the choice: freeze with their children or evacuate as soon as possible. But where? How? At whose expense?

My fifth "mistake": military reform. When the state owes the army six trillion rubles in salaries alone, and the Defense Ministry owes its suppliers twenty trillion, how can anyone deny that our military is in crisis? I did everything I could to restructure the military leadership, to pick people who were really capable of building a new army. I worked out realistic projects to get more funding for the army, including the use of the state arms monopoly *Rosvooruzhenie*, and the income from selling arms. It was like another bypass operation,[4] but this time for the army's weak heart.

What scared the official Kremlin was my prediction that the army was on the brink of mutiny. There are 125,000 families in the armed forces without housing. The programs to build more housing have been held up. And the amount of money spent on the average soldier is less than half the minimum acceptable level. Due to insufficient funding, Russia's defense capability is declining to the point

---

[4] Lebed is sarcastically alluding to President Yeltsin's quintuple bypass surgery at approximately the same time.

where the collapse of our armed forces, military infrastructure, defense industry, and Russia's status as a great power will soon be inevitable. Again, 1917 comes to mind. When will we start learning from our mistakes?

My sixth "mistake": the more I came to know people from the Kremlin, the more clearly I understood where I had to start my fight against corruption and crime.

In working on the presidential decree, "On Urgent Measures to Strengthen Law and Order and Step Up the Fight Against Crime in Moscow and the Moscow Oblast," I came to understand that if someone was a co-author, it did not necessarily mean that he was on the same side as I was. Yes, the decree envisioned hiring more policemen and strengthening the judicial branch, in part by using money confiscated from criminals. Special detachments were created in the prosecutor's office and the tax inspectorate to fight organized crime. A mechanism was proposed for immediately removing corrupt officials, regardless of their rank, from their posts. But when the leaders of the top federal law enforcement agencies all have their hands in the cookie jar and spend their time creating the illusion of frantic activity, it is impossible to implement any decisions that are made, even those made with the best intentions.

The head of the Ministry of Internal Affairs[5] reports that the crime rate is falling. This is a lie. The unenforced decree, together with the new criminal code, only a couple of dozen articles of which are really enforced, have merely made "His Majesty the Law" a "gofer" for the Kremlin elite.

My seventh "mistake" was my trip to NATO headquarters in Brussels. How can the West avoid thinking of us as a helpless old man if Russia is not represented at NATO headquarters? At the headquarters of the "Partnership for Peace," our flag is there only out of polite-

---

[5] Interior Minister Anatoly Kulikov, the man whom Lebed named as the person chiefly to blame for the war in Chechnya, and whose later accusations against Lebed formed the pretext for his dismissal.

ness. Out of fourteen sessions, we have taken part in two. We sent three officers there. Nobody asked any questions.

But so many vitally important questions have to be asked! For example, who and what threatens Hungary today? Where will Belgium, with its population of ten million, stand on the hierarchical ladder, once Poland, with its fifty-two million, becomes part of the system? What effect will the admission of new members have on the already complex set of tensions within the bloc? Who will pay for the development of an infrastructure? For unifying the arms systems? How will decisions be made? Who will be responsible for carrying them out? What form will our relations take in the transitional period? A treaty? A charter? An agreement?

It's stupid to stand outside the process, stamping our feet and showing everyone how helpless we are. We have to exert influence on the process, both externally and from within. If you try to build a European security system, and everyone but Russia, which occupies half of Europe, agrees that it should be built, the system will be fundamentally defective. Taking part in NATO would lead to better security. Russia must strengthen its authority, not just by nuclear weapons, but by hundreds of international ties.

What else the president had in mind in accusing me of "intolerable mistakes" remains a secret. But I would like to say, without any false modesty, that other people are now developing the ideas—especially about military reform—that I advanced.

After being fired, I had time to draw some lessons from my brief experience in high-level politics.

My first and main conclusion is that our present leaders are incapable of rebuilding Russia in the interests of the people, to bring it to the level of economic and social progress that has been reached in the most advanced countries of the modern world. Capitalism, as it is being practiced by the present Russian bosses, is missing its most attractive side—free competition.

My second conclusion is that Russia is not evolving toward a more complete or more profound democracy, but toward oligarchy—a government based on the fusion of state institutions with finance capital. In the new Russia, power, money, natural resources, and real estate are all flowing into the hands of a few "financial-political corporations." And these are waging a no-holds-barred fight to swallow each other up.

The government, which is nothing but a representative office of the same "corporations," is torpedoing direct foreign investment into the Russian economy, denying investors elementary security guarantees, and offering them schemes and financial opportunities that will inevitably fail. Private investment is strictly monitored and restricted to projects controlled by quasi-governmental groups.

And our already heavy tax burden, which stifles healthy competition merely to feed voracious bureaucratic budgets, is getting heavier.

Criminal organizations are increasingly becoming social "regulators," destroying lives and corrupting our politics.

In short, the illusion of free capitalist development has been shattered; the dreary reality is that this "Time of the Seven Bankers"[6] has no future. The economic growth of medium and small business is being artificially restrained; the young, growing managerial class is fading away; the formation of a middle class in the country—the guarantor of stability and positive changes—is being postponed or canceled. As a consequence, broad strata of the population, forced to

---

[6] Lit. *semibankirshchina*. Lebed is drawing an analogy to a chaotic time in seventeenth-century Russian history, called the *semiboyarshchina*, or the "Time of the Seven Boyars," when a council of *boyars*, or Russian nobles, ruled Russia after the overthrow of Czar Vasily Shuisky in 1610. The *boyars* put a Pole on the throne without the approval of the Orthodox Church. Conflict ensued, and in 1612 the Poles were driven from Russia. On February 21, 1613, Mikhail Romanov (the founder of the Romanov dynasty) became czar.

This period in Russian history—dating approximately from the death of Ivan the Terrible in 1584 to Mikhail's accession to the throne—is called the "Time of Troubles." In Russian, *smutnoe vremya*. It is popular in Russia today, especially among the radical opposition, to draw parallels between contemporary Russia and this period.

feel the pain of "wild capitalism," without any hope of alleviation, are getting angry.

The Russian state is getting weaker before their eyes, eaten away by the lawlessness and corruption that have affected all levels of government. The rivalry between the president's administration and the legislative government, which intensified during Yeltsin's illness, has reached the point where a state of "dual power"[7]—which is really no power—has been created in the country.

The present regime's authority in the eyes of the population is extremely low. According to the pollsters, 80 percent of the people rate the government's performance as "poor" or "extremely poor." The drop in the government's authority is the result of the government's inability, or unwillingness, to keep its word to the people. The overwhelming majority of the president's promises issued during the campaign were not carried out and will not be carried out in the foreseeable future. The money just isn't there.

Nowadays, average Russians are just as far from the real levers of power as they were when the CPSU was in control. Perhaps even farther. The chasm between rich and poor has reached dangerous proportions. Oligarchic rule and deep social stratification are two factors making the achievement of civil peace in Russia unrealistic. And no "days of national reconciliation"[8] will change the situation. It can be changed only by implementing reforms in the people's interest (not like now, at their expense), by developing the political system along

---

[7] Lit. *dvoevlastie*. This word was used to describe the state of affairs between the February and October revolutions, when there were, in effect, two governments in power in Russia, the Provisional Government, formed on the basis of the former State Duma, and the so-called "Soviet of Workers', Peasants' and Soldier's Deputies." This situation came to an end when Lenin overthrew the Provisional Government on November 7, 1917, ostensibly in the name of the Soviet of Workers', Peasants', and Soldiers Deputies.

[8] Boris Yeltsin renamed the November 7 national holiday, previously celebrated as the anniversary of the "Great October Socialist Revolution," the "Day of National Reconciliation."

truly democratic lines, and by establishing order and legality in all areas of public life.

The nationwide miners' strike, among others, and demonstrations, more and more often accompanied by political demands, such as that the government step down, are evidence that the people recognize the need for fundamental change.

So are the results of the regional elections. The election of opposition representatives in a number of regions is a sign of the people's disillusionment with local leaders who zealously carry out government policies.

My third conclusion is that Russia is going through an economic, social, political, and moral crisis which could lead to social and political upheavals. Our country in the twentieth century has exceeded all others in the destructive force and cruelty of its revolutions. Another revolution would simply annihilate the country. Most Russians understand this and will not let themselves get involved in a new round of bloodshed.

The ineffective policies and the general disorder in the country are made worse by the extreme unpopularity of those who represent the current regime in its harshest form. I am speaking, above all, of Chief of the Presidential Administration Anatoly Chubais, Finance Minister Aleksandr Livshits, Prime Minister Viktor Chernomyrdin, and the new financial oligarchy.

But the situation is still far from hopeless. Our Motherland has not lost the ability to revive itself relatively quickly and guarantee a life with dignity to its people.

But first, let me make it perfectly clear that we Russians will have to accomplish this mission through our own efforts. The idea that the West will pour its money into Russia is pure fantasy. Serious investments only go to countries where the economic, political, and legal situation is secure, and the risk minimal. We are not yet such a country.

In this connection, it is better to put off all arguments about which system suits Russia best—socialism or capitalism—until better times. No one knows exactly where we are headed or what we will build.

There is as yet no clear or attractive goal, no positive ideology, no faith in the future. These things—the goal and the ideology—must be created, and the faith must be revived. We need to concentrate the energies of all parties and political movements interested in a strong and flourishing Russia.

I am even more convinced than before that Russia's revival must begin with the establishment of order. Order does not mean dictatorship or heavy-handed, arbitrary rule. By order, I mean above all strict obedience to the law by all, and I mean *all*, citizens. Everyone must be equal in the eyes of the law, not only in words but in fact.

But as we restore order, I am against restoring the old, centralized, unitary Russian state, whether it is the Russian Empire or the Soviet Union. That form of government, which stifles any initiative on the part of the local authorities or the rank-and-file citizens, has outlived its usefulness. But I am also against the present chaotic condition of the Russian state.

How did the situation get so bad?

First. The regions, seeing that the center is incapable of helping them solve their socio-economic and political problems, are moving away from the center. They have virtually been thrown on the mercy of Fate, in accordance with the well-known principle, "let those who are drowning save themselves." And many regions do not agree with the way the center views reform.

Second. The new government, having abandoned the ideas of a centralized state, of Russian nationalism, of Russia as a great power, has proposed a political model based on Western liberalism. But this ideology has no roots in our history or spiritual heritage. The ideas of individualism and confrontation, or alienation, between man and the state, or the center and the regions, which are part of this doctrine, are foreign to the overwhelming majority of Russians. It is not surprising that, under Russian conditions, this attempt to follow Western liberal models has led to disintegration. What *is* surprising is that the government stubbornly pretends that it doesn't notice, and continues to follow this mistaken course.

Third. A group of people commonly called the "regional elites" has found a mutual interest with federal authorities in loosening the bonds of the Russian state and profiting from the redistribution of property. In exchange, the regional leaders guarantee their loyalty to the president and the government.

This destruction of the Russian state must be stopped. Local legislation must be brought into harmony with all Russian legislation.

One of the most painful questions we face is constitutional reform. In my view, constitutional reform must envision long-term measures that are not linked to the next presidential elections. The constitutional reform most acceptable under present conditions would be to transform our existing "super-presidential" republic into some sort of presidential-parliamentary republic. This would somewhat curtail the authority of the president. But he should remain in charge of the armed forces and foreign policy, and should continue to name the head of government.[9] The president would keep his official status as the nation's political leader. But the real leadership of domestic policy and the country's socio-economic development would pass into the hands of the government, which would be responsible to the lower house of Parliament and would itself depend on the results of parliamentary elections.

To give the whole federal government more balance and solidity, it would make sense to create a special organ—the State Council—appointed by the president. Its authority would include giving opinions on constitutional laws submitted to it after being passed by the Parliament, and making plans for the country's economic development, government programs, doctrines, and so on. The State Council could prepare the drafts of presidential decrees and work out recommendations about implementing a national policy. Such a body would include the most authoritative politicians, economists, and legal scholars in the country who were not members of the government or deputies of the Parliament, and other worthy statesmen.

[9] Here, "government" is being used in the sense of ministers, under a prime minister.

Of course this is not the only course that constitutional reform could take. I touched only on some of the most urgent problems that beset the modern Russian state. There are others. Many know of them; President Yeltsin knows about them as well. His last term is drawing to a close. So I call on President Yeltsin to initiate constitutional reform. This would create a favorable background for his departure from political life.

The Russian people want an alternative to the communists and to the "democratic *nomenklatura.*" They see the battle between "communists" and "democrats" as an internal struggle within a semi-criminal regime, and want nothing to do with it. This explains Russians' temporary political apathy. But Russia's people have reason and will on their side, and they will have their affirmative path. They love their Motherland. For them, life outside of Russia would be unthinkable.

CHAPTER 24:
MY COUNTRY, THE WEST, AND THE FUTURE

DESPITE THE LONG HISTORY of mutual suspicion and competition, I believe that Russia can cooperate with the West—and America—in all aspects of international activity. Indeed, cooperation is essential, because a country like Russia that occupies one-sixth of the globe cannot be ignored. If people try to fence such a country in, she will always break those barriers. We need to make sure that she breaks out not like a wild beast, but in a civilized way.

No country should completely defeat another. Yes, the Cold War is over and the West was victorious. This is an indisputable fact. But if the fruits of this victory are not used productively, if our national dignity continues to be degraded, German history could repeat itself in Russia. In 1918, Germany was crushed. Fifteen years later, Germany was again in uniform and had rearmed.

It is important to think about how Russia and the West can build mutual relations in this complicated world. With all due respect to the United States, it is not possible for one power to be always powerful in every corner of the globe. We need to find ways to avoid possible confrontations, and I see no obstacles to our cooperating to achieve this.

The world needs a strong Russia. This is part of my political program. History shows that satisfied and successful countries are not belligerent. Russia needs to be allowed to put her economy in order and join the ranks of civilized states. But if Russia is continually bowed, conflict will break out.

NATO, as we know, is expanding. The United States and NATO are powerful, they are the winners, they feel their moral superiority. Today, Russia is weak. But this is a temporary phenomenon. NATO will expand as it desires. For Russia, it is simply a question of limiting the damage, nothing more. This is what President Yeltsin did on May 27, 1997, when he agreed to NATO expansion and gained Russia a small contributing role. But Yeltsin's agreement does nothing substantial to improve relations between Russia and NATO. Rather, it is addressed to the Russian people; it is an attempt to save face.

> **"S**ome say that Western culture is a threat to Russian traditions—and I believe that is true.**"**

I support Yeltsin in this agreement. But in the long run, it doesn't address the real issues confronting NATO and the Russian Federation.

NATO is not monolithic. One needs only to look at Greece and Turkey to see that. And there is still the question of who will pay for its expansion and to what end. One American senator told me confidentially that "We are tired of supporting Yeltsin. But we don't know what to do with such a politically unpredictable, wild country."

The Poles, for sure, will not pay for NATO. They are too poor. I have the impression that they as well as the Czech Republic, Slovenia, and Hungary want to join NATO in order to gain access to Western markets and capital that will rebuild their infrastructure and their armed forces.

But these hopes are, to my mind, groundless. The West has its own problems. The Germans are not going to pay. They are concerned with eastern Germany. In France, unemployment is high. The

French have spent enormous sums increasing their social spending and now they don't know how to cut it. The English are traditionally conservative; they have an island mentality; and they have their own internal discord to deal with. I believe NATO expansion is driven by ambition, particularly by the ambition of the president of the United States.

In Soviet times, the authorities liked to open things—like new Metro stations—to celebrate the anniversary of the revolution. They would open the station and take home their awards, bonuses, and decorations. The new station would operate for one day. Then they would shut it down.

I think something similar is taking place with NATO's expansion. The year 1997 is the fiftieth anniversary of the Marshall Plan. So the expansion agreement is made this year. And 1999, when the expansion will really take hold, is the fiftieth anniversary of NATO itself. So it is sort of a gift to themselves. But when the ceremonies are over, there will be a structure without much substance.

Instead of devising a well thought-out plan to build European security, the NATO powers declare something—like NATO expansion—and then seek justifications for what they have done. The pragmatic Americans usually know how to count their money, but not this time. The latest serious entry into NATO was Spain in 1986. But now expansion has become a populist gesture proclaiming: "We are strong, we are big, we'll expand, we can handle it."

I think the tensions with NATO will increase because of expansion; in fact expansion might even destroy NATO. The lines of communication are overstretched, the interests are contradictory, the system of cooperation is friable. I can draw another analogy with the Soviet Union: outwardly big and strong, it fell to pieces in three days. That is the danger the West faces in rushing forward with half-baked plans.

There are other ways to achieve European stability. While there have always been those who fear that Germany will upset European equilibrium, especially after two world wars, Germany deserves to be respected. A half-century ago Germany was a devastated country, with an economy in tatters and ten million dead. It rose from its knees through economic and political reforms and with the help of the Marshall Plan. Today it occupies the second position in the world and the first in Europe. We should give credit to people who had the will to overcome their devastating problems.

History teaches us that when the three continental powers—Russia, Germany, and France—have good relations with one another, peace and order reign in Europe. That peace is more important than any ideology.

There are differences between us, of course. Some say that Western culture is a threat to Russian traditions—and I believe that is true. Unfortunately, Russia has become a refuse pit for low-grade Western art: action movies where thirty or forty people are killed in a variety of ways, or pornography, or other mass-produced, formulaic rubbish on television. When you take people like our own, whose work ethic has been destroyed, and give them television programs that show how to rob a bank, you're creating a very explosive mixture. This is not culture; it is mass consumption trash. It doesn't present the great masterpieces of art and literature that have been produced in countries like the United States; it provides the nightmare fantasies of the dregs of human beings.

I should also mention that the West is not our only neighbor. We have a 2,400 kilometer joint border with China. China is growing day by day, while we are now weak. So we need to maneuver and deal with a big, strong neighbor to the East as well as the West.

And needless to say, we have our own internal difficulties. For three years the government has been talking about fighting corruption—and nothing has been achieved. Yes, they are trying to fish Sergei Stankevich—a former Yeltsin aide and deputy mayor of Moscow accused of taking a $10,000 bribe—out of Poland; and yes, Alexei Ilyushenko—a former prosecutor general—has been jailed on corruption charges (though not yet tried). But these are small fry—not nobodies, but far from important.

The government has declared its intentions to root out corruption. But since the political elite is collectively responsible for the corruption, nothing can happen. We have an old joke that describes the situation. The chairman of a collective farm is arguing with a priest. The chairman doesn't want to provide the bricks for a new church. The priest says, "If you don't give me the bricks, I won't provide the nuns for your sauna entertainment." The chairman replies, "Okay, then I won't provide pioneers from the Communist Youth League for your choir."

There is another problem, which is the sheer inefficacy of the government. For example, in 1995, 447 presidential decrees were promulgated—and ignored. Nothing happened, despite there being a Main Control Department of the administration whose job it is to make sure these things do happen. A roughly equal number of decrees were eviscerated, with, say, only one of ten points being acted upon first because it was in someone's interest.

First Deputy Premier Boris Nemstov has promised a decree that will force state officials to declare their incomes and property. This makes me feel sorry for him. He is saying appealing, showy things, but they are not based on anything and they will have catastrophic consequences. Everyone in government who has had the chance to buy prestigious apartments, dachas, and yachts has already done so. The new "accumulators" made use of pyramid schemes and banks that have since gone bankrupt; and they did so with the help of Yegor Gaidar, the former acting prime minister, who reduced people's savings to dust and ashes.

We've reached the point where people cannot trust the state. They view it as an enemy, a looter, a robber. So now money is being hidden, hoarded in boxes. The people have up to $30 billion in cash that is not being invested. And at the same time, we consider ourselves fortunate to receive another $300 million tranche from the International Monetary Fund or other international lending institutions. We must create an economic climate and provide guarantees in order that cash be invested for the good of the country.

Boris Nemtsov's proposals will only drive our economy further underground, as people try to escape the tax police. During the Soviet period, the shadow economy occupied a narrow band of the spectrum. But now our entire economy has gone underground and the entire policy of the state is to force people either to stop producing or hide their profits. Most people are doing the latter, and our economy is quickly becoming criminalized.

The government is trying to seize ninety-two kopecks out of every ruble. I believe in a tax rate of 35 percent so that people can feel confident that if they work, if they create, if they manufacture, if they invest, they will profit.

I believe in common sense, but we have been driven into a surrealistic situation where the more you work, the poorer you become. Manufacturing long ago stopped making economic sense; so instead, enormous capital is simply shifted between banks. That money pile grows, but because it is not invested, our economy is falling apart, and at some point will shatter completely.

And not without consequences. There will be social explosions, cataclysms. Russia has a huge reserve of strength, an underestimated reserve of stability. Other nations would already have exploded and swept away their governments. But any patience has its limits, and we are fast approaching them. And that patience is not helped by a government that last year produced a budget it claimed we could be proud of and then six months later we discovered that it had to be cut by at least 30 percent. Where will the cuts fall? On education, health care, science, culture—where they will cause the most harm and inflict the most pain. If we invest in education, science, health care, and culture, then we will have a healthy, cultured, educated, creative nation. But we have no such thing.

Power in Russia lies in the hands of four groups—the government, the banks, organized crime, and the monopolies, from the railroads to the giant state energy monoplies like Gazprom and United Energy systems.

But to speak of the power of the government is wrong. The government is a power vacuum; government, in the civilized understanding of the term, does not exist in Russia. What we have is a kind of administrative mutant built on the ruins of the Soviet Union. It redistributes property and retargets financial flows. These manipulations are a game played by 5 percent of the population. Some get rich, others go broke. And the other 95 percent of the population are made beggars. Their savings evaporate, their futures are ruined, and no money is made from work. Even if our people were as patient as camels, at some point they will rebel.

What triggered the February Revolution of 1917? There was no fresh bread in the St. Petersburg market. The lesson: the trigger can be anything, any stupidity that in a normal society would not even be noticed.

The Soviet Revolution took place eighty years ago. It collapsed in 1991 because the system had exhausted itself and no one—not one secretary of a local Party committee, let alone the 100 percent Communist KGB or the 80 percent Communist army—rushed outside with a machine gun to defend it.

Everyone wanted a new, improved life. But the only improvement we received was freedom of speech. That has been the first and, so far, the last achievement of a post-Soviet Russia. And even now, Boris Berezovsky, deputy secretary of Yeltsin's Security Council and head of a financial empire, and Vladimir Gusinsky, the banking mogul with ties to the Kremlin, are separately buying up the media. Thus our one democratic achievement is under threat.

Instead of improving, people are losing hope. Their lives are deteriorating. And President Boris Yeltsin, who has promised reform, has been sidelined.

So far, what have the Russian people received from our immensely rich country? A piece of paper, a voucher from Anatoly Chibais, now first deputy premier, that represents our share of the privatized Soviet Union's property. Its value? Nearly nothing, thanks to a plummeting ruble and two years of runaway inflation. Its face value? Ten thousand rubles—the price of three loaves of bread. My grand-father went to war, my father fought, and I fought too, and this was all we three generations ever received. And yet someone like Berezovsky acquired Aeroflot, Russia's main television channel ORT, and the financial-industrial combine LogoVAZ. What has he done to deserve this, while others have nothing? Unless steps are taken to achieve social justice, there will be an explosion with such enormous reverberations that the whole world will want to stop it, but it won't be possible.

The West has been confused about the situation in Russia because Chubais, whose popularity in Russia is at 2 percent, speaks the lan-guage of the West when he goes abroad. He describes a model of reform that he knows is effective in America. He acts as a proponent for Western ideology. But the Russian people don't believe Chubais; and they won't be driven by force. The key, again, is providing guar-antees that labor will be protected, that taxes will be low, and that rob-bery will be punished. The state should not be the enemy of the people—it should help the people protect themselves. Right now in Russia we have that exactly backwards.

But things cannot stay that way forever. Whatever turmoil we may undergo, I am convinced that sooner or later, with or without help from the West, Russia will revive. We have a tremendous population and territory. We just need to develop the skills to manage our own resources and find a way to integrate ourselves into the world econ-omy without pain, without confrontations, in a civilized manner.

I should also mention that I have no intention of trying forcibly to restore the union of former Soviet republics. That is not Russia's future, and there is no need for it. In the past we were united by a party, the Communist Party, and its huge fist, the KGB. When the Party collapsed and the fist unfolded, there was nothing left to unite us. And because of the so-called Leninist nationalities policy, each republic had its own party, its own government structures; thus there was no fight in 1991 because they already had established elites who could take over.

Russia has neither the money nor the force to bring the republics back, and it makes no sense to do so. It's much easier and cheaper to rebuild relations with neighbors by respecting their sovereignty and independence. Certainly, when the republics thoughtlessly cut well-developed economic ties, everyone suffered. But to force everyone under the same roof, to create a new USSR, is senseless. I reiterate: I have no plans to do this.

But neither should Russia totally abandon places such as Chechnya. Peace is more profitable than war, and we should provide common sense help to the Chechens. In the Soviet period, 42 percent of Chechen men made a living doing seasonal work of which there was never enough. Now these people have arms and combat experience. If we leave them to the mercy of fate, we leave them to a future of armed robbery. There is another option—invest small amounts of money there, rev up the engine of the Chechen economy, start drilling oil, and create conditions for productive labor.

So far this hasn't happened. Grozny is not being rebuilt, money has not been invested, and in Chechnya business is conducted by idiots running around with machine guns robbing people.

We should know better; all of us have peasant roots. We should know the importance of work. We should know that when people are allowed to work productively, good things happen. Before the Bolshevik revolution, Russia exported food. We fed ourselves, Europe, and one-third of the world. In 1913 Russia had no shortage of bread; it had a shortage of sacks and bread was sometimes stored in pits. But by the 1930s the peasantry in Russia was devastated. Today, our agriculture is in total ruins.

We must develop not only a middle-class of small businessmen, but of farmers. It is a class that will cement our society and protect it from revolutions, riots, and other stupidities. If you are an owner, you have something to work on and hand down to your children. You don't need to fight. This is my task and my goal; this is why the political party I have founded, the Russian Popular Republican Party, is a party of the middle class.

But the challenges ahead are great. If Russia continues to crumble, it will not be like Albania. Here, the revolutionaries will not only seize machine guns. Disorder in Russia risks the loss or purchase of nuclear weapons, and therefore, the unleashing of nuclear terrorism. It is our mutual responsibility—Russia and the West's—to ensure that this doesn't happen, that nuclear, chemical, and biological weapons do not proliferate and do not fall into the wrong hands. If a time should ever arrive when this tremendous arsenal of extermination has no owner and the population becomes more and more criminalized, it won't be good for anyone. Russia's great task is to make sure our situation does not leap over civilized boundaries. Should it do so, we will fall into a ditch of chaos. Or we can avoid it. If we avoid it, then we can talk of Russia's bright future.

INDEX